Popular television drama

Critical perspectives

MANCHESTER
1824

Manchester University Press

Popular television drama
Critical perspectives

edited by
Jonathan Bignell and **Stephen Lacey**

Manchester University Press
Manchester and New York
distributed exclusively in the USA by Palgrave

Published by Manchester University Press
Oxford Road, Manchester M13 9NR, UK
and Room 400, 175 Fifth Avenue, New York, NY 10010, USA
www.manchesteruniversitypress.co.uk

Distributed exclusively in the USA by
Palgrave, 175 Fifth Avenue, New York,
NY 10010, USA

Distributed exclusively in Canada by
UBC Press, University of British Columbia, 2029 West Mall,
Vancouver, BC, Canada V6T 1Z2

British Library Cataloguing-in-Publication Data
A catalogue record for this book is available from the British Library

Library of Congress Cataloging-in-Publication Data applied for

ISBN   0 7190 6932 7   *hardback*
EAN   978 0 7190 6932 1
ISBN   0 7190 6933 5   *paperback*
EAN   978 0 7190 6933 8

First published 2005

14 13 12 11 10 09 08 07 06 05   10 9 8 7 6 5 4 3 2 1

Typeset in Minion with Rotis Semi-Sans display
by Northern Phototypesetting Co Ltd, Bolton
Printed in Great Britain
by CPI, Bath

Contents

Notes on contributors

Jonathan Bignell is Reader in Television and Film at the University of Reading, and Director of the Centre for Television Drama Studies. He is the author of *Postmodern Media Culture* (2000), *Media Semiotics* (2002) and *An Introduction to Television Studies* (2004). He is the editor of *Writing and Cinema* (1999) and joint editor of *British Television Drama: Past, Present and Future* (2000). He is a series editor of 'The Television Series' of studies of television screenwriters and co-wrote the volume *Terry Nation* (2004) for the series. He recently completed his book *Beckett on Screen: The Television Plays* and is currently working on a study of Reality TV. He is also co-director of an AHRB-funded research project, 'Cultures of British Television Drama, 1960–82'.

Peter Billingham is Subject Leader for Drama Studies at Bath Spa University College and is also a writer and dramatist. He has won awards for his playwriting and made his full London debut with *Perfection* at The Barons Court Theatre (2003). His publications include *Sensing the City Through Television* (2000) and *Theatres of Conscience* (2002). He has specialist research and teaching interests in the plays of Edward Bond, postwar British political theatre and contemporary British and American television drama.

Steve Blandford is a Professor and Head of the Department of Arts and Media at the University of Glamorgan. His research interests are centred on identity in relation to film, television drama and theatre, particularly the response by writers, performers and filmmakers to the rapidly evolving nature of British national identity. He edited *Wales on Screen* (2000) and co-authored *The Film Studies Dictionary* (2000). He has also written for theatre and television.

Mark Bould is Senior Lecturer in Film Studies at the University of the West of England. He is an editor of the journal *Historical Materialism* and an editorial consultant for *Science Fiction Studies*. He is currently completing books on John Sayles and *film noir* and co-editing the collected essays and reviews of M. John Harrison.

Lez Cooke is the author of *British Television Drama: A History* (2003). He is currently writing a book on Troy Kennedy Martin for Manchester University Press and is researching regional British television drama at Manchester Metropolitan University as part of an AHRB-funded project on 'Cultures of British Television Drama, 1960–82'. He is also the programmer for Stoke Film Theatre.

Julia Hallam teaches film and television studies at the University of Liverpool. She has written widely on questions of aesthetics, identity and representation including *Nursing the Image: Media Culture and Professional Identity* (2000); *Realism and Popular Cinema* (2000). She is joint editor of *Medical Fictions* (1998) and *Consuming for Pleasure* (2001) with Nickianne Moody (1998) and currently writing a book on Lynda La Plante.

Stephen Lacey is a Principal Lecturer in Contemporary Arts at Manchester Metropolitan University. His main research interests are postwar British drama/theatre and television drama. He is co-director of an AHRB-funded research project, 'Cultures of British Television Drama, 1960-82'. Publications include: *British Realist Theatre: The New Wave in its Context 1956–65* (1995), *British Television Drama: Past, Present and Future* (2000) (joint editor) and articles on Arnold Wesker, Augusto Boal, John McGrath and the relationship between theatre and television for the journal *New Theatre Quarterly*. He is currently working on a book on Tony Garnett.

Barry Langford is Lecturer in Film and Television Studies at Royal Holloway, University of London. His recent publications include essays on Siegfried Kracauer, Walter Benjamin and the Holocaust; 'revisionist' Westerns; narrative reversal as redemption in Holocaust film; Chris Marker; and suburban sexualities. His forthcoming books include *Film Genre: Hollywood and Beyond* (Edinburgh University Press) and *America First? Naming the Nation in American Cinema* (co-edited with Mandy Merck).

Máire Messenger Davies is Professor of Media Studies and Director of the Centre for Media Research in the School of Media & Performing Arts, University of Ulster at Coleraine. She has written widely about television and young audiences. Her books include *Television Is Good for Your Kids* (1989, 2nd edition 2002); *Fake Fact and Fantasy: Children's Understanding of Television Reality* (1997) and *Dear BBC: Children, Television Storytelling and the Public Sphere* (2001).

Robin Nelson is currently Head of Department and Professor of Contemporary Arts at Manchester Metropolitan University. He is currently working on a new book on British and American contemporary television cultures. Other recent television publications include contributions to G. Creeber, ed., *The Television Genre Book* (2001) and *Fifty Key Television Programmes* (2004) and his television books include (with Millington) *'Boys from the Blackstuff': The Making of TV Drama* (1986) and *TV Drama in Transition* (1997).

Helen Wheatley is a Postdoctoral Research Fellow at the University of Reading, working on the AHRB-funded project, 'Cultures of British Television Drama, 1960–82'. She is the author of *Gothic Television* (2005) and is currently editing a collection on television historiography. Alongside ongoing research into British television drama (particularly drama for women and questions of quality, creativity and experimentation), she has also published work on natural history and lifestyle television.

Acknowledgements

Many of the essays in this book come out of the work of a research project, 'Cultures of British Television Drama: 1960-82'. The editors would like to acknowledge the support of the Arts and Humanities Research Board, who generously fund the project.

Editors' introduction

This book aims to provide resources for critical thinking about key aspects of television drama in Britain since 1960, including institutional, textual, cultural and audience-centred modes of study. It comprises original essays on aspects of British television drama which our contributors believe have not yet been adequately theorised or researched in existing scholarship. The book presents and contests significant strands of critical work in television drama studies, using case study examples to show how critical approaches are in dialogue with specific problems, programmes and issues. Thus, the book aims to function as an organic whole, which examines existing approaches to the study of television drama and lays down markers for new directions in the subject. We have also added a concluding Afterword discussing how the arguments in these essays bear on the directions that studies of television drama are taking, or should take. So, although the book is a collection of diverse contributions, the arrangement of the essays into parts, each prefaced by a brief editorial introduction, offers ways of linking the contributions and creating a dialogue between approaches and issues. This introduction suggests further connections that link essays in different parts, as well as highlighting some of the links that are noted in our editorial introductions to each part.

The book is intended as a response to existing work on television drama, which tends to examine programmes and categories in isolation or subsumes them into a more general cultural or media analysis. The essays consider many popular and significant programmes, some of which have been marginalised because of their lack of fit with dominant paradigms, and the contributors seek to raise questions about what studies of television drama address, and how attention to both well-known and less studied topics and programmes might offer new insights that enrich existing critical work or suggest new lines of enquiry. Contemporary studies of popular television largely address contemporary programmes, but this book has a historical dimension, and we hope this will enhance the emergent research agenda in television drama studies that rediscovers and revalues popular television drama as well as engaging with contemporary material. As critical methodologies and theoretical approaches change, new insights and problems appear that create the need for further work on issues or material that had seemed exhausted by former interpretations. The continual generation of new objects of analysis in the ongoing production of television drama produces both new points of discussion but also new marginalisations (see Nelson 1997).

Historically, the academic study of television drama has placed the single television play and the segmented episodes of the prime-time high-profile television serial at the centre of its curriculum and at the head of its hierarchy of canonical programme texts (see Bignell *et al.* 2000; Brandt 1993; Caughie 2000). Although we have used the term 'drama' in the title of this book, few of our contributors have written about these television forms. Instead, many of the essays draw attention to the much broader field that could be called 'television fiction', and discuss programmes in the series form whose individual episodes are largely free-standing narratives and are often written and directed by different people. We have devoted one part wholly to situation comedy, where the essays by Robin Nelson, Barry Langford and Julia Hallam focus less on the aesthetic value or authorship of programmes in this generic drama form than on their cultural significance for audiences and how they work with the generic constraints of the sitcom form itself. Langford, in particular, refers to a wide range of sitcom examples including both the much-repeated *Steptoe and Son* (BBC 1962–65 and 1970–74) and the contemporary 'classic' *The Office* (BBC 2001–3). His essay shows how the very restrictions that the genre conventions of this popular television form entails provide a productive tension which makes possible an exploration of the politics of the genre and of the characteristic pairings and groupings of characters that it focuses on. In the seemingly very different context of the television adaptation of a literary source, included in a different part of the book, Helen Wheatley's analysis of *Rebecca* (ITV/Carlton 1997), *The Wyvern Mystery* (BBC 2000) and *The Woman in White* (BBC 1997) distinguishes the gendered concerns of the Gothic as a mode that encompasses literary and cinematic realisations of narratives that reflect on the politics of domesticity and the home. Here, a genre that began as a popular and devalued literary form makes continual appearances in the context of television, equally as popular and devalued in contrast to literature or cinema, and equally marked by an address to female audiences and placed in a domestic space. Like the work on sitcom in our genre part, Wheatley's essay emphasises the relationships between the television drama text and its contexts of production and viewing. Bignell's essay on *Doctor Who* (BBC 1963–96) also investigates how the programme's production and realisation negotiated the possibilities that television offered for realising both conventional 'pulp fiction' monster stories and also the more aspirational claims for 'serious' speculative and educational drama in the genre of science fiction. In these and other essays, contributors show how television drama works with its own conventions and connects them with, and differentiates them from, other media.

The title of the book includes the significant and problematic word 'popular', a term whose paradoxes and problems are a useful way into the range of ideas about television that we represent in this book. Recent approaches to television and the media in general have valued 'the popular' because of its engagement with the day-to-day cultural experience of the citizens of modern societies, and its use as a set of means for locating the social subject in a culture. This contrasts with thinking about the popular that developed in the formative period of the 1960s in British theatre, as Stephen Lacey's essay shows by discussing the work of writers and producers adopting a Brechtian position that drama should both analyse society and also engage a broad audience. The development of political drama in theatre was in part a reaction to the widespread belief that television undermined the family, encouraged audience passivity, smuggled American values into British culture and displaced an organic working-class culture. Lacey explores the role of social realist television drama as a response to this complex of ideas about the politics of dramatic forms. Lez Cooke's essay on social realism in the contemporary drama series *Clocking Off* (BBC 2000–3) demonstrates how related concerns in more recent times have opened up television drama to reconfigured versions of politically engaged drama for popular audiences.

In this respect, one strand of work in these and other essays in the book is constituted by the connections between the aesthetic forms of television drama and their cultural and political relationships with ideas of nation and region. The ways in which community is formed as a spatial construct is developed in the essay by Steve Blandford on BBC drama in the Northern Irish, Scottish and Welsh regions in the 1990s. Blandford shows that, while both Belfast and Glasgow achieved some kind of network presence in television drama, and some critical success in the 1990s, Cardiff simply experienced the turmoil of rapid changes of senior personnel and repeated failures in its attempts to produce popular drama with nationwide appeal. The essay accounts for the different levels of success experienced by each region, particularly in terms of mainstream popular drama, and goes on to examine the possible impact of broader cultural differences in the representation of the three national regions in drama programmes. Blandford's essay, like Robin Nelson's on 'Englishness' in *Dad's Army* (BBC 1968–77) and Peter Billingham's on *Queer As Folk* (C4 1999–2000), shows how imagined geographical and political spaces, where the ideological and aesthetic representations of space combine in particular programmes and programme categories, intersect to shape the meanings of programmes and reflect on questions of sociopolitical belonging and responsibility.

The significance of what is 'popular', in the different terms of television institutions (which measure it by ratings or audience share) and television analysts, illuminates the different stakes of the groups that have shaped notions of 'popular' television drama in connection and distinction to notions of seriousness and taste. Television drama has both reproduced distinctions between 'serious' drama and 'popular' forms and also challenged them. A key debate that focuses this issue is that over the existence and value of a canon of television drama. The idea of a canon is convenient in its suggestion of fixity and allows for a hierarchy of what is of interest and of significance. Yet is also useful as a permeable boundary that allows for the arguments of those who want to change it, enlarge it or redefine it. Canonical status can derive from the association of television with cultural forms that have been accorded greater prestige, such as the adaptation of 'classic' literature and theatre, or the related value given to authorship in the prestige television play or authored serial. To many academic commentators, and some personnel in the television industry, the canon is slanted towards drama that claims, or can be argued to claim, political engagement or to work on the aesthetics of television by adopting new formal conventions. With some exceptions, this association of the canon with either political intervention or formal experiment has taken place around high-profile prime-time programmes that are peripheral to the generic closure supposed to delimit series and serial drama in the popular genres of fantasy or comedy. Furthermore, the mutual definition of the canonical and the popular against each other produces an illusory boundary. There are certainly programmes that transgress this boundary. In devising entries in his edited collection of 'key' television programmes (perhaps not quite the same as a canon), Glen Creeber (2004) included three programmes discussed in detail in this book, namely *The Prisoner* (ITV/ITC 1967–68), *Doctor Who* and *Queer As Folk*. It is no accident that the essays on each of these programmes appear in our part on approaches to the issue of 'quality', since canonicity and quality have a relationship although the essays in the part seek to problematise some of the grounds on which evaluations of quality have been made, such as the significance of authorship and genre. There is no necessary separation, then, between the 'canonical' and the 'popular', and each term shifts in its meaning according its referent, its user's critical agenda and the discursive context. The essays in this book variously concern programmes that might form part of a canonical curriculum in academic studies of television drama, that could be considered 'good' or even 'the best' example of a particular genre or television form, or that are or have been among British television audiences' favourites. But since these kinds of valuation are made by different groups for different purposes, and refer to different selections of programmes, this book participates in the selection and evaluation process rather than aiming to close it down or complete it.

The contributors to this book have each selected a topic or programme for discussion that is popular with audiences, but this does not always mean large or mass audiences. As Raymond Williams (1977) noted a long time ago in his analysis of the drama-documentary *The Big Flame* (BBC 1969), the television audience comprises viewers from all social groups, and is not therefore a mass audience in the Frankfurt School's sense of a univocal and homogeneous group. The audience is internally differentiated and television offers the possibility of differently accented reception among its constituent viewers. The crucial role of scheduling, and the transmission of programmes on one channel rather than another, contributes to this. For the drawing of audiences across the schedule from, for example, news to sitcom to an episode of a police series itself produces interactions between programmes that are not determined by the expectations that a form or genre sets up. Programmes can therefore shift across the boundaries of 'quality' and the popular as a result of their relationships with each other and with the different audiences attracted to them, relatively independently of their textual features. Work throughout the book on aesthetics and ideology, including the representation of class and gender, deals with the connections and tensions between production values, questions of 'quality' and the variant forms of realism, fantasy and comedy.

Television has long been regarded as a medium that has a special relationship with its viewers' everyday lives. In a sense, the scholarly study of
television – in particular what we could call the aesthetic study of television drama – is a process of 'making strange' the most familiar of media,
of attaining some kind of critical distance from that which is quotidian
and taken for granted. Yet it is television's very familiarity, and its conventional focus upon the familiar, the present time and the everyday, that
opens up alternative formal and stylistic possibilities. So television is
well-placed to offer humorous, wry, reflective and/or radical defamiliari-
sations of familiar sights, ideas, places and moments. Fantasy, science fiction and horror are established modes which television has adopted for
this purpose, and the essays by Jonathan Bignell, Mark Bould and Helen
Wheatley address these kinds of programmes.

But 'the popular' also carries the meaning of a kind of production by
'the people' themselves, an organic culture which seems to conflict with
the industrial, institutional and technological facts of television. The
important work on the agency and activity of the television viewer can be
regarded as an attempt to capture some of the attractions of organic and
resistant 'popular' culture, and this is especially true of feminist studies
that focus on the active use of television by women viewers (see Brunsdon *et al.* 1997 or Brunsdon 2000 for example). Much of the work of the
last decade and a half that has dealt with drama has focused largely on
audiences and an approach to television that is closely related to the study
of popular culture generally. In the 1980s interests in audiences and how
real viewers gained pleasure from their viewing overtook the issue of the
progressiveness of particular television texts. This approach to television
drama by considering its reception by audiences is central to the essays by
Julia Hallam, Robin Nelson and Máire Messenger Davies. Audience studies have had a persistent concern for how the pleasures of watching television play a role in identity-formation, and in that respect Hallam's,
Nelson's and Messenger Davies's essays draw on that agenda. Messenger
Davies shows how children's viewing of *The Demon Headmaster* (BBC
1995–96, 1997, 1998) is part of their valuation of their own generational
identity, not simply against that of adulthood but also as a licensed space
that seems to be both open to their own independent activity and a corrective to what they perceive as the injustice and mismanagement of society by adults. Messenger Davies makes a powerful case for the value of
both children's television drama and *The Demon Headmaster* in particular. Hallam's and Nelson's essays draw in different ways on issues of
memory and nostalgia. *Butterflies* (BBC 1978-83) functioned for some of

its women viewers, Hallam argues, as a way of negotiating changing roles for women and attitudes to domesticity, and this response to the programme was documented by respondents to her requests for memories about the programme. Nelson discusses how older viewers of *Dad's Army* saw the programme as a validation of ideas about national solidarity and community, contributing to memories that informed their sense of the present. Younger viewers without that memory understood the programme somewhat differently, and this issue of television drama's role in the marking of time and the shaping of ideas about the self connects to broader debates about television and nostalgia. Nostalgia frequently informs both the viewing of television and the study of television, offering a potential route through which to re-engage with and re-evaluate that past. Some contemporary programmes hark back to a collective viewing experience, and comment on television's appeal as a medium, such as the BBC sitcom *The Royle Family* (BBC 1998–2000). In the context of today's multi-channel environment, where, for example, UK Gold and Granada Plus have restored popular programmes of the past to visibility by repeating them, diverse forms of drama have proved their enduring popularity. The legacy of repeated and 'classic' programmes contributes to television viewers' sense of television history, and one of the questions addressed by many of the essays in this book is why some past programmes were, and remain, as popular as new productions.

References

Bignell, J., S. Lacey and M. K. Macmurraugh-Kavanagh (eds) (2000), *British Television Drama: Past, Present and Future*, Basingstoke: Palgrave Macmillan.

Brandt, G. W. (ed.) (1993), *British Television Drama in the 1980s*, Cambridge: Cambridge University Press.

Brunsdon, C. (2000), *The Feminist, the Housewife and the Soap Opera*, Oxford: Clarendon.

Brunsdon, C., J. D'Acci and L. Spigel (eds) (1997), *Feminist Television Criticism: A Reader*, Oxford: Oxford University Press.

Caughie, J. (2000), *Television Drama: Realism, Modernism, and British Culture*, Oxford: Oxford University Press.

Creeber, G. (2004), *Fifty Key Television Programmes*, London: Arnold.

Nelson, R. (1997), *TV Drama in Transition: Forms, Values and Cultural Change*, Basingstoke: Macmillan.

Williams, R. (1977), 'A lecture on realism', *Screen* 18:1 (1977), 61–74.

Part I

The boundaries of genre: the sitcom

Editors' introduction

The sitcom has a history that spans most of the postwar period, and is one of the most popular and enduring of television programme formats. Not only do new sitcoms figure prominently in the schedules of terrestrial television, but 'old' examples of the form (and the idea of 'old' programmes in an age when television has ceased to be, by its nature, ephemeral is one that needs revisiting) are a staple of cable and satellite channels as well. Indeed, as Robin Nelson notes in his essay, certain sitcoms have such a hold over the popular imagination that they can still gather audiences in the millions some time after their first screening (a repeat showing on BBC1 of a one-off episode of *Dad's Army* (1968–77) in 2001 attracted 6.6 million viewers).

However, academic interest in the sitcom has been fitful – though not always unsympathetic – and it has not received the kind of critical attention that has focused on other popular genres. Some genres are more visible than others, it seems, and it is interesting that even *The Television Genre Book* (Creeber ed. 2001), one of the most comprehensive accounts so far, has only limited space for sitcoms; there are essays that deal with particular series, but 'sitcom' is not identified as a specific category.

Before considering this absence further, it is worth exploring the concept of genre itself, which has become increasingly important to the study of television, led, no doubt, by the dominance of generic programming in the schedules. This has produced both a more sophisticated notion of genre as a critical category and a more sympathetic treatment of particular programmes and programme categories. *The Television Genre Book* considers genre in a complex way and summarises critical approaches to the field, and its emphases are revealing in this context. The selection of material reminds us that it is not just popular television that can be con-

sidered 'generic'; there are contributions on the single play, documentary
and drama-documentary – all programme categories that are often seen
to exist in opposition to the 'generic', which is sometimes seen as a syn-
onym for the 'formulaic'. 'Serious', or canonical, television drama, it might
be argued, is authored, is ambitious and exists within a world of its own
making; generic drama by contrast is featureless, safe and predictable.
However, if genre is understood as the sharing of expectations between
audience and programme makers as to the type of programme being
viewed, then there is no reason why a great deal of television should not
be thought of as generic. It may also be thought of as 'popular', for, as the
writer David Edgar has observed in another context, genre 'involves a
transfer of power. It is the viewer saying to the producer, I possess key elements of this event before it's begun . . . If foregrounding the customer is
the end, genre is the means' (Edgar 2000: 75). This democratic aspect of
genre is clearly important and is one reason why generic television is so
often linked to the kinds of popular television that are the focus of this
book

   Yet suspicion of generic television in general, and of sitcom in particular, remains. As Barry Langford argues here, critics have often demonstrated either muted embarrassment at the genre *per se* – and a consequent
attempt to validate those examples that seem to be somehow 'untypical' –
or a desire to legitimate sitcom in terms of its sociological significance and
its ability to reveal the mores and values of the culture that produced it.
Other forms of popular drama have been reclaimed for serious attention
– see Julia Hallam's discussion of feminist criticism of the soap opera –
along with the popular audience that watches it; sitcom, however, has not,
by and large, attracted such a sustained and spirited defence.

   One of the main criticisms of sitcom has focused on its ideological
conservatism. Dominated by the family, or family substitutes such as
workplace networks, and located in domestic, or domesticated, settings,
traditional sitcom has often seemed impervious to the social changes that
affect its audiences (and which are represented elsewhere in the television
schedules). The view of Britain seen through the lens of, say, *Terry and
June* (BBC 1979–87) is a curiously outmoded one, in which traditional
masculinities and class identities have survived the onslaught of feminism and affluence. British sitcoms have often been compared
unfavourably with those from the US, which, as Hallam points out, seem
to have recognised the need to engage with cultural shifts, especially the
changing position of women, if only out of a desire to deliver a new generation of high-spending, liberal feminists to advertisers.

As many critics of the genre have noted, the conservatism of sitcom has a formal aspect. The obsessive circularity of the dominant narrative model, in which the situation that gives each series its peculiar identity must be returned to unaltered, constrains the possibilities for change; no matter what the threats and challenges of the specific episode, the status quo must be re-established by the final credits, and only a limited degree of narrative progression, of linear plot development that might carry on beyond the frame of the episode, can be tolerated without destroying the form. However, as Langford points out in an essay that is concerned with how the 'boundaries' of sitcom operate at an ideological level, certain sitcoms (his examples are *Steptoe and Son* (BBC 1962–65 and 1970–74), *Porridge* (BBC 1974–77) and *The Office* (BBC 2001–3)) have accommodated a degree of narrative progression that has both drawn attention to, and threatened to destabilise, the series' premise; it is often at these points, where circularity seems more than a mere generic feature, that the sitcom seems at its most subversive.

A great deal of criticism of other popular forms has acknowledged, if not explicitly focused upon, the complex relationships between programmes and their audiences, often engaging with actual viewers in their own viewing contexts. This has given a much-needed corrective to the kind of textual criticism that ascribes fixed 'meanings' to texts without acknowledging the role of the spectator, or the position of the critic, in the process. Relatively little academic attention has been paid to the audiences of sitcoms, however. The essays of both Julia Hallam and Robin Nelson seek to remedy this in different ways and for different purposes, drawing on their own audience research. This is offered not for its statistical validity but because it offers a sense of how 'real' audiences respond to, and engage with, actual programmes in specific social situations, and how important television characters can be to the construction of popular memory. The result, in both cases, is that dominant conceptions of the social meanings of *Butterflies* (BBC 1978–83) (Hallam) and *Dad's Army* (BBC 1968–77) (Nelson) are challenged and renegotiated. Linking audience response to ideological or textual criticism and a nuanced account of modes of acting and performance, the analysis contained in both essays is complex and politically aware. For Hallam, *Butterflies*, for all the narrowness of the comfortable, affluent and middle-class social world it portrays, nevertheless engaged its (largely female) viewers with real-life dilemmas and was appreciated for this, often by women of differing class backgrounds and ages. Nelson's research into the way that contemporary viewers of varying class and ages watch *Dad's Army* demonstrates the

unexpected survival of the 'family' viewing audience in the multi-channel era, suggesting that accounts of the series as a straightforward exercise
in nostalgia and faded patriotism catch only one element in its enduring
appeal. He uncovers a 'utopian' element in viewer responses, a desire for
a 'collectivism' that works in tension with both a celebration – and ironic
subversion – of the series' nostalgia and a decidedly un-ironic celebration
of a wartime concept of 'Englishness'.

All three essays in this part, therefore, explore the continuing popularity of the situation comedy, in both its historic and contemporary forms,
and make a convincing case for considering sitcom as a key popular
genre. They also provide evidence of the elasticity of the sitcom format;
the conventions of the genre may seem clear-cut, even rigid, but, as Langford argues in relation to *The Office*, this does not mean that it cannot
address the new working realities and social hierarchies of post-industrial
Britain.

References

Creeber, G. (ed) (2001), *The Television Handbook*, London: British Film Institute.
Edgar, D. (2000), 'Playing shops, shopping plays: the effect of the internal market
    on television drama', in J. Bignall, S. Lacey and M. Macmurraugh-Kavanagh
    (eds) *British Television Drama: Past, Present and Future*, Basingstoke: Palgrave
    Macmillan, 73–7.

1

'Our usual impasse': the episodic situation comedy revisited

Barry Langford

> The question of what counts as an innovative feature in the development of a sitcom is difficult because in some ways we are talking about a framework so simple and so easy to recognise that the sitcom is, literally, child's play. (Feuer 2001: 69)

This essay takes a second look at the apparent simplicities of the situation comedy, comparing some 'classic' 1960s and 1970s British sitcoms with a more recent example, *The Office* (BBC 2001–3), with the aim of clarifying the relationship of narrative form to ideological and historical content. I have chosen to focus on the question of linear narrative development in sitcom: a vexed question in a genre that has traditionally been marked by, and has indeed in important respects relied on, a distinctive episodic circularity. One group of situation comedies in particular struck me as striving to find ways of exploring their own horizons of narrative possibility without having explicit recourse to standard modernist tactics of 'baring the device'. In the process they produce a pull-me-push-you relationship of linearity and seriality, realism and reflexivity. The essay grew in the writing, finally emerging as an attempt of sorts to explore situation comedy's political unconscious.

Taking sitcom seriously

By comparison with other forms of popular television drama, and notwithstanding its eternal popularity with programmers and audiences, sitcom remains notably underdiscussed. It may no longer be true that, as Mick Eaton asserted, 'there has been virtually nothing written about television situation comedy as a specifically televisual form' (1981: 26); none-the-less, a great deal of writing about sitcom still seems slightly embarrassed by what Paul Attalah characterises as 'the unworthiness of [its] object . . . It appears that in an undeserving medium, situation comedy constitutes a particularly undeserving form equalled only perhaps by the game show and the locally produced commercial' (2003 [1984]: 95). The standard critical strategies for relieving this embarrassment include, firstly, *the redemption of the exceptional object* – the discovery of an underlying seriousness of moral and ethical concerns, a depth of characterisation, high production values and quality of writing and performances and, not least, a strong degree of 'realism' in treatment of character that can 'elevate' a series such as *M*A*S*H* (CBS 1972–83) to 'a higher status than mere sitcom' (Mintz 1985: 113). A more sophisticated alternative approaches sitcom, in keeping with an influential strain in film genre theory, as *popular myth and social ritual*. Anthropologised, sitcom proves to reveal – through parodic articulation – social norms and dominant ideological values (see, for example, Marc 1997). The best of such readings avoid the uninflected 'reading-off' of political and sociocultural events and trends from the evolving characterisation of, say, women or ethnic minorities in sitcoms; nevertheless, they will always tend to limit sustained consideration of sitcom's formal or aesthetic properties.

An analysis organised around the social construction of genres will frequently prefer to treat the *forms* of sitcom as transparent givens through which socio-cultural *content* is encountered. This essay, by contrast, is primarily concerned with understanding sitcom form itself as the principal means whereby ideological encounters are staged and worked through. My discussion will focus on selected well-known popular sitcoms that have also drawn critical praise for their 'realistic' qualities. But rather than emphasising this 'realistic' dimension in order to redeem their lowly generic status – which would in fact merely replicate their own protagonists' futile aspirations – I will propose that these texts are characterised by an exploitation of sitcom's highly marked formal constraints as a means of exposing the very social truths on whose exclusion sitcom is formally predicated, and which its formal structures are engineered to obscure. It appears to me that this movement can be historically and ideologically situated in useful ways that can help us better understand the interplay of popular media forms with their socio-historical situation. I will approach this complex relationship through a discussion of sitcom's most obviously distinctive formal attribute, its narrative – or rather, non-narrative – structure.

Sitcom and narrative form

According to John Ellis, television narrative is principally constructed according to a principle of seriality rather than linearity, since 'the series implies the form of the dilemma, rather than that of resolution and closure' (1992: 160). Exemplifying Ellis's argument in a condensed way, sitcom poses problems for any narrative analysis that takes linearity as its presumed starting point, inasmuch as sitcom traditionally depends heavily on an unusual degree of circularity and even stasis in its basic situation. According to Lawrence Mintz, 'structure is the inevitable point of departure' for analysing sitcom (1985: 114), and most analyses comment on the ways in which the 'classic' sitcom pushes the general narrative tendencies of episodic series television to an extreme. What above all distinguishes sitcom is its obsessive circularity: the way in which week-in, week-out, it works through an adapted form of Todorov's equilibrium-disequilibrium-new-equilibrium model of narrative – a movement, not towards a *new* equilibrium but rather to a forceful restatement of the *existing* equilibrium, the narrative *status-quo-ante*. '[T]he sit-com relies upon a different form of repetition from the soap-opera serial – the situation is not allowed to *change* but is rather subjected to a recurring process of destabilisation-restabilisation in each episode' (Neale and Krutnik 1990: 235). Depending on the particular sitcom and/or the extremity of the narrative predicament the episode has imposed on the recurring characters, this restoration may be accomplished by (or behind) the closing credits, or in the indeterminate and textually unremarked – indeed unspeakable – period between episodes; accomplished, however, it must be. This is indeed what generically typifies the *situation* comedy: that the narrative events that occur during a given episode must not interfere with the central *situation* (or premise), once established at the start of a series, to the point of that situation's dissolution. This cyclical structure induces a peculiar amnesia, in which whatever lesson has been learnt one week is forgotten the next. In other words, even though teaching the principal character(s) a (moral, ethical, social) 'lesson' may be the central thrust of the series, it is the generically obligatory incorrigibility of the characters that underpins the continued life of the series itself. In 'The Builders', a first-season episode of *Fawlty Towers* (BBC, transmitted 26 September 1975), the shrewish Sybil Fawlty skewers just this, quite literally *foolish*, incapacity for growth on Basil's part:

> SYBIL: I'm sick to death of you! You never learn, do you?? You never, ever, learn! (*Hurls metal cashbox at Basil's head, narrowly missing him.*)

This situational crux has generally been interpreted in reference to hegemonic social ideologies. Sitcom's circularity betrays its inherent conservatism: narrative energies are directed towards containing transgression and reasserting norms (see Eaton 1981). This echoes Adorno's argument that the element of narrative 'predestination' in television generally expresses the movement under advanced capitalism away from free competition towards 'a virtually "closed" society into which one wants to be admitted or from which one fears to be rejected' (Adorno 1991 [1954]: 138). However, Virginia Wexman has argued interestingly that narrative analysis of sitcom, in laying a misplaced emphasis on linearity as a putative source of comic frustration (the protagonist's frustrated desire to change self and/or circumstances), overlooks sitcom's specific textual pleasures for the spectator, rewards that might better be understood synchronically and in terms of performativity:

> an analysis that attends to the effect of contrasting performance styles within individual programs is in a position to construct a more complex narrative model in which the issue is not simply beginnings and ending but tensions surrounding the development of the story as a whole, which are generated by the styles of its various characters. (Wexman 2003: 66)

Wexman's observations open up an important new field for formal narrative analysis of sitcom, grounded in the specific relationship of narrative structure and humour. Of course, humour is notoriously difficult to explain and unrewarding to analyse. None-the-less, it is striking how little attention has been paid to the way that what makes sitcoms funny – which is after all why people watch them – arises not only out of the basic situation and or premise (the mismatched couple or group, for example, or the dysfunctional or anomalous organisation) but also from the *formal* requirement for the premise to remain a narrative invariant whatever the specific plot complications of a given episode. Sitcom's formal properties do more than preserve the performative space for the comic interplay of pre-established types and characters. It is precisely *because* the characters are locked into (what would in 'real life' be) pathologies, compulsions and obsessions from which they have no capacity to escape or learn, that situations which might otherwise be experienced by audiences as painfully as they are by the characters themselves, are released into comedy. As in the classic cartoon *Tom and Jerry*, the absence of consequentiality – the assurance that pain will not persist, that regrets, guilt, shame and other psychic costs will not be exacted, and finally that growth is an impossibility – all liberate and legitimate our laughter. Thus, much humour in sitcom depends on, and is sustained by, the audience's assumptions of circularity.

Naturally, there are numerous exceptions to such a 'rule'. As *Yes, Minister* (BBC 1980–82, 1984) developed into *Yes, Prime Minister* (1986–88), for instance, the initial characterisation of neophyte minister Jim Hacker as altogether callow and easily defeated was modified to allow the cannier campaigner, seasoned by his progress through the corridors of power, to emerge at least temporarily triumphant from the odd skirmish with Sir Humphrey. In fact, a number of classic episodic sitcoms incorporated elements of developmental narrative. We may subdivide these into two types.

In the first, significant adjustments are made to the basic situation (premise) itself. Because of their gravity for the sitcom's fictive universe, such situational realignments typically take place at end of a season or 'between' seasons, the better to allow the viewer to absorb their implications and integrate them into the previously established diegesis. Once enacted, they constitute a new situational given, with no specifically serial element ensuing. While superficial shifts in location – for example, the redeployment of the Royal Artillery Concert Party from India to Burma for the third season of *It Ain't Half Hot, Mum* (BBC 1976–80) – barely qualify, the repeated changes to principal personnel over the three decades of *Last of the Summer Wine* (BBC 1973–) provide one obvious example of how this works. Another is the 'sequel series' – for example, *Whatever Happened to the Likely Lads?* (BBC 1973–74) or *George and Mildred* (Thames 1976–79) – which takes established characters and not only relocates them in space and/or time but also in some important way alters the relational dynamic. Even though a relationship of temporality and at least some measure of causality (to the earlier series and the characterisations established therein) is implied by the idea of the sequel, the newly or re-established situational parameters themselves enjoy the genre's characteristic non-progressivity.

A second class comprises serial elements 'proper', that is, ongoing narrative threads whose unfolding and resolution has consequences for the characters and situation (although such elements are problematic and need to be carefully controlled). In general, there is a correlation between a sitcom's aspirations to some degree of social and/or psychological realism and the consequent emergence of serial elements; that is, the broader and more grotesque the comic vein, the less a sitcom is likely to deepen and round out its characters in the name of psychological realism. The seaside-postcard stereotypes of *Are You Being Served?* (BBC 1973–83) for instance, any more than the pop caricatures of *Absolutely Fabulous* (BBC 1992–95, 2001–), neither require nor receive any suggestion of an 'inner world'. By contrast, the more comedy is generated from the interaction of dimensional individuals, the more their personalities, motivations, emotions and perceptions are explored in conventional dramatic fashion. Here 'comedian comedy' (heavily performative, often physical and gag-oriented) can be helpfully differentiated from 'character comedy' (comedy mediated through the relatively realistic rendering of dramatic characters and situations). It is axiomatic of 'character comedy' that the characters who are the object of comedy never themselves recognise the humour of their situation. To do so would in a sense place them in an impossible textual position as the audience of their own performance – a gesture that would seem to require the definitive transgression of the kinds of formal barriers that character-based sitcom, in common with other realist dramatic forms, maintains as a textual given. Such 'postmodern', non-character-based sitcoms as *The Young Ones* (BBC 1982–84) or the various *Blackadders* (BBC 1983–89), which in their different ways revel in reflexive, polysemic and intertextual display, have licence to dismantle such barriers more or less at will.

As Jane Feuer (1992) has pointed out, the movement from the 'classical' episodic model towards serial form may also be read in terms of ideological and market positioning: the pretensions to greater character dimensionality and growth marking both a claim on the kinds of sophistication and complexity traditionally valorised in 'serious' drama and an appeal to a specific and desirable audience demographic – upscale, affluent, sophisticated – whose own tastes are presumed to privilege 'depth'. Feuer's analysis of US sitcoms identifies a return of sorts during the 1990s from the 'thick' social universe of 1980s shows such as *Family Ties* (NBC 1982–89) to the flattened characters of early 1970s social satires such as *The Beverly Hillbillies* (CBS 1962–71). In both *Roseanne* (ABC 1988–97) and *The Simpsons* (Fox 1989–) 'the stars . . . are flat cartoon figures, in the case of *The Simpsons* quite literally. Roseanne Barr has been criticised for not knowing how to act, but that kind of criticism is probably more applicable in [a] sitcom that emphasizes fully developed characters' (Feuer 1992: 155).

Interestingly, Feuer also notes that such non-empathetic, two-dimensional characters might be ascribed a Brechtian 'estrangement' function in relation to the kinds of social conflicts and pathologies they parody and explore. Such devices – which were a favoured reference-point for 1970s screen theory intent on the construction of radical alternatives to 'classic realism'[1] – would typically be considered incompatible with any form of naturalism. Brecht's own preference for the comic mode as fundamentally anti-empathetic clearly chimes with the account offered above of sitcom circularity making possible humour through comic distancing. There is, however, a class of sitcom that produces a kind of estrangement not by recourse to the flattened characterisations Brecht himself favoured but rather through a deepening of comic naturalism, and which simultaneously intensifies both linearity, with its concomitantly extended psychological interiority, *and* episodic circularity. Such sitcoms manage to square the generically mandated impossibility of significant (psychological, emotional) growth with a drive towards a naturalistic exploration of character psychology. Moreover they do so, as paradoxical as it may seem, through introducing a linear narrative element in the only available way – via a degree of formal reflexivity more usually associated with the more freewheeling forms of comedian and 'disruptive' (modernist) comedy. In so doing, their protagonists are rendered *viewers* of their own situation rather than trapped, hamster-like, within the cages of their own predicament. All of this not only helps produce that specific combination of pathos and humour that typifies the British sitcom but also confronts sitcom's own narrative possibility, which in turn opens up a new field of political reference. I will explore this argument through a discussion of one of British sitcom's recognised 'classics', *Steptoe and Son* (BBC 1962–65 and 1970–74), treat *Porridge* (BBC 1974–77) in less depth, and conclude with a consideration of the award-winning *The Office* (BBC 2001–3), focusing on the persistence across these texts of similar formal concerns, understood as a response to sociohistorical conditions. Firstly, however, we will need to consider the key motif whereby this interaction of form and thematic content is accomplished in all three of these examples – the image of the *trap*.

Entrapment

It has been observed that the nature of British social experience – historically bound by particularly rigid and intractable class (hence lifestyle) structures – lends a particular intensity to sitcom's characteristic circularity. 'It is no coincidence that the themes of many (particularly British) sitcoms centre around social entrapment and frustration' (Baker 2003: 40). Whereas many US sitcoms from *I Love Lucy* (CBS/ITV 1951–61) to *The Cosby Show* (NBC 1984–92) and even, making due allowance for irony, *The Simpsons* aim to reveal the compensating power of love, friendship and familial solidarity in even the most limiting of circumstances, their British counterparts have typically allowed their protagonists to register unassuageable resentment, even rage, at their frustrated ambitions and thwarted desires. Forms of white male pathos, in particular, abound, even (perhaps especially) in the ostensibly complacent suburban sitcom (Medhurst 1997). The matter of British sitcom thus crystallises form and (social) content in the repeated dynamic of frustrated movement. From Hancock onwards, British sitcom has focused on protagonists whose ineradicable yet unrealisable desire to be different encounters its ultimate horizon of impossibility in the very limits of the form in which they have been conceived. *The Fall and Rise of Reginald Perrin* (BBC 1976–79) articulates this longing for transcendence very clearly, not merely in the details of Reggie's efforts to escape from and/or transform the Poets' Estate but importantly in the series' overall narrative arc, which enacts a kind of eternal return: at the end of each series (as well as behind the credits of each episode) Reggie finds himself re-enacting the same foredoomed emancipatory gesture – emblematically, abandoning his clothes on a Dorset beach. This not only returns Reggie to where he, and the series, started out (after each faked suicide and new identity or social role, Reggie is drawn ineluctably back to corporate suburbia), but in so doing locks the series itself – presented for these purposes as a serial – firmly back into the unforgiving generic logic of sitcom (Fox 2000).

Sitcom's structuring opposition between what is and what may (not) be centres on the contrast between 'inside' – reliable, comfortable and familial, but also limiting, stifling and regressive – against an 'outside' that is rarely actually seen but is mainly figured primarily in the protagonist's (and the audience's) imagination. In classic 1970s and 1980s sitcom this finds a key formal articulation in the use of the studio for the main action, with standing sets and three-camera setups, and – usually brief – interpolated sequences shot on 16mm film for the characters' ventures into the world outside the domestic, workplace or familial space.[2] The world outwith the studio is charged with a heterotopic allure: it is a place where different rules might apply.[3] Yet equally it is a space where the sitcom protagonist manifestly does not belong.

The rigidity of such a structure, variously iterated across visual style and narrative structure as well as narrative content, thus sets clear spatial and narrative boundaries to the possibilities for growth that sitcom characters can experience, limiting the 'evolution from flat to round characters over the life of a situation comedy' that helped secure, for example, *M*A*S*H*'s critical reputation (Mintz 1985: 113). Yet those British sitcoms in which the situational 'trap' is most emphasised are the same ones whose 'realistic' depictions of character have been singled out in their critical reception. It is through the apparently paradoxical textual process thus set in play that the core ideological concerns of this kind of sitcom finally stand revealed.

The comedy of limits and the limits of comedy: *Steptoe and Son* and *Porridge*

Steptoe and Son's considerable reputation relies importantly on the perception that its creators, Ray Galton and Alan Simpson, were committed to a version of what Peter Goddard terms 'sitcom naturalism':

> Galton and Simpson again clung firmly to the notion of 'reality', reinforced with the casting of straight actors in the leading roles, to the extent that *The Times*' television correspondent could write in 1962: '*Steptoe and Son* virtually obliterates the division between drama and comedy'. (Goddard 1991: 86)

Neale and Krutnik's fine analysis of the show, however, stresses not only the naturalism but the also unusual formal rigidity – specifically, the emphatic circularity – of *Steptoe*'s episodic plot structures, which raise this generic convention to the status of a natural law: whereas 'in the majority of sit-coms the implications of this structural necessity are played down, in *Steptoe* they are frequently made explicit' (1990: 255). One of Harold Steptoe's speeches from the 1972 seventh-season episode 'Divided We Stand' exemplifies this structural self-consciousness:

HAROLD: We seem to have reached our usual impasse, don't we?

ALBERT: If you like.

HAROLD: You won't give way on anything, will you? You don't give a toss what colour we 'ave. You just got to go against me, don't you? If I wanted flock wallpaper in the bog, you wouldn't. Whatever I want, you don't.

ALBERT: I'm entitled to me opinion.

HAROLD: (*Angrily*) I mean, it's not just the decorations, it's – it's *everything*. Every idea I have for any improvements – improvements to the house, improvements to the business – you're agin' it.

(*Beat. Harold starts to walk menacingly towards Albert.*)

You frustrate me in everything I try to do. You are a dyed-in-the-wool, *fascist*, reactionary, spoiled little know-your-place, don't-rise-above-yourself, don't-get-out-of-your-hole, complacent little *turd*!

This speech neatly encapsulates many of the qualities that have made *Steptoe* intriguing to critics since the series first aired – not least the complex transmutation into comedy of quite realistically imagined (and performed) and readily recognisable experiences of familial frustration and hostility. Both content *and structure* mimic Harold's repeated narrative predicament – the aspirational grandiosity of his rhetoric (paralleling his socially upwardly mobile affectations) brought firmly back down to working-class earth by the concluding coarse demotic ('little *turd!*'). Neale and Krutnik (who also quote this speech) note that 'often behind the broadest comedy in the show are actions which would ordinarily be branded disturbing and cruel', and that the series generally is typified by 'its combination of crudity, cruelty, and revenge' (1990: 259–261). In fact, the fine line between humour and grim psychological realism trod by *Steptoe*'s comedy of frustration and entrapment was immediately and predictably seized upon by critics as a means of redeeming the series from sitcom status. (The series has often been the object of flattering 'high culture' comparisons, for example to Artaud's Theatre of Cruelty[4]).

What I want to stress here, however, is not the series's psychological acuity but its reflexive intensity. What, after all, is 'the usual impasse' invoked by Harold if not the very series premise itself? Harold's bitter outburst reflects the edge of growing desperation that by 1972 increasingly appeared to sharpen the – now nearly forty–year-old – Harold's tirades as he saw the dreams of freedom that had already eluded his decade-younger self receding yet further beyond the domain of the possible. Might it also be that Harold's frustrations are intensified by the atemporality of the classic sitcom that disallows any direct reference to the inescapable and visible passing of time across the series's twelve–year run (on television and radio)? In fact, this inadmissible linearity does find masked expression – through the increasingly baroque nature of the show's plots and narrative situations and through the growing reflexive dimension that accompanies them. In 'Divided We Stand' Harold's response to the 'impasse' he protests here is the patent absurdity of physically dividing the house into two 'separate but equal' areas. Quite apart from the possibilities this offers for inspired comic business – the television control knobs are on Albert's 'side', for instance, thus enabling him to frustrate Harold's planned high-cultural prime-time communion with Margot Fonteyn and the Bolshoi – this extravagant device materialises the series's premise, of intolerable yet unalterable proximity.

In the next broadcast episode, 'The Desperate Hours', deservedly amongst *Steptoe*'s most celebrated, the Steptoes find themselves first hostage, then hosts, to a pair of escaped convicts whose circumstances exactly mirror their own – Johnny, the younger felon (played appropriately enough by the future Reginald Perrin, Leonard Rossiter) inescapably and ruinously bound to a succubus-like older man. The episode relies heavily on intertextuality (a more unusual strategy in the pre-video age than subsequently, as for instance ubiquitously in *The Simpsons*), invoking and inverting the eponymous 1955 Bogart melodrama: whereas the film's self-destructive trio of convict brothers represent a parodic inversion of the bourgeois family they hold hostage, the escapees from Wormwood Scrubs hold up a clarifying rather than a distorting lens to the Steptoes. Recognising their own situation reprised in the relationship between the two convicts, Harold and Albert become empathetic viewers of their own, decidedly uncomic, drama. Harold urges Johnny to abandon the older man, whose continued company will doom them to be recaptured; Albert urges youth's obligation to age. Each urges on 'his' counterpart as a means of securing vicariously the definitive victory that in their own world – here constituted as a recurring 'real' against the 'reflection' of the guest performers – is necessarily denied. At the end of the episode, the convicts accept the inevitable and set off to turn themselves in, a resolution experienced by Harold as (yet another) painful defeat.

> ALBERT: They've gone.
> HAROLD (*quietly*): Yeah . . .
>   (*The howling of the wind outside increases.*)
> ALBERT: I'm glad they stayed together.
> HAROLD (*bitterly*): Yeah. I expect you are. (*Long pause*) Well . . . better go lock up the cages . . . (*heads out into the yard*)

Behind the closing credits a parallel montage depicts the Steptoes and the convicts bedding down for the night in their respective – literal and figurative – prisons.

The prison metaphor that hovers around *Steptoe and Son* and is briefly crystallised in 'The Desperate Hours' provides the literal premise of another much-praised 1970s BBC sitcom, *Porridge*, and a brief comparison might be instructive. In general, Dick Clement and Ian La Frenais's humour in *Porridge* (and elsewhere) is a good deal more benign than Galton and Simpson's. The convicts in *Porridge* are less persistently oppressed by their actual confinement than Harold Steptoe is by his social or familial shackles; the series emphasises old lag Fletcher's canny manipulation of the ostensibly 'closed' system rather than his subjugation by it.

Yet on occasion *Porridge* touches the desperation that was *Steptoe*'s abiding keynote; and, when it does, it is striking that the fabric of the 'sitcom naturalism', to which otherwise the series cleaves more consistently than *Steptoe*, is breached, inviting in a kind of inherently reflexive imaginative play. In episode three, 'A Night In', old lag Fletcher explains to his novice cellmate Lennie Godber, pining for the freedoms of a Saturday night, his strategy of imaginative survival:

> If you're keen, we could go out, you know. Oh yeah, I could ring up a couple of birds, you know . . . couple of them darlings that dance on *Top of the Pops*, know what I mean? . . . We could ring up and meet them at an Italian restaurant, couldn't we, eh? Up West? Lovely. Then we could go on somewhere from there, nightclubs, know what I mean? Dance till dawn. Then back to their luxurious penthouse flat and wallop!
> (*Beat*)
> Trouble is, I done all that last night and I'm a bit knackered. Anyhow, we'd have to get all ponced up, you'd have to darn the 'oles in me socks, wouldn't you? Nah, why don't we just have a – a quiet night in, eh?

Fletcher's recourse to escapist fantasy as a strategy for enduring the reality of incarceration can also be seen as a reflexive gesture that by rendering 'outside' (of Slade Prison and of the sitcom) as something available only in fantasy reinforces the viewer's consciousness of the operative constraints of the 'inside' (at once diegetic and generic). Noticeably, for a sitcom widely praised for its character realism, *Porridge* mostly ignores the obvious, indeed the sole, important temporal dimension one might expect to structure the prisoners' lives – the duration of their incarceration. While the credits remind the viewer of Fletcher's five-year sentence ('the maximum term allowed for these offences'), elsewhere any sense of progress towards parole is emphatically downplayed. Lennie's rueful rejoinder that 'I've got 698 quiet nights in to go' is exceptional in the first and second seasons. In the third and final season – Fletcher never served out his full five years on screen, being released into the sequel series *Going Straight* (BBC 1978) having apparently had two years lopped off his sentence – Lennie's approaching parole introduced a progressive narrative element. Upon Lennie's release, Fletcher announces his intention to serve out his own remaining time quietly and trouble-free – a declaration upon which *Porridge* ended its run. It is as if the incorrigible recidivist Fletcher's new acquiescence in constraint paradoxically signals a release into temporality that 'liberates' the circular sitcom narrative into a linear progress it cannot support. Although nothing in the concrete situation has irrevocably changed (Fletcher is promised a new young cellmate upon Lennie's release, a device that seems to herald a traditional change of personnel in a new season), by explicitly anticipating a future that, unlike Harold Steptoe's, will definitely arrive, the series fractures the circularity upon which its fragile balance of drama and comedy relies. Once Fletcher accepts the linear momentum of his sentence, he ceases to resist – and he stops being funny.

Porridge and *Steptoe and Son* both foreground sitcom's circularity by centring their narratives on acts of resistance to a diegetic snare that explicitly analogises the genre's paradigmatic structure. In each, the 'naturalistic' deepening of characterisation encounters those limits through the protagonist's dramatic experience of frustration and constraint. In each, the release into movement, the flow of temporality after which Harold and Fletcher both in their different ways strive, takes on an unexpectedly ambivalent coloration. For Fletcher, as we have seen, while temporality will release him from the suspended time of prison, entering the flow of time entails acquiescence in the coercive forms of authority that his play of fantasy has hitherto resisted. For Harold, the case is subtly different: while the moving world 'outside' remains the unattainable focus of his desire, it is also true that it is time's passing – the unmentionable passing of the years not only of the Steptoes but of *Steptoe* itself – that lends his drive to escape its edge of growing desperation. The limited freedom accessible in these sitcoms is to be found neither in escape nor in submission but rather in the *tension* that holds movement and stasis in an unstable and delicate equilibrium and allows these sitcom protagonists to encounter a fleeting and unstable liberation from both the conventions that bind them and those they seek to adopt.

What remains is the more difficult task of pinning down the political valences of these formal articulations. It is something of a cliché – which does not mean it is untrue – to note that *Steptoe*, like other 1960s and early 1970s sitcoms, reflects concerns around 'class and social mobility or the lack of it' (Bowes 1990: 129). I would argue, however, that, while class is certainly at the heart of the painful laughter these programmes so often inspire, the root cause lies deeper than superficial improvement of material or social circumstances. And perhaps the question can best be addressed from the perspective of a contemporary social world where we are repeatedly asked to believe that, in the struggle of social life, class 'no longer matters'.

The sitcom at the end of history: *The Office*

> You can't change circumstances. (Tim, episode six, *The Office*, second series)

Superficially, both *Steptoe* and *Porridge* are working-class sitcoms, a category that flourished throughout the 1970s, across the ideological (and quality) spectrum from *Citizen Smith* (BBC 1977–80) to *On the Buses* (LWT 1969–73) and *Love Thy Neighbour* (Thames 1972–76). Such series – usually urban, sometimes quite aggressively proletarian – offered a strong contrast to the cosy (though perhaps equally stifling) middle-management world of the suburban sitcom. Yet the abjection of the subjects of both *Steptoe* and *Porridge* at once accentuates and problematises this class identity. Both the near-destitute Steptoes and the inmates of Slade Prison stand to an extent outside of the interpellations of an expanding consumer society even as they also testify to its human costs.[5]

The most successful 1980s sitcom, *Only Fools and Horses* (BBC 1981–), displayed obvious continuities with the working-class sitcom tradition even as its narratives reflected Thatcherite preoccupations with individual self-advancement at the expense of class or traditional workplace solidarity. By the time Tony Blair's 'New' Labour government took power in 1997, however, the partial destruction of British industrial and manufacturing capacity, and of the working-class culture those industries had supported, ensured that sitcom naturalism would also have to shift its social orientation. Under New Labour, the ideology of the 'meritocratic' society encouraged the shift in aspirations towards white-collar jobs, however insecure and low-skilled, in the ever-expanding service and financial sectors. The language of ministerial speeches and official publications promoted an image of a constantly changing, always evolving workplace that required a comparable willingness to re-educate and re-invent on the part of the employee – a social universe of restless mutability apparently far removed from the lumpen stasis of *Steptoe* and *Porridge*. Over two series airing in 2001–2, *The Office*, the BBC's most highly praised sitcom for several years, seemed perfectly to capture this renovated milieu.[6]

Depicting life in the offices of Slough-based paper manufacturers Wernham-Hogg, the series – written by Ricky Gervais, who also starred as office manager David Brent, and Steven Merchant – not only captured the distinctive suburban trading-estate world of early twenty-first-century southern England but in the process updated the sitcom's time-honoured visual style. Abandoning the straight studio-bound mode of the classic sitcom, *The Office*'s key conceit was that the series was an office-based documentary, or 'docusoap' – a ubiquitous genre of the late 1990s that had in some measure displaced sitcoms from their traditional dominance of prime-time entertainment. Focusing typically on quotidian rather than glamorous or unusual workplaces and professions – driving instructors, trainee nurses, airport service personnel (not airline crews), even parking attendants – docusoaps blended 'fly-on-the-wall' observational techniques with direct-to-camera interviews in highly structured narratives that, soap-style, edited together several clearly identifiable simultaneous narrative lines, often focusing on individuals encountering and (not invariably) rising to professional and personal challenges. Unapologetically interventionist, docusoaps sidelined traditional documentary preoccupations with objectivity in favour of a clear agenda to render reality as entertainment (Bruzzi 2000: 75–98). *The Office* is, therefore, a clear act of generic reterritorialisation, inasmuch as it folds the new fashion for reality-as-entertainment back into traditional light entertainment's champion genre.

The series centred on the character of office manager David Brent, a self-styled 'maverick' whose self-image as entertainer and motivational firecracker was predictably undermined by his incompetence in both roles. Brent's façade of brio and self-confidence was easily penetrated to expose wells of insecurity and fear of failure, experiences that became increasingly and painfully central to the second series, when Brent was confronted by the arrival of a new boss and an intake of unimpressed staff from another branch of the firm. The most important supporting character was Tim, a university drop-out now on the cusp of his thirties, whose insistent wry self-deprecation arose out of his own candid awareness of his aversion to personal or professional risk.

The Office situated itself firmly in the *Steptoe* tradition of 'painful' comedy: many if not most of the scenes of Brent's very public failures made for deeply uncomfortable viewing (the absence of a studio audience and laughter track underlined this), and the second series in particular drove towards a conclusion of quite astonishing bleakness. This bleakness in turn drew heavily on the series' abandonment of the sitcom's traditional episodic circularity for a progressive narrative development of the work and personal relationships at Wernham-Hogg befitting the docu-soap style the show so acutely aped. The second series focused on two narrative lines: Brent's hastening downward spiral into eventual redundancy, and the simmering but unacknowledged romance between Tim and office receptionist Dawn. Brent's foregrounded – and increasingly vital to his crumbling self-regard – attempts to cast himself as a (comic) *performer*, through either his disastrous workplace stand-ups or his short-lived and predictably catastrophic second career as a motivational speaker, recall the reflexive aspects of Harold Steptoe's desperate attempts to break the cycle of sameness and entombment, while Tim's self-mocking awareness of his own endemic timidity, the flipside of Brent's blind self-aggrandisement but fuelled by the same desperation, suggests that in *The Office*'s zero-sum world, to stay is as self-destructive as to go.

In the series's bitterly ironic conclusion, generic constraints are explicitly foregrounded by moments of dramatic crisis that threaten to break them. Dawn's resignation and stated intention to 'start over' in Florida with her lumpish fiancé Terry finally impels Tim to confront Dawn with their hitherto inadmissible mutual desire and plead with her to stay – a scene that unfolds mutely, half-glimpsed through Venetian blinds, as Tim has taken off his body-mike and drawn Dawn out of camera range (the documentary fiction is maintained as the camera frantically searches for a vantage point). We seem on the verge of a denouement of romantic redemption and transcendence. Dawn, however, says no to Tim, choosing the satisfactions and security, however limited, of life with Terry. The last shot of the entire series shows a dejected-looking Dawn answering the phone at the reception desk once again – 'Hello, Wernham-Hogg' – in a coda that recalls the bleak restoration of the familial status quo at the end of *Steptoe*'s 'The Desperate Hours'. Brent, on the other hand, is compelled into a self-reinvention he fears and recoils from, reduced to begging tearfully for a stay of execution. Our assumption of course is that Brent will be annihilated by the world 'outside', a world we glimpse briefly in the weekly opening montage –significantly, devoid of a single human figure – before returning to the sanctuary, however sterile, of the office. Brent's exclusion not only definitively fractures *The Office*'s situational premise, terminating the series, it also recalls key moments from *Steptoe* in that it is played entirely 'straight'. Brent's final desperation is hard to watch and impossible to laugh at; unlike, say, Harold Steptoe's speech in 'Divided We Stand' quoted above, there is no concluding gag or verbal slip to qualify the grimness of the situation.

In this way, *The Office* recalls both *Steptoe* and that earlier white-collar comedy *Reginald Perrin* both in its setting, its serial dimension and its ultimate reimposition of an inescapably circular narrative arc. Moreover, it shares with those 'serious' sitcoms a large degree of formal self-consciousness – primarily through the 'mockumentary' format. *The Office*, however, differs in that it quite explicitly locates the source of sitcom's characteristic circularity not in an unspecified social pressure but as an undisguised reflection of the working environment itself. The airless, timeless quality of the office is repeatedly stressed in interstitial general shots of the office floor, bathed in artificial light and oblivious to climate or time of day, like an underground dystopian city in a science-fiction film. In these shots, the open-plan work-stations are frequently and inexplicably abandoned, underlining the uncanny quality of the scene; when staff are visible, they are often all but immobile – scrolling screensavers provide the only motion in the frozen underworld. A repeated close-up of the photocopier's output tray cycling for ever in mid-collation encapsulates this image of the post-industrial workplace, all human agency rendered redundant in a society governed by the quiet, undemonstrative adjustments of computer-based decision-making. In this static, sterile environment, the jargon of career development and the shifts in status (newly arrived Neil as Brent's new boss, creepy nerd Gareth duly replacing Brent upon the latter's redundancy) cruelly belie the realities of a marginal post-industrial business.

Conclusion

In Trevor Griffiths's 1975 play *Comedians* veteran comic Eddie Waters urges his class of aspiring stand-ups to forgo the cheap laughter that caters to prejudice and social convention, and to pursue a humanist comic vision that challenges such values head-on: 'A true joke, a comedian's joke, has to do more than release tension, it has to *liberate* the will and the desire, its has to *change the situation*' (Griffiths 1975: 20; emphasis in original). To some extent the sitcoms considered in this essay clearly relate to the ideal Waters invokes. Yet of course, as we have seen, 'changing the situation' is the one thing that sitcom *cannot* achieve, not if it is to remain a sitcom. It is as if, in a world of surface and stereotype, the aspiration to anything deeper itself constitutes a transgression that must be punished by its visible and perpetual frustration. Harold Steptoe's aspirations go beyond self-improvement: he longs not only to be the kind of person that 'someone like him' can never be, but above and beyond that to be a *person*. Even David Brent's pathetic vanity and aggression betrays the reality of his humiliation and terror, qualities that like Tim's self-contempt render him acutely and vulnerably human in a social universe where quotidian 'reality' denies human experiences and replaces them with myths of professional fulfilment. Situation comedy articulates the longing to be fully human in a world that denies full humanity.

Notes

1 See Stam (2001: 140–5) for a summary of these debates.
2 There are obvious exceptions in both directions (excessive enclosure or free-dom of movement): for example, *Are You Being Served?* almost never ventures outside the studio, while most of the action in *Last of the Summer Wine* takes place outdoors on the Yorkshire Dales, and on film.
3 On the 'heteretopia' see Foucault (1986).
4 Neale and Krutnik cite Stefan Zweig's novel *Beware of Pity* as well as the *Arabian Nights* tale 'The Old Man of the Sea'; without especially wanting to add to this list of elevating parallels – and Galton and Simpson themselves have always derided and denied such 'high culture' models – I would suggest that one obvious point of comparison for the Steptoes' inextricable compact is Beckett's coupled clowns, handcuffed in mutual loathing and utter dependency, in his plays of the previous decade, for example Lucky and Pozzo in *Waiting for Godot* (1954) and still more Clov and Hamm in *Endgame* (1958).
5 Fletcher twice makes reference to his youthful 'Marxist phase' (his eldest daughter was conceived behind Karl Marx's tomb in Highgate Cemetery).
6 A one-off Christmas special edition of *The Office* aired in 2003.

References

Adams, P. (1993), '*Yes, Prime Minister:* "The Ministerial Broadcast"': social reality and cosmic realism in popular television drama', in G. W. Brandt (ed.), *British Television Drama in the 1980s*, Cambridge: Cambridge University Press.

Adorno, T. W. (1991[1954]), 'How to look at television', in J. M. Bernstein (ed.), *The Culture Industry: Selected Essays on Mass Culture*, London: Routledge.

Attalah, P. (2003 [1984]), 'The unworthy discourse: situation comedy in televi-sion', in J. Morreale (ed.), *Critiquing the Sitcom: A Reader*, Syracuse: Syracuse University Press.

Baker, J. (2003), *Teaching TV Sitcom* London: BFI.

Bowes, M. (1990), 'Only when I laugh', in A. Goodwin and G. Whannel (eds), *Understanding Television*, London: Routledge.

Bruzzi, S. (2000), *New Documentary: A Critical Introduction*, London: Routledge.

Eaton, M. (1981), 'Television Situation Comedy', *Screen* 22, 61–89.

Ellis, J. (1992), *Visible Fictions* (rev. ed.), London: Routledge.

Feuer, J. (1986), 'Narrative form in American network television', in C. MacCabe (ed.), *High Theory/Low Culture: Analyzing Popular Television and Film*, Man-chester: Manchester University Press.

Feuer, J. (1992), 'Genre study and television', in R. C. Allen (ed.), *Channels of Dis-course, Reassembled*, London and New York: Routledge.

Feuer, J. (2001), 'Situation comedy, part 2', in G. Creeber (ed.), *The Television Genre Book*, London: BFI.

Foucault, M. (1986), 'Of other spaces', *Diacritics* 16:1, 22–27.

Fox, C. (2000), 'The emancipatory strategies of Reginald Perrin', in J. Bignell, S. Lacey and M. Macmurraugh-Kavanagh (eds) *British Television Drama: Past, Present and Future*, Basingstoke: Palgrave Macmillan.

Goddard, P. (1991), '*Hancock's Half-hour*: a watershed in British television comedy', in J. Corner (ed.), *Popular Television in Britain: Studies in Cultural History*, London: BFI.

Griffiths, T., (1975), *Comedians*, London: Faber.

Grote, D. (1983), *The End of Comedy: The Sit-Com and the Comedic Tradition*, Hamden, Connecticut: Shoestring.

Jameson, F. (1981), *The Political Unconscious: Narrative as a Socially Symbolic Act*, Ithaca: Cornell University Press.

Marc, D. (1997), *Comic Visions: Television Comedy and American Culture*, 2nd ed, Oxford: Blackwell.

Medhurst, A. (1997), 'Negotiating the gnome zone: versions of suburbia in British popular culture', in R. Silverstone (ed.), *Visions of Suburbia*, London: Routledge.

Mintz, L. E. (1985), 'Situation comedy', in B. G. Rose (ed.), *TV Genres: A Handbook and Reference Guide*, Westport, Connecticut: Greenwood.

Morreale, J. (ed.) (2003), *Critiquing the Sitcom: A Reader*, Syracuse: Syracuse University Press.

Neale, S., and F. Krutnik (eds) (1990), *Popular Film and Television Comedy*, London: Routledge.

Seidman, S. (1981), *Comedian Comedy: A Tradition in Hollywood Film*, Ann Arbor: University of Michigan Research Press.

Stam, R. (2000), *Film Theory: An Introduction*, Oxford: Blackwell.

Wexman, V. (2003), 'Returning from the moon: Jackie Gleason and the carnivalesque', in J. Morreale (ed.), *Critiquing the Sitcom: A Reader*, Syracuse: Syracuse University Press.

Internet sites

The complete scripts of the *Steptoe and Son* episodes quoted in this essay, 'Divided We Stand' and 'The Desperate Hours', are available online at: www.mgnet.karoo.net/steptoeepdividedwestand.htm and www.mgnet.karoo.net/steptoeepdiesparate.htm.

2

Remembering *Butterflies*: the comic art of housework

Julia Hallam

In the autumn of 2000 the original cast of Carla Lane's *Butterflies* (BBC 1978–83), Wendy Craig (Ria Parkinson), Geoffrey Palmer (Ben Parkinson), Nicholas Lyndhust (Adam Parkinson) and Andrew Hall (Russell Parkinson), reassembled to celebrate Ria's sixtieth birthday as part of the BBC's annual charity appeal *Comic Relief*. *Butterflies* was a domestic situation comedy centred on the boredom and frustration of a 'typical' 1970s suburban housewife (white, middle-class and southern English) who teeters on the brink of having an affair but, overcome by guilt, finds herself unable to commit adultery. Initially screened on BBC2, it was a surprise hit that ran to four six-part series between 1978 and 1983; subsequently the series has had numerous reruns on UK terrestrial and cable satellite channels. The constant recycling of 'old' situation comedies and their apparently enduring appeal has provoked surprisingly little academic interest; the complex pleasures of viewing, re-viewing and remembering *Butterflies* are discussed in this essay. Watching *Butterflies* again after a period of more than twenty years, I was surprised by the vehemence of Ria's frustration with her comfortable lifestyle; by comparison with other British domestic sitcoms of the day, such as *Bless This House* (ITV 1971–76) and *Terry and June* (BBC1 1979–87), *Butterflies'* focus on the point of view of a female character was uncharacteristic. Usually in these sitcoms, the wife was the butt of her husband's discontent and disappointment; themes of ageing, domestic entrapment and frustrated desire are fertile ground for verbal gags and one-liners delivered at her expense. In *Butterflies*, writer Carla Lane breaks the frame of traditional situation comedy to explore these themes from the wife's perspective, juxtaposing the comedy of Ria's situation with elements of romance and melodrama. This account explores the historical contexts of production of this ground-breaking series and the socio-cultural contexts in which it was watched and enjoyed, drawing on research in the BBC's written archives and comments solicited from a small group of viewers about their memories of the series.

Work on television audiences has focused on questions about the ways in which specific programmes and genres appeal to different audiences, with feminist work in particular exploring the feminine and feminist pleasures and anxieties of watching soap opera. A few studies have sought to rediscover the female audience for different genres and earlier periods, such as notable accounts of the US context from Spigel (1992), D'Acci (1994) and Haralovich (1992), with Thumim (1995, 2002) contributing studies from a British perspective. In her work of reconstructing the gender positions of the 1950s television audience, Thumim emphasises that 'we can't really know how it was, but we can propose: and here we are obliged to recognise what interests are served by one set of propositions or another ... we need to note not only what is "known", "named", "remembered", and by whom, but also why' (Thumim 1995: 54). The materials assembled for analysis here are part of a pilot project designed to offer a tentative glimpse of why viewers remember and re-view 'old' television: what pleasures did or does *Butterflies* offer its viewers, what do viewers remember about the series and why? The focus here is on memories from letters and questionnaires solicited from female viewers; these are used, in the spirit of my original request, as contributions to a history of the programme.

There is little doubt that *Butterflies* appealed primarily to a female audience; the BBC's in-house audience research department tracked responses to *Butterflies* during the transmission of the first two series on BBC2 in 1978 and 1979; *Butterflies* was watched by more than eight million people, 59 per cent of whom were women (BBCWA SP 84/44/84/19). In 1982, the BBC's light entertainment department was interested in finding out whether women watched situation comedies and what their preferences were; in 1984, the Broadcasting Research Department compiled a full review of their data on audiences for situation comedy. These accounts, although not without problems in terms of how data was collected and analysed, were compiled to provide the BBC with information about the role of situation comedy in meeting their public service remit through 'penetration' of the audience (their term).[1]

These official accounts are usefully complemented by a second body of material, memories of *Butterflies* solicited from female viewers in 2001 through the tried and tested means of advertising in a women's magazine.

Readers were invited to write to me if they wanted to contribute to a project that would write *Butterflies* into television history.[2] Twenty-eight women responded either by letter or by e-mail; given the nature of my request, it is no surprise that these respondents are full of praise for *Butterflies* and eager to convey what they liked about the series. Their responses were used to formulate a questionnaire that was completed by a further self-selected random group of women; the aim of this questionnaire was to extend the invitation to comment on the programme outside the framing context provided by the magazine letter. Questionnaires were snowballed amongst three small groups of respondents: office workers on Merseyside, members of Yorkshire Women's Institute and self-identified lesbian women, generating a further seventeen respondents.

The letters and questionnaires were used to identify the principal themes for commentary and discussion based on each respondent's comments and observations; principal issues to emerge that were mentioned by virtually everybody include praise for the writing and performances, questions raised by maternal redundancy and ebbing confidence due to loss of physical attractiveness and ageing and the ongoing conflict between personal desire and family responsibility. The exercise was not designed to constitute self-selected respondents as 'typical' viewers of *Butterflies*; there was no attempt to ensure that the respondents were a representative sample either of women 'in general' or of those who may have watched the series. There were some surprises, however. I expected a clear generational difference to emerge between the letter writers (readers of *Woman's Own*) and the office workers. This was not the case; only a small number of the letter writers claimed to be fifty-five or older, indicating that most respondents were in their twenties or early thirties when the series was broadcast initially. There were no obvious differences between this group's memories and those of older respondents; nor were there significant differences between married and single women or heterosexual and gay women. The most notable differences between respondents' interpretations of *Butterflies* surfaced through perspectives informed by class-consciousness, although there was no necessary link between this perspective and the commentators' own attribution of their social status. Respondents were asked whether they considered their position in life to be similar to Ria's in terms of material circumstances, personal situations and cultural background; the majority of respondents claimed they were similar, although a significant minority claimed they had been working-class or had become middle-class. Changes in material, personal and cultural circumstances make little difference in how *Butterflies* is remembered *in general*; the themes frequently commented on by the majority of respondents (most commented on more than one) are issues such as freedom, entrapment, guilt, responsibility and choice, and the ways in which these are explored through the central motifs of the script, fear of ageing and romantic fantasy. For some women, the initial invitation to write to me about *Butterflies* was perhaps an opportunity to demonstrate their knowledges and competencies as cultural critics, while other respondents regretted that they did not consider themselves equipped with what they considered the 'formal' tools of critical appreciation but wanted to demonstrate their support for the series because, in the words of one respondent, 'it brilliantly exposed the situation that many of us so-called happily married women found ourselves in'.

Sitcom and the female audience

Most respondents consider *Butterflies* a 'superior' domestic sitcom in comparison with other popular favourites such as *Terry and June, George and Mildred* (Thames 1976–79) and *The Good Life* (BBC1 1975–78) although these shows were also considered enjoyable. Several people termed *Butterflies* 'an all-time favourite'; Hazel Hawford thought it 'the best comedy of its time' and Pam Gamble insisted that 'the programme has a place in TV history and must be recognised'. Critical concerns are framed within traditional humanistic evaluations and judgements that seek to recognise writers and performers as talented individuals. Major sources of pleasure in *Butterflies* are the writing (Carla Lane's script) and the actors' performance skills, particularly those of Wendy Craig and Geoffrey Palmer; everyone, irrespective of age differences or other obvious variables such as social class, commented on the high quality of the writing and acting. The former was regarded as 'excellent – unlike modern sit-coms', 'the best thing Carla Lane ever wrote', 'the combination of comedy and drama a truly brilliant piece by Carla Lane', 'funny but equally sad', 'a wry slice of life excellently written'. For many of these respondents, Wendy Craig's depiction of a woman fast approaching middle-age was the key to the series's success: A. Hanson comments that 'thousands of us menopausal so-called happily married women could associate with her'; Glenda O'Donnell, 'Ria portrayed something we all feel but pretend we don't'. Evaluations oscillated between reference to the series's 'believability' (expectations of the ways in which someone like Ria might behave if she was in a similar situation in everyday life) and the professional skills drawn on by Lane, Craig and the ensemble cast to create the script in performance, some comments emphasising the symbiotic relationship between the writer and the actors (only one person mentioned direction).[3]

Feminist analysis and interpretations of sitcom have consistently pointed to the tension between the performance of the characters and the (simplistic) narrative form of the genre, particularly in sitcoms dominated by 'unruly' female characters such as Lucy in *I Love Lucy* (CBS/ITV 1951–61), Roseanne in *Roseanne* (US 1989–97) and Patsy and Edina in *Absolutely Fabulous* (BBC 1992–5, 2001–). Jane Feuer argues that the unruly woman sitcom forms a persistent thread in the genre since the 1950s, with the unconventional and disruptive behaviour of the female clowns at their centre a source of potential transcendence from the containment of the form. Drawing on arguments that posit the ideological containment of the sitcom formula, she suggests that the outrageousness of the physical gags may overcome the return to domesticity that inevitably closes the series every week and that these are often the moments that one remembers (Feuer 2001: 68). Arguably, however, Wendy Craig's performance lacks the absurdist element of slapstick and anarchic carnivalesque disruption to everyday life that typifies this strand of sitcom; Ria is a more timid, conventional character whose actions and thoughts reside squarely in the realms of the possible. Domestic sitcom in 1970s Britain was considered by some academic critics to be one of the most conventional of all television genres, its repetitive return to the same situation week after week reinforcing the white, male-dominated heterosexual status quo in a society slow to adjust to the changing order of the postwar world. Medhurst and Tuck, for example, argue that most sitcoms ignore the fragmentary nature of modern life, envisaging an idealised organic nation by sanitising a past era (*Dad's Army*, BBC1 1968–77) or by removing any disturbing contemporary issues from the 'timeless nowness of television situations' (*Terry and June*). These programmes are stuck in a pre-Wolfenden, pre-'permissiveness', pre-feminism 1950s time warp that effaces broader, more inclusive notions of 'Britishness' by perpetuating outmoded forms of entertainment (Medhurst and Tuck 1982: 45). By comparison, imported US sitcoms such as *The Mary Tyler Moore Show* (CBS 1970–77, BBC 1971–72) and *Rhoda* (CBS 1974–78, BBC2 1974–81) seem positively ground-breaking with their focus on the working and domestic lives of their leading female protagonists and inclusion of Jewish characters. Drawing on liberal definitions of feminism as personal freedom and individual choice, they define the liberation of their female heroines in relation to woman's traditional place in the domestic confinement of the home or in the surrogate family of the workplace (Bathrick 1984). Developed by US network executives to target growing numbers of white, middle-class professional women as audiences that could be delivered to advertisers, comedies such as these became the site of a generic feminist address to affluent female viewers over the age of twenty-five (Rabinovitz 1999).

In Britain, with the BBC and commercial ITV network companies constituting a 'comfortable duopoly' governed by public service standards of quality, taste and decency, situation comedy faced no such market-driven imperatives; patriarchal and paternalistic concerns continued to dominate the majority of programme output. Television was primarily a male enterprise; there were few women in senior management and few women in creative positions as producers, writers or directors. Sitcom writing at this time was an exclusively male preserve apart from one-off contributions by women authors to new talent slots such as Comedy Playhouse and one-off series. Carla Lane was the first female writer to break through this glass ceiling; after cutting her teeth working alongside other writers on long-running sitcoms such as *The Liver Birds* (BBC1 1969–78) that she created with Myra Taylor, *Bless This House* and *And Mother Makes Three* (ITV 1971–73, 1974–76, which starred Wendy Craig), *Butterflies* was her first stand-alone script. She claims it took her three years to persuade the BBC that the theme of potential adultery explored in *Butterflies* could be remotely funny even though she had a proven track record in writing female-centred comedy.[4]

Lane's interventions in a genre where women invariably played second fiddle to their male partners and her development of leading roles for women received surprisingly little attention from feminist critics at the time. At best, Lane's sitcoms were regarded as mildly controversial, at worst as perpetuating an infantile dependence on men through their conventional representations of white bourgeois femininity and support of dominant heterosexual values. This was in part a response articulated through feminist work that situated the 'housewife' as a woman oppressed by patriarchy who needs to liberate herself from enforced domesticity.[5] Within this context, Ria is entirely conventional, just another giddy housewife dreaming of having a romantic affair; Gray (1994), for example, sees Ria as a woman defined by the men in her life who has no independent identity outside of these relationships. Andrews (1998) is one of the few critics to note Lane's intervention in domestic sitcom, arguing that this 'housewives comedy' at least makes women the focus of the text as well as referencing contemporary feminist concerns such as the 'wages for housework' campaign. Later commentators agree that although *Butterflies* may not offer a 'liberating' vision of a woman's life, it does offer an interpretation of married life different from that of other sitcoms of the day through its reference to the stifling pressures of conventional femininity that, according to some of my respondents, was still considered 'the norm' for many women in the 1970s.

Lane's sitcoms frequently feature women struggling with everyday life, their domestic and working lives torn by conflicting desires and needs, duties and expectations. Lane claims that she writes situation tragedies rather comedies, explorations of distressing situations enlivened by humour; she wrote *Butterflies* for women who, like her, grew up in the 1940s and 1950s and were 'galloping towards forty with so much to do, so little time to do it'.[6] Little has been written about Lane's work in spite of the enduring popularity of some of her comedies and official recognition of her contribution to British television comedy (she was awarded the OBE in 1989). In one of the few published overviews, Frances Gray argues that one of the problems facing female writers of comedy is that they are never taken seriously by critics or commissioners; they are seen as 'one-offs', eccentric oddballs rather than as talented and skilled individuals, people whose 'quirkiness' is the source of their popularity as writers (Gray 1994: 89). The press coverage surrounding Lane's divorce certainly served to enhance the image of her as a bizarre, unconventional character. The tabloids published stories of wild parties, naked romps in the garden and her passion for animals; reports commented on her eccentric family living arrangements that included housing her grown-up sons and their spouses as well as her mother and ex-husband under one, albeit very large, roof.[7] Lane claims that she had considerable difficulty persuading the BBC to commission *Butterflies*, not least because her own private life was the subject of much tabloid speculation at the time. The intimate and private nature of the subject matter was deemed the stuff of women's magazines and their problem pages, not at all the kind of thing that could be the subject of comedy shown on prime-time television even on the 'experimental' high-culture channel, BBC2. *Butterflies'* success was a surprise to the BBC's light entertainment commissioner; the audience for BBC television in the 1970s was generally conceived as a family one dominated by a male head of the household who dictated what the family watched through his control of television set top buttons or the remote control. Women were the principal audience for soap opera, and it was assumed that situation comedy was watched by a male, predominantly working-class audience (Neale and Krutnik 1990).

In-house BBC audience research throws further light on the composition of the sitcom audience by the early 1980s through its reports on selected programmes compiled on a regular basis. In response to a request that asked researchers to find out whether women watched situation comedy, senior audience researcher Eleanor Cowie concluded that only 'a few comedies, depending on their setting or particular brand of humour, attract more men or have roughly equal appeal'.[8] The rest appealed more to women, particularly on ITV, 'because the audience to ITV is predominantly female for most programmes except sport'.[9] The data indicate that *Butterflies* was one of the BBC's most popular situation comedies, increasing its audience from 3.7 million viewers to 8.2 million during the run of series two from October to December 1979; 66 per cent of these viewers were in the A and A+ social category (professional, teaching and managerial, attributed at the time by husbands' profession), whilst 26 per cent were in the B and C categories that included sub-professional groups such as nurses, police and skilled tradespeople. *Butterflies*, they concluded, appealed primarily to middle-class and lower-middle-class groups, particularly women; of this significant audience share, only 23 per cent of *Butterflies* viewers were aged over fifty-five in 1983 – a lower percentage than for any other sitcom. Indications of the extent of *Butterflies'* popularity are hinted at in that it succeeded in attracting an audience of 7.5 million to BBC2 following a programme that only achieved 1.6 million; 6 million people switched on or switched channels to watch it, rather than just leaving the television on the same channel (BBCWA SP 84/44/84/19). *Butterflies* also had the highest Appreciation Index rating of all BBC sitcoms, surpassing even the highly popular and perennially repeated *Only Fools and Horses* (BBC1 1981–83, 1985–86, 1989, 1990–91) and *Last of the Summer Wine* (ITV 1973–2004) (BBCWA SP 84/44/84/19). There was general agreement amongst BBC respondents that *Butterflies* was very enjoyable, the humour subtle and low-key, the situation true to life and very well observed. Poignancy in the scripts was considered the strength of Carla Lane's writing, and the cast were highly regarded. Comments include 'humour subtle, low key, true to life, well observed', 'Lane's scripts excellent'; the themes of the series were 'not only amusing but said something about the frustrations and uncertainties of a woman approaching middle age'. Those who disliked the series felt that Carla Lane's opinions tended to dominate the script and that Ria was too neurotic and more than a little fey.[10]

Butterflies and femininity

Butterflies' themes of marital boredom and frustration have strong similarities to Betty Friedan's interpretation of the discontent and dissatisfaction experienced by white middle-class US housewives in *The Feminine Mystique* (1963), the book often dubbed the 'founding' text of second-wave feminism. Friedan's best-selling text was first published in Britain in 1963 and reprinted seven times by 1982; the publication dates indicate that, although written in the early 1960s, the book (and its ideas) remained in circulation in Britain until the early 1980s. Referring to the unhappiness of her respondents as 'the problem that has no name', Friedan describes affluent white suburban domestic life in the late 1950s as a comfortable concentration camp where the constraints and barriers are not material but social and symbolic, constructed by cultural products such as magazines and advertising that have content and subject matter designed and controlled by men (Friedan 1963). Viewers remembering *Butterflies* identify Ria's lack of confidence, feelings of failure and entrapment, uselessness and frustrated desire as ongoing themes; the series negotiates a comparable range of symptoms to 'the problem that has no name', including 'The happy housewife heroine' (Ria's long-suffering attempts to cook), 'The crisis in woman's identity' (with her sons grown up, Ria is unsure of her role in life) and 'Housewifery expands to fill the time available' (vacuuming and dusting the furniture even though she has a cleaner).

In *Butterflies*, Ria is, as she often declares, 'happily married but not excitingly married'. She has everything expected of a successful 1970s television wife and mother: a large semi-detached house in the suburbs that could be in any affluent part of Britain, a loyal husband, healthy teenage sons, a cleaner and no need to work to earn a living. In spite of her obvious material comfort (or perhaps precisely because of it), she is plagued by inner conflicts between her sense of duty and the feeling that her life is passing quickly by. Virtually all respondents mentioned Ria's awful cooking and her escapades in the kitchen as one of the defining images of their memory of the series; Ria hates housework and loathes cooking, she seems unable to perform the simplest of domestic tasks and the ghastly food she dishes up to the family is a source of much of the series's amusement. Like Friedan's 1950s US suburban housewife, Ria is dissatisfied and unhappy, bored by the monotony of housework and, with the children grown up, depressed about the uselessness of her life and her ageing body.

Lane's awareness of many of these issues is apparent in the shooting script of *Butterflies*: 'Why do I have to spend my days in this brick prison (pointing to the hoover) pushing that thing around?' Ria grumbles to a photograph of her husband on the sideboard.[11] Lane is precise about stage directions, placing Ria's commentary as she walks home with her shopping in deliberate contrast to her surroundings: Lane's stage direction states that 'We must notice the tidy, almost "to attention" semi-detached houses – the net curtains, the grass verges – all the *desperate* signs of suburbia' (my emphasis).[12] Ria wants to paint her house purple, to have naked gnomes in the front garden, a rude door knocker and to hoist her knickers on the television aerial while she mows the lawn without any clothes on. At heart, however, Ria remains an old-fashioned girl, quizzical about the changes brought about by the 'swinging sixties' but not an enthusiastic advocate of them. Lane rejects obvious images of female freedom in the 1970s, such as 'the hippy' (arguably played by Felicity Kendall in another popular 1970s staple, *The Good Life*) or 'the feminist' (often represented on television talk shows through the persona of Germaine Greer). She disassociates herself from feminism because she feels guilty about the effects of her personal success on her family and had 'for too long . . . been practising and perfecting the art of being sacrificial'.[13] Instead she draws on a notion of romantic freedom imaged around the gypsy; Ria's low-necked peasant-style tops and flowing scarves flirt with the idea of the exotic, ethnic 'Other', an idealised image of freedom found in British women's films of the 1940s such as *Madonna of the Seven Moons* (GB 1944) and *Caravan* (GB 1946). As was noted by critics at the time, the series also has blatant similarities to one of the most well-known British films of the 1940s, *Brief Encounter* (GB 1945); like the suburban housewife Laura Jesson (Celia Johnson), who pours out her feelings of frustration and guilt in her internal monologues, Ria voices her innermost feelings in soliloquies addressed to photographs of her husband or own image in the mirror.

Performing femininity

Wendy Craig plays Ria as a Laura Jesson for the 1970s, a conventionally married middle-class woman who relieves the boredom of her days by engaging in 'brief encounters' with her potential lover in the café and the park. The contrast between her 'real' life as a wife and mother and her 'ideal' life as the subject of romantic adoration is enhanced by the series's production format; 'home life' is shot in the studio in front of a live audience, whilst the romantic interludes are shot on film with a laughter track added in post-production. These different settings have implications for

Craig's performance: in the studio, she plays to the front much as she might have performed on the stage, pacing dramatic delivery to the measure of audience response. On location, her performance is less theatrical and more fluid; the dramatic staccato outbursts and physical gags performed in front of the family are counterbalanced by a more relaxed soul-searching as she talks to God in the local church, for example, after guiltily meeting Leonard in the park. In these latter sequences, Ria enacts the kind of English femininity that is sometimes characterised by the term 'restraint'; in her gypsy-style clothes carrying her shopping bag she projects an image of demure respectability. Although she yearns to shake off the shackles of respectability, to lower her necklines, to have an affair, to make passionate love on the rug in front of the fire rather than in the bedroom, like Laura Jesson before her, Ria cannot bring herself to commit adultery. Her sense of guilt ensures she remains firmly married to home and duty: 'my wedding ring is glued to my finger'.

Butterflies presents domesticity as a trap, a literal dead end, that can be relieved only by romantic fantasies and daydreams; 'I feel like one of your specimens', Ria says to her butterfly collector husband, 'caught and put on public display as a trophy'. Ria is acutely aware of herself as an image. She performs femininity through constant anxiety about the state of her appearance: the shape of her nose, the suitability of her clothes and her physical signs of ageing. In numerous sequences, she talks to the mirror about ageing as she examines her face and body for visible evidence of change. Feminist sociologists provide evidence that many of Ria's internal conflicts were part of broader female experiences in Britain in the 1970s. During the course of long in-depth interviews with married women, Anne Oakley found that 70 per cent of them claimed they were dissatisfied with their domestic role (Oakley 1974: 182). Whole areas of Britain were designated 'valium valleys'. Described at the time as 'mother's little helper', valium became the prescription drug of choice for depression; in 1978 a study found one in three women in south London was clinically depressed and taking the drug. Some women were less prepared to put up with the unhappiness of a failed relationship and miserable home life; owing to relaxation of the divorce laws, the incidence of divorce trebled between 1966 and 1976.

Remembering *Butterflies*

In the questionnaires, I asked women whether they thought the success of the series was primarily due to Wendy Craig's depiction of Ria; around 75 per cent of respondents answered with an unqualified 'yes'. For those who commented further, Craig's facial expressions and her body language captured a combination of naivety and knowingness, externalising internal emotions that were recognisable and familiar, particularly to those who had experienced similar discontents and frustrations in their everyday lives: 'I strongly identified with Ria and her problems'; 'thousands of us menopausal so-called happily married women could associate with her'; 'she hit home to so many women at the middle stage of life'; 'I was like that, searching for my own identity'. A couple of people commented that the series helped them to see life in a deeper way, 'she made you question the point of it all'. For these respondents, Ria's growing discontent with her domestic role was more than just a joke; one of the pleasures of *Butterflies* was its articulation of a female viewpoint in the public realm of television where it was shared with their families: 'I willed her "to do it" but in the 1970s, you didn't, not on a family TV show'. Of the respondents who were in partnerships at the time, most watched *Butterflies* with their husbands and families; a minority commented that their husbands and children also found it funny, a few that their husbands refused to watch it because it was a 'women's programme'.

Although respondents remembered Ria and most named her as their favourite character, around a quarter named Ben, Ria's husband, as their favourite because they liked Geoffrey Palmer and found him attractive. This did not prevent them being critical of Ben as a husband; he was remembered as grumpy, bored and indifferent, someone who didn't understand the younger generation or his wife but was prepared to tolerate them (one person called him a male chauvinist pig). A major source of pleasure in the series was Ria's romantic affair with Leonard (Bruce Montague) which was 'dangled in front of the viewer to torment – Yes Ria, go for it! No, stay with your family'; it was the hook on which to hang her questioning of her 'place', 'it showed her vulnerability', 'it was her/our escape'. A couple of people commented on the 'unrealistic' and 'dream-like' quality of these sequences, another that the romance 'showed how Mills and Boon fantasies sustain women in the face of real life men and real life relationships'. Most agreed that without the romantic sub-plot *Butterflies* would have been 'just another mediocre sitcom'.

Respondents to the questionnaire were more critical of Ria and the series as a whole than the letter writers were. Many of them were working during the early years of their marriages and thought Lane's depiction of the housewife as a dizzy, stupid frustrated woman who needed 'to get out more' old-fashioned and backward-looking, reiterating well-worn jokes about female incompetence. Those who were most critical of Ria thought that the representation of married life marginalised those with different experiences and expectations because it was too personal. Several people raised the question of class, commenting that the series projected a 1950s image of women's lives, that poorer people had always had to work, that Ria's cleaner, who worked for a living, was more independent than she was; another respondent knew a couple of women who were regularly beaten up by their husbands – 'Ria seemed like a spoilt brat by comparison'. Class perspectives were not always divisive, however; one older respondent commented that 'it was reassuring to know that Ria felt like us (working-class women), irrespective of her class and income'. A couple of respondents envied Ria; for one, newly married in the early 1980s, Ria's middle-class lifestyle was the pinnacle of her aspirations . . . 'she seemed to have it all – lovely home, family, car, no need to work, a cleaning lady and a rich man after her. An ideal life or what! . . . I would still settle for what she had.' For another, living in a flat with two young children, Ria's boredom and frustration showed that money and material possessions were no guarantee of happiness.

Asked whether they thought *Butterflies* reflected changing images of women in the 1970s, twenty-three respondents replied with an unqualified 'yes' – women wanted more fulfilment and opportunities, women were beginning to find their own identity: 'it showed women had a right to expect more from their lives', 'it was more intelligent, it questioned her life' and 'dealt with feelings rather than situations'. One person commented that these changes had started earlier, but the series was one of the first to address them. Asked whether they remembered any other images of discontent amongst women circulating in 1970s magazines, on television or in books, most said no – this programme appealed because it was the only one that directly addressed their situation. A few women had heard of *The Feminine Mystique*, and one remembered seeing Germaine Greer on a chat show; another woman had read Fay Weldon's *The Fat Woman's Joke*, but overall there was little familiarity with recognisable sources of early second-wave feminist ideas and attitudes. Several people commented that political correctness was boring in entertainment and that *Butterflies* was a comedy and should not be taken too seriously.

These memories challenge textual critiques of the day that claim that all British sitcoms in the late 1970s and early 1980s were ideologically hidebound by retrospective depictions of contemporary life. Although this was certainly true of some British sitcoms such as *Dad's Army*, others such as *Butterflies* drew on images of the past for their commentary on life in the present. The past that is drawn on in *Butterflies*, however, is not an 'authentic' past but an imaginary one; *Butterflies* uses images of feminine fantasy and escape commonly found in 1940s British films, images probably familiar to a generation of women of a similar age to Carla Lane from family trips to the cinema and television reruns. Here, these images may serve to reiterate and reinforce outdated depictions of popular fantasy; on the other hand, they can also be interpreted as gently mocking the traditional image of white middle-class femininity from which such dreams were wrought. Through location filming and performance, Ria's harmless liaisons with Leonard are perceived (and remembered) by many viewers as escapist fantasy. Ria's frustrations gave shape and substance to the dissatisfactions that many women living with paternalistic husbands in male-dominated households recognised. Although some people found Ria irritating and lacking in self-assertion, everyone remembered her because her problems were seen as not untypical of women of a certain age who find themselves in similar circumstances. Viewers' memories of *Butterflies* suggest that, rather than projecting an ideologically conservative commentary on women's lives and times, as some critics have argued, the programme indicates the ways in which popular forms of drama and entertainment can express personal tensions masked by a deceptive veneer of social conformity.

These respondents may not be 'typical' of all viewers who remember *Butterflies*; their memories of Ria's situation are suggestive, however, of the role that television characters play in popular memory. Memories of *Butterflies* were articulated through two discursive frameworks: objective, detached commentary that judged the writing and acting skills of Lane and the actors, and a more personal commentary on how the series negotiated recognisable feelings and emotions previously unexplored in sitcoms. All the respondents commented on the quality of Carla Lane's writing; most agreed that it was excellent, with a number of people commenting in more depth on Lane's ability to develop characters with plausible emotions. As well as acting as a linchpin in memories of a particular programme or series, Ria and her family reminded many respondents of broader debates about women's work in the home. Cooking may no longer be an issue but feelings of frustration and dissatisfaction continue to reverberate amongst many female viewers as they juggle their modern roles as breadwinners and 'captains of the domestic ship'.

Notes

Thanks to all those who participated in the project: Brenda Beardsley, Gina Brooks, Barbara Ann Bryan, Liz Campbell, Joyce Carter, Rita Coxon, Janet Davies, B. Fell, Beverley Fleming, Penny French, Pam Gamble, Edna James, J. James, Hazel Handford, A. Hanson, Jan Hughes, Jocelyn James, J. Knight, Ria Lewis, Audrey Lobely, Judith Lobely, Claire MacDonald, H. S. McEwan, Rosemary Medland, Gina Mildren, Pat Mulcahy, Glenda O'Donnell, Val Orford, Jean Pearson, J. Penman, Susan Peston, Joan Rendell, B. Rhodes, Hilary Riordan, K. Tucker, A. Stephenson, Ms Whitesand and those who chose to remain anonymous. Special thanks to Natalie Chubya and Wendy Phillips for sharing unpublished accounts of Carla Lane's work, to the editor of *Women's Own* and to the staff, BBC Written Archives, Caversham.

1 The BBC was aware that its daily survey results were at variance with BARB audience data owing to differences in survey design; see, for example, BBCWA memo from Graham Field, 'The audience to situation comedies: differences between age groups', 3 September 1982.

2 'Do you remember the popular TV series *Butterflies*? And would you like to help the programme earn a place in TV history?' Extract from the brief letter printed in *Woman's Own*, 9 April 2001, p 53.

3 In Hobson's (1981) account, the women she discussed *Butterflies* with distinguished 'between what was believable and likely in the situation depicted in real life and what was believable for a character played by Wendy Craig' (Hobson 1981: 23). In these accounts, there is no mention of Craig's other roles in popular sitcoms such as *Not in Front of the Children* (BBC 1967–70) and *And Mother Makes Three/Five* (ITV 1971–73, 1974–76).

4 Interview with Martin Jackson, *Daily Mail*, 25 November 1978.

5 See, for example, Oakley's discussion in *Housewife* where she argues that women need to break the circle of oppression (1974: 222–41).

6 Carla Lane, 'The elusive butterfly of love', *Radio Times*, 4 November 1978, 11–13.

7 See, for example, *Daily Express*, 22 March 1976, *Daily Mail*, 24 September 1977, 5 October 1977.

8 Eleanor Cowie, internal memorandum, 29 July 1982, courtesy BBCWA

9 Ibid.

10 BBCWA Audience research reports for *Butterflies*, 3 December 1979 and 11 January 1980.

11 BBCWA 1158/2381, *Butterflies* shooting script, scene 6, 25 June 1978.

12 Ibid., scene 4, p. 44, 25 June 1978.

13 Carla Lane, 'The elusive butterfly of love'.

References

D'Acci, J. (1994), *Defining Women: Television and the Case of Cagney and Lacey*, Chapel Hill: University of North Carolina Press.

Andrews, M. (1998), '*Butterflies* and caustic asides: housewives, comedy and the feminist movement', in S. Wagg (ed.), *Because I Tell a Joke or Two: Comedy, Politics and Social Difference*, London: Routledge.

Bathrick, S. (1984), '*The Mary Tyler Moore Show*: women at home and at work', in J. Feuer, P. Kerr and T. Vahimagi (eds), *MTM: 'Quality Television'* London: BFI.

BBC Written Archive: BBCWA SP 84/44/84/19 'Situation comedies: a review of audience data', June 1984.

Feuer, J. (2001), 'Situation comedy, part 2', in G. Creeber (ed.), *The Television Genre Book*, London: BFI.

Friedan, B. (1963), *The Feminine Mystique*, Harmondsworth: Penguin.

Gray, F. (1994), *Women and Laughter*, London: Macmillan.

Hallam, J. (2005), *Lynda La Plante*, Manchester: Manchester University Press.

Haralovich, M. B. (1992), 'Sit-coms and suburbs: positioning the 1950s homemaker', in L. Spigel and D. Mann (eds), *Private Screenings: Television and the Female Consumer*, Minneapolis, University of Minnesota Press.

Hobson D. (1981), quoted in T. Lovell, 'A genre of social disruption', in J. Cook (ed.) (1982), *Television Sitcom*, BFI Dossier 17, London: BFI.

Medhurst, A., and L. Tuck (1982), 'The Gender Game', in J. Cook (ed.), *Television Sitcom*, BFI Dossier 17, London: BFI.

Neale, S., and F. Krutnik (eds) (1990), *Popular Film and Television Comedy*, London: Routledge.

Oakley, A. (1974), *Housewife*, London: Penguin.

Rabinovitz, L. (1999), 'Ms-representation: the politics of feminist sitcoms', in M. B. Haralovich and L. Rabinovitz (eds), *Television History and American Culture: Feminist Critical Essays*, Durham and London: Duke University Press.

Spigel, L. (1992), *Make Room for TV: Television and the Family Ideal in Postwar America*, Chicago: University of Chicago Press.

Thumim, J. (1995), '"A live commercial for icing sugar": researching the historical audience: gender and broadcast television in the 1950s', *Screen* 36:1 (1995) 48–55.

Thumim, J. (ed.) (2002), *Small Screen, Big Ideas: Television in the 1950s*, London: I. B. Tauris.

Further reading

Banks, M., and A. Swift (1987), *The Jokes on Us: Women in Comedy from Music Hall to the Present*, London: Pandora.

Barreca, R. (ed.) (1988), *Last Laughs: Perspectives on Women and Comedy*, London: Gordon and Breach.

Finney, G. (1994), *Look Who's Laughing: Gender and Comedy*, London: Gordon & Breach.

Kirkham, P. and B. Skeggs (1998), '*Absolutely Fabulous*: absolutely feminist?', and in C. Geraghty and D. Lusted (eds), *The Television Studies Book*, London: Arnold.

Rowe, K. (1995), *The Unruly Woman: Gender and the Genres of Laughter*, Austin: University of Texas Press.

3

They do 'like it up 'em': *Dad's Army* and myths of Old England

Robin Nelson

> Who do you think you are kidding, Mr Hitler,
> If you think Old England's done?[1]

On reflection, the lyric of the famous signature song to *Dad's Army* may be read as carrying an unintentional ambiguity with regard to British involvement in the Second World War. First and foremost, the Allies were of course fighting to defend 'Old England' from Nazi invasion and the world-domination of fascism. At the same time, the conclusion of the war in a presumed Allied victory was intended to see the end of 'Old England' as a highly stratified society, riddled with class prejudice.

> MAINWARING: Things'll be very different after the war, you mark my words! The common man will come into his own. This country will be run by *professionals*: doctors, lawyers . . . bank managers . . .
> WILSON: You mean people like you?
> MAINWARING: All right, yes: people like me.
> WILSON: (*smiling mischievously*) You mean 'common'?
> MAINWARING: Now *watch* it Wilson!
> WILSON: I didn't know you were a socialist, sir . . .
> MAINWARING: I said nothing about 'common men'! I said the common *man*! People who've got somewhere by their own efforts – not because their father had a title. *Their* day's over!

Though this dialogue treats the topic in the series's distinctive comic way, the idea of a classless society in Britain gained impetus as the war progressed. Mr Hitler was indeed 'kidding', however, if he was predicting the imminent demise of 'Old England' in this latter sense. Though much has undoubtedly altered in social history between the ending of the war in 1945 and the opening of the twenty-first century, the English class structure, on which *Dad's Army* is founded as we shall see, has not yet been dissolved. At the time of writing this essay in late 2003, well over half a century since the end of the Second World War, hereditary peerage in the House of Lords is only just undergoing reform.

Though it is impossible to be po-faced for too long when writing about such an engagingly humorous comedy as *Dad's Army*, this essay takes the programme somewhat seriously in trying to account for its extraordinary success and longevity. Without resonances beyond the series' undoubted comic appeal, the argument runs, it is unlikely that the show would have sustained the long-term following it has achieved. Unless it is simply assumed that great comedy has universal qualities which transcend time and place, the relationship between social circumstances and *Dad's Army* over time invites an explanation.

Outline genealogy

It is true, as Victoria Wood amongst others has observed, that a sitcom set in the past does not date as quickly as a comedy of the moment,[2] but this alone cannot explain why *Dad's Army* has stood the test of time in defiance of popular television's noted transience. The comedy series built and sustained a strong following through the nine series and eighty episodes (BBC 1968–77) of its first transmission,[3] and many subsequent reruns over a thirty-five-year period. At its height in series five, *Dad's Army* averaged an audience of 16.3 million and for 'Brain versus Brawn' (first transmitted 8 December 1972) drew its biggest ever audience of 18,634,500. In 1978, the audience for a repeat of series nine rose progressively over the six episodes from 6.9 million to 9.6 million, by the late 1980s reruns were watched by as many as 11 million people and, as late as January 2001, a repeat showing of a one-off episode on BBC1 at 6.45 on a Saturday evening still attracted 6.6 million viewers.[4] The series, its creators and its performers have won many accolades and awards and, in a BFI poll of the hundred best British television programmes conducted in 2000, it was 'placed thirteenth, and the only surprise was that it had not been rated even higher' (McCann 2002: 223).

Dad's Army first aired in 1968, an iconic year in the history of English social liberation, and a time sufficiently distant from the Second World War to allow laughter at it. At this moment, an iconoclastic treatment of war might have been expected since *Dad's Army* was the first comedy series to be set in the Second World War, and the mood was to reject the past.[5] Unlike later anti-Vietnam-War comedies such as *M*A*S*H* (1970) or *Catch-22* (1970), however, *Dad's Army* is not deeply satirical. Indeed, it balances laughter at its characters and situations with a reiterated respect for the readiness, if necessary, of Home Guard members to sacrifice their lives just as much as their counterparts in the regular military. In the seminal 'Battle of Godfrey's Cottage' (first transmitted 8 March 1969), for instance, Captain Mainwaring (Arthur Lowe), believing himself to be isolated with just Jones (Clive Dunn) and Frazer (John Laurie) to defend Walmington-on-Sea, remarks without irony, 'It'll probably be the end of us. But we're ready for that, aren't we men?'. When Jones and Frazer assent, Mainwaring adds, 'Good show' with a genuinely stiff upper lip. Whilst, then, Mainwaring is himself frequently a comic butt in the series for his pomposity about the Home Guard's role and his own place as a commander in it, the writers, Perry and Croft, do not debase the efforts, indeed the bravery, of the Home Guard platoons, and by implication the war effort in general. The final episode of *Dad's Army*, 'Never Too Old' (first transmitted 13 November 1977) contrived to end with Mainwaring, on Wilson's suggestion, proposing a toast to 'Britain's Home Guard!', repeated with: 'ALL (*turning to face the camera*) "To Britain's Home Guard!"'.

Jimmy Perry, originator and co-writer (with producer, David Croft) of *Dad's Army*, had himself joined the Home Guard as a young man and subsequently served in the army, albeit mainly in the Royal Artillery Concert Party (see Perry 2003). His experiences from Oswestry to Deolali proved fruitful in his writing career and, with regard to *Dad's Army*, were crucial to its success. Firstly, the comedy series is indeed underpinned by Perry's unmistakable patriotism, which licenses it to laugh at the ineptitude of this particular aspect of the war effort. Secondly, many of the episodes have a ring of authenticity in spite of the comic treatment, since they draw directly on Perry's experience, or on incidents he learned of at close hand. For example, as Graham McCann relates, Mainwaring 'was a composite of three people from Perry's past' and Corporal Jones 'owed much to the elderly raconteur with whom Perry had served in the Home Guard, and a little to a bellicose sergeant at Colchester barracks who had taught him bayonet drill' (2002: 53). Jones's famous catch-phrase referencing the unwelcome insertion of cold steel, for example, is drawn from this encounter ('Any doubt – get out the cold steel, 'cause they don't like it up 'em!').

History, authenticity and discursive position

Though not in any significant sense a documentary, *Dad's Army* is nevertheless based in an important historical moment and on a specific
wartime phenomenon. Perry and Croft's creation, though fictional, is historically accurate. It deals with a disparate group of people brought
together, like many in Home Guard platoons, between 1940 and 1945.
The age range in the comedy series, from young Pike (Ian Lavender) to
doddering Godfrey (Arnold Ridley), reflects the official seventeen to
sixty-five (actually fourteen to eighty) age range of the volunteers. The
Land Defence Volunteers (subsequently renamed the Home Guard) was,
however, largely comprised of older men who fell short of the standards
required for regular military service. Hence the platoons attracted the
derisory nickname of 'Dad's Army'.

In production, *Dad's Army* was effectively treated as a costume drama
shot partly in the studio but substantially on locations near Thetford, East
Anglia, particularly in the town itself and on Stanford, a nearby Military
Training Area. Efforts were made to achieve historical authenticity in costumes and settings, exemplifying the BBC's cherished reputation for
attention to detail as typically applied to period drama. The designers
undertook meticulous research, and period brand foods (e.g. Camp
coffee, Orlox beef suet and Sunlight soap) and utility furniture were
either found or made (see McCann 2002: 70). Vintage vehicles, such as
greengrocer Hodge's 1939 Bedford truck and the 1935 Ford box vehicle
customised by the BBC to serve as Jones's navy and white butcher's van,
lent period authenticity to the series (McCann 2002: 164–165). Although
this essay is ultimately interested less in aspects of authenticity and more
in how the programme may have tapped into the social imaginary for
shifting reasons over several generation-spans, the specific development
of *Dad's Army* in respect of its credibility is important to both aspects (see
Webber 2001: 17). As will become evident in the discussion of viewer
responses below, the credibility of the characters in situation and the
period detail contributes much to the enjoyment of different members of
the audience.

In respect of historical authenticity, however, *Dad's Army* understandably avoids those aspects of Home Guard experience which would defeat
laughter. The hundreds killed and the thousands injured, mainly by accident and 'friendly fire' in Home Guard service, are reflected only in the
ramshackle nature of the Walmington-on-Sea platoon and its members'
often misguided preparations for defence.[6] Indeed, *Dad's Army* is selective
about history in ways that assist in more precisely identifying its discur-

sive position and perhaps its success. For, though it might have come to nothing even without Churchill's intervention,[7] in actual history some of the early established Land Defence Volunteer platoons had a tendency to put themselves above the law. Moreover, the only available training of the actual Home Guard at Osterley Park gravitated towards republicanism, being in fact led by socialists, some veterans of the Spanish Civil War, notably Tom Wintringham, who might have sought social change by another route.[8] Thus another treatment of *Dad's Army* material based authentically in history might be imagined which would offer a different version of the Home Guard and, depending upon political stance, possibly not be comedic at all.

In this alternative light, the specific discursive position of *Dad's Army* becomes even clearer. It is the undoubted base of patriotism on which *Dad's Army* is founded that, besides licensing the laughter at the bumbling incompetence of the Home Guard as noted, aligns the series with a liberal-conservative tradition which has frequently been identified with 'Englishness' (see, for example, Richards 1977). In the two possibilities noted at the outset for a fundamental change to Old England as a result of the Second World War, any shift towards a classless society envisaged in *Dad's Army* would be slow and gradual rather than radical and revolutionary.

If the success and longevity of *Dad's Army* lies in its capacity to tap into a disposition which might be constructed as characteristic of 'Englishness', it goes beyond the Brits' alleged capacity to laugh at themselves, and beyond the amateur's pleasure in taking part as distinct from aiming to win at all costs. *Dad's Army*, I suggest, taps into a largely tacit, but deeply enculturated, sense of Britain's durability through periods of historical change. For historical good or ill, change in British history has been brought about piecemeal and largely constitutionally. From its discursive position of gentle ridicule grounded in unquestioned patriotism, the discourse of *Dad's Army* invites an attitude of gradualist change which will turn out right in the end rather than the wholesale inversions of radical revolution. I will return to this point in relation to audience responses to the series. Firstly, I propose briefly to comment on the form and content of *Dad's Army* and their interrelationship.

Comic form and content

In *Dad's Army* there is a happy consonance between the content and the form of the comedy, which invites gentle laughter at aspects of social life but leads to a happy ending. Viewed from a wide angle, the series is not concerned with war but is about human interactions in a specific cultural context. In the manner of traditional television comedies, the framework of *Dad's Army* is highly formulaic. Typically, the episodes involve the platoon either getting into a scrape which is likely to show Walmington-on-Sea's Home Guard in a bad light with the military hierarchy of the regular army, or losing out to one of its rivals. The day is saved at the eleventh hour often by chance or by an action of one of its inept members which inadvertently proves productive

Dad's Army might formally be classed as a sitcom in that each episode is set in the Home Guard situation which equates with both family and workplace sitcoms, the staples of the genre (see Creeber 2001: 65–72). An established pattern of sitcom, so simple and familiar that, according to Hartley, it serves to teach 'two important skills: how to watch television (media literacy) and how to live in families with tolerant mutual accommodation, talking not fighting (life skills)' (Creeber 2001: 66), is repeated in each episode. In achieving formal harmony in their conclusion, the story arcs of episodes return us to the status quo at the outset and constrain the potential for any hurtful and destructive mockery. An assurance, derived from the known comedic formula, prevents any fears in the audience that the platoon might, for example, actually be drowned in the local pumping station as the waters rise around them ('Asleep in the Deep', first transmitted 6 October 1972).

A feature of sitcom, however, is the lack of character development. Humour arises from observing known characteristics responding typically to variations within a given situation. *Dad's Army* for the most part adheres to this formula, but, as the series matured, Croft and Perry pushed against the framework to allow real emotion at least momentarily to surface. Though some of the characters began as comic stock – the character of Frazer, for example, was initially no more than 'Scotsman' – others were more fully formed at the inception. Jones, as noted, was drawn on Perry's experiences as was the relation between Mainwaring and Wilson (John le Mesurier) which emerged to be a cornerstone of the series. In an episode entitled 'Mum's Army' (first transmitted 20 January 1970), homage is paid to the popular war film *Brief Encounter* when Mainwaring is smitten by one Mrs Grey to the point that her departure by train back to London, complete with a scene at a table in the station buffet, leaves him tearfully bereft. The attraction between the two is class-based. Mrs Grey is a 'good-looking-for-her-age', well-dressed, well-spoken, middle-class English lady, just the kind of partner bank manager

Mainwaring in his social aspiration would have preferred to his wife, the daunting 'Elizabeth'. A class-consciousness expressed in subtle social distinctions is a part of Perry's middle-class suburban upbringing which remained with him throughout his life. It is evident in the subtle detail of a stratified class-based culture in the corps of men drawn up by Perry, no doubt partly unconsciously.

Jane Feuer suggests that 'the sitcom has been the perfect format for illustrating current ideological conflicts while entertaining an audience' (Creeber 2001: 70), both aspects of which observation will be pursued in this essay. In Home Guard actuality, rank, based on class rather than skill, was introduced with the aim of bringing some discipline to what were initially loose associations of confederates in towns and villages. Perry's decision to make grammar-school boy, Mainwaring, Captain of the Platoon instead of the public-school-educated Wilson, his Sergeant, was destined to create a core comic tension. The decision can be located in Perry's sense of his own social position. As he relates:

> I'd been a sergeant myself you see, and one day while I was serving in the Far East, this major had come up and said to me: 'Sergeant Perry, why do you speak with a public school accent?' And I'd replied: 'Well, I suppose because I went to public school.' So he said, 'Oh. But still; a *sergeant* speaking like *that* – it – it's *most* strange!' Well the man was an idiot. (cited in McCann 2002: 53)

The incident clearly offended Perry, and he wanted to get away from what he regarded as social stereotyping in his casting of Mainwaring and Wilson. That it went against general expectations is reflected in BBC executive Paul Fox's[9] surprise on visiting the *Dad's Army* set to find the small, stout Arthur Lowe with the bespectacled, petit-bourgeois demeanour of a bureaucratic, rural bank manager cast as Mainwaring, against the sleek, silver-haired, debonair litheness of his chief clerk, Wilson, in the form of John le Mesurier.[10] Fox had known that Lowe and Le Mesurier were to be cast but this distribution defied his expectations. As Fox recalls, 'I had done the casting wrongly in my own mind ... I was delighted [by the inversion]. It was the first note of unpredictability' (cited in McCann 202: 76). The inversion sets up a series-wide running gag based on a very English class antagonism between the bourgeois and the aristocracy. The meritocrat, Mainwaring, has gained his professional and social status through application. He is reminded daily of his achieved, as distinct from 'natural', standing by the very presence of Wilson, whose lightly worn air of superiority is rooted in his class pedigree and educational background. As noted above, 'Things [were supposed to] be very different after the war'.

Dad's Army's reflection of the gradations of the English class-structure continue down the social scale. Vying with Mainwaring more overtly than Wilson for top notch in Walmington-on-Sea's civil defences is greengrocer Mr Hodges (Bill Pertwee), who as Chief Air Raid Warden runs a competing outfit of volunteers. From a similar background to Mainwaring, he has failed to make the leap into 'the professions', and the small social distance between them reflects another 'nicety' of English class distinction. Hodges is a comic butt of the series, serving as 'other' to the Home Guard platoon, a device which works particularly well with those who recall the war years because the ARP were something of an officious irritant, since their role was to ensure blackout and they thus interfered in domestic life.

Further down the hierarchy – though he might not see it that way – is Walker (James Beck), who, operating very successfully in the black market outside the official Establishment, represents business talents unrecognised in official culture but commercially effective none-the-less. Not aspiring to established values, Walker is a threat to Mainwaring only in that his unorthodoxies are not readily contained within respectable codes of conduct, and they frequently prove embarrassing. The treacle and raisins causing inappropriate bulges in the breast pockets of Walker's uniform on parade, for example, turn out to be a delivery for Sergeant Wilson. Tensions between church and state are handled with bathos in terms of conflicts over the use of the village hall, HQ to Mainwaring's platoon but also the meeting-place of Mr Hodges's ARP. The vicar (Frank Williams) and his verger (Edward Sinclair) are frequently drawn into the squabbles. Overall, *Dad's Army* seems to confirm that 'Old England' is certainly alive and well in the second sense noted above. Whilst popular television comedy quite often serves as a vehicle through which cultural change is negotiated, the framework of *Dad's Army* and the audience responses to it (see below) seem to affirm the status quo rather than to call it in question.

Broadly speaking, the core viewing pleasure taken in watching *Dad's Army* would seem to lie in its very predictability, in getting more of the same, though the actors grew into the characters in time to give highly skilful, nuanced performances. In the raise of an eyebrow (Lowe as Mainwaring), a louche posture (Mesurier as Wilson), a wild eye and sonorous voice of doom (Laurie as Frazer), a vacant yet interrogative face (Lavender as Pike), however, the performances generally reinforced key traits. No doubt, pleasure is taken in the ensemble of actors whose increasing

rapport placed the comedy as much in reaction shots as in the comic situations and the dialogue itself. Similarly, the gags are repeated. There is a
fair amount of light physical business, for example Jones's contrivance, in
defiance of his emphasis upon proper discipline, always to fall to attention fractionally after the others. In visual terms, Private Pike (Ian Lavender) sports a knitted woollen Aston Villa scarf with his uniform, and
Arthur Lowe always contrived to surface from a physical put-down with
Mainwaring's spectacles aslant on his nose and his cap askew. Indeed,
Lowe and Lavender developed this physical comedy into stock business
(see McCann 2002: 198). Many phrases, most notably Mainwaring's
'stupid boy'[11] addressed to Pike, were likewise repeated to the point where
the catchphrases have been absorbed into everyday English speech. Other
examples include 'we're doomed' emphatically articulated in the deep
accent of Scots undertaker Private Frazer and 'don't panic, don't panic'
along with 'they don't like it up 'em', the pronouncement when under
pressure of Lance-Corporal Jones, constructing himself as a bayonet-
toting veteran of earlier wars.

There is, for sure, a pleasure to be taken by the *Dad's Army* initiate in
small deviations from the norm as the comedy matured, for example,
Frazer's 'we're entombed' (instead of 'we're doomed') as the water rises
around the platoon trapped in the pumping stations. But significant
departures from the norm are few and are variations on a theme located
in the circular narrative sitcom form, as noted. Sustained interest would
not therefore appear to lie in the series's novelty. It is the mechanics of the
means to the anticipated end that please, perhaps, rather than unexpected
plot outcomes. Particularly in the case of the many repeats, viewers know
what they are going to get, and still they watch.

Indeed, the longevity of *Dad's Army* would seem to lie in its very familiarity and predictability and in the relations between its characters,
notably in the comic treatment of English class tensions. The situation is
male-dominated and, other than in the exceptional 'Mum's Army'
episode, *Dad's Army* does not offer overt positions of identification to
women by featuring female characters.[12] Unlike in the television soap
genre, there are no strong women with whom to bond in sorority. Pleasures distinctly available to women beyond the sheer enjoyment of the
comedy perhaps lie elsewhere, and yet some women, young and old, do
undoubtedly enjoy the series.

Audience research findings

The idea of undertaking a small viewer response survey initially arose from casual conversation with friends in which a trend emerged of fathers watching *Dad's Army* with their younger teenage sons. I wondered whether this might be true also of mothers and daughters and became interested in the difference of response across generations. Accordingly, as part of the reflection on *Dad's Army* as a popular phenomenon under-taken for this essay, a viewer questionnaire was devised and some small viewing and discussion groups were set up. The questionnaire sought to establish broad age-bands, sex, frequency of viewing and relationships with people with whom the respondent watched *Dad's Army*. Invitations to comment on favourite characters and memorable incidents from the series led on to the questions 'what is it about the programme that amuses you?' and 'what does *Dad's Army* say to you about being British?'. The opportunity to offer additional comments on the programme, or the enjoyment in watching it, was afforded at the end.

From the 120 questionnaires printed, a high rate of 82 (anonymous) returns was achieved largely through specific targeting of the over-sixties, who may have remembered the war years, and the twenty to thirty age range, to whom the Second World War may seem ancient history. Assisted distribution to groups of university students of television produced the bulk of responses (54, predominantly female) in the twenty to thirty age range. The assistance of my eighty-three–year-old father afforded access to small discussion groups in the fifty-plus age-range, and an additional 12 questionnaire responses subsequently received from friends of people in these focus groups. Broadly, there was a keenness to respond wherever I mentioned my interest in *Dad's Army*. People requested blank copies to pass on to friends and family, and a trickle of responses continues as I write. The youngest respondent was six years old (his answers written by his grandma) and thirteen responses were received in the thirteen to nineteen age-range. The audience research claims no scientific validity and is presented here as qualitative, anecdotal even. In addition to the above, observations are drawn from many conversations involving people of all ages who were keen to share their views. With regard to humour, the findings bear out the points made above. Typical comments on why view-ers enjoyed the programme included: 'it's as comforting as a cup of tea'; 'relationships between characters'; 'complicated relationships between M & W [Mainwaring and Wilson], due to their different backgrounds'; 'eccentricity of characters'; 'cheesy humour; set pieces'; 'the confusion';

'farce, slapstick, humorous obvious jokes'; 'in-jokes, such as Elizabeth not openly on camera'.

The last comment instances a discernible, though not widely reflected, sense amongst younger viewers of the contemporary, ironically distant disposition towards television in which media-savvy viewers seek out in-jokes and intertextual play and even laugh at, rather than with, the programme. One respondent in the thirteen to nineteen age-range, for example, related that she 'watch[ed] it with my sister and we take the piss'. The overwhelming majority of responses from young people in the twenty to thirty age-range, however, indicated a sincere appreciation, but very frequently enjoyment was refracted in a family context. Specifically, young women, as well as young men – as my initial findings had led me to believe – watch with their fathers. The following responses were characteristic: 'it is a bonding with father's programme'; 'I watch with my dad: he was in the marines and he can relate to it'; 'his enthusiasm makes me laugh'; 'it's set in an age when neither of us was alive . . . hence we both laugh at the same jokes'; 'the one programme we used to watch as a family. We all like it and it's funnier if you can all laugh together'; 'there are no points which would be embarrassing with them [parents]'; 'I like to see my parents laugh'. This response from young people was mirrored amongst the over sixties: 'I used to watch it with my children when they were young, also my husband and father'; 'very clean, no bad language; you could watch it with the children'; 'it's nice to appreciate traditional, old-style comedy with the family'; 'when I go to Canada to stay with my sister, we have a night of *Dad's Army* videos'.

In the early twenty-first century, when niche marketing targets specific programmes to micro-cultures rather than a generic product to a mass audience, *Dad's Army* appears to sustain a virtually obsolete notion of 'family viewing'. Respondents watched with their grandparents, mothers, brothers, sisters or friends, but the majority watched with their fathers. As in the first comment above, many were aware that the shared viewing experience offered a 'bonding' opportunity, now rare in respect of television. A sense also may be detected that some young people enjoyed the bonding experience more than they directly enjoyed *Dad's Army*. The idea that 'he was in the marines and he can relate to it' perhaps suggests access to a domain of specific male experience from which he (the respondent was male, twenty to thirty) was otherwise excluded.

Other research findings suggest that some women brought up in the postwar years when men continued to be valorised for the war achievement, effacing women's substantial involvement, find a comic release in laughing at Mainwaring's pomposity. The dryly delivered phrase, 'he reminds me of my father' of one respondent summed up a reaction to a disposition for a military order imposed on everyday life and the assumption of dominance that characterises dismissive attitudes to women. As indicated in the 'Mum's Army' episode, from the wartime male point of view women should stay out of things until called upon to assist, since, with the exception of the idealised Mrs Greys of this world, they would prove largely incompetent. In the drill of the female recruits in 'Mum's Army', only Mrs Grey, in the eyes of Captain Mainwaring, could execute the manoeuvres with precision. To the developing strains of feminisms between 1968 and 2003, the archetypically 'male' attitudes might be off-putting, offensive even. However, the balanced approach of mockery and affection in the series seems to soften critical attitudes, though it may license derisive laughter at men generally, and fathers of a particular generation in particular.

Characters and their eccentricities were recalled more than incidents in reflections on the series. Few respondents, when asked, recalled specific episodes and referred more to incidents: 'bomb at bank during dinner at Mainwarings'; 'Walmington and Eastgate platoons in competition'; 'assault course'; 'Germans dressed as nuns'; 'retrieving flag from clock-tower'. The only episode identified by more than one person as a favourite was 'the one with the German PoWs' ('The Deadly Attachment', first transmitted 31 October 1973) in which Mainwaring defeats his own highest objective of resistance to Hitler's forces at all times by giving the game away in the memorable line, 'don't tell him, Pike!' when the German officer wishes to make a note of the young private's name.

The politics of enjoying *Dad's Army*: communal viewing in postmodern families

With regard to the idea of 'Englishness', the weight of response reflects an apparently contradictory sense of individualism in the frame of the collective. Character eccentricity, noted frequently with approval, appears to reflect a notion of the libertarian tradition in British culture, which affords individuals the right to be or do what they like providing it does not interfere with the liberty of others. The negotiation of a reluctance to be regimented in conflict (the platoon) with a disposition to well-managed uniformity (Mainwaring) might illustrate the play of English tolerance. The Walmington-on-Sea Home Guard presents a collection of individuals, but it is also made clear that they would come together and stick together if their freedoms were under threat. The following typical observations reflect, besides the above, a readiness to recognise 'ourselves' as genial buffoons who nevertheless have an 'irrepressible fighting spirit' when roused: 'Bumbling idiots'; 'We panic, we're stupid and we're funny'; 'Even the people who are supposed to protect the country can be stupid'; 'We have sense of humour with a serious subject like war'; 'Proud but stupid'; 'Good sense of camaraderie'; 'We stick together'; 'We can pull together and act as a nation if necessary'; 'Strength in solidarity'; 'Accidental triumph in the face of adversity'; 'Determination, dedication, high sense of duty'; 'Irrepressible fighting spirit'; 'Strong-willed, slightly dopey but determined'; 'Very patriotic and eccentric'; 'Patriotic, a bit daft, eccentric'; 'Old men take pride about being British during the war'; 'Proud'; 'Traditional and pompous'; 'United, the British will overcome'.

Though, as acknowledged, these findings are qualitative rather than quantitative, they gain additional force through their correspondence with previous observations about the success and longevity of *Dad's Army* (see, for example, Richards 1977). As McCann remarks, '*Dad's Army*, deep down, was not really about the war. It was about England. It was about us' (2002: 6). Whilst the unified 'we' might be a recognisable (though not unquestionable) signifier for English people who actively fought in or directly experienced the Second World War, namely those now well over sixty years of age, it can scarcely be assumed to function in a highly consumerist, individualist, multicultural Britain in 2003. What, then, is particularly noteworthy in the findings above is the consonance between the remarks of the over-sixties and those of much younger people.

McCann anatomises 'Englishness' as follows: amateurism; faith in good form; willingness to help out; reluctance to be regimented; cosy eccentricities; irrepressibility; playfulness; loyalty; caution; courage; deep-rooted distrust of outsiders; chronic consciousness of class (see 2002: 6–7). All these characteristics are evident in aspects of the series and/or the comments above made upon it. But, although only one respondent (male, twenty to thirty) suggested that *Dad's Army* offered 'a clichéd look at British life', it is hard to accept in 2003 that what amounts to a mythology (in Barthes's 1972 sense) of Englishness is widely sustainable.

Texts in popular culture frequently function, however, outside social realism and rationality. As Rapping has observed of melodrama, 'it suggests recognisable depths of the human spirit that ring true on some level and that defy the language and scope of mere reason' (1992: 67). Perhaps comedy can function similarly. The utopian visions of popular texts often dismissed as 'escapist', it is implied, may have deep cultural resonances. Richards goes further to propose that 'Nostalgia is a vital force, passionate, active, committed to the ideal of reviving and preserving the best of the past' (1977: 363). The political significance of *Dad's Army* in Richards's view is that, 'it is not just a picture of an idealized past, it is also an image of an imagined future' (1977: 364–365). To express such a view today, however, is unfashionably to posit universal values ('the human spirit' or 'timeless comedy', or 'Englishness') in defiance of the dominant tropes of scepticism and relativism. Though it may afford a utopian vision of the future, such a view may equally express a deep English liberal-conservatism. Richards's assertion that, 'wherever you turn, people are looking back to the past and finding things that work' (1977: 365) betrays an uneasy slippage between traditionalism and his conception of nostalgia as a vital force for future good. The idea that the popularity of *Dad's Army* evidences a sustained tradition of sound English values would seem to embody an untenable notion of textual fixity, as well as an essentialism of national character, which scarcely maps on to the fragmented micro-cultures of the UK in the early twenty-first century. To account for the continued popularity of *Dad's Army* across the ages requires more nuanced analysis.

Popular drama on the domestic medium of television has historically been centred on the ideology of the family (see Feuer 1986 and Rapping 1992: xxxviiff). A constant tension between cohesion and a tendency to fragmentation in nuclear families of earlier television drama (and still in the major British soaps) has been followed with parallel tensions in the surrogate 'families' of the workplace and friendship networks. This dynamic itself reflects what Feuer identifies as 'television's dual ideological compulsions: the need to repeat and the need to contain' (Feuer 1986: 114), and this in turn is an analogue of a play between broader social cohesion and fragmentation. This nexus of ideas applied to *Dad's Army* mobilises an account of the longevity of the comedy series, even if it cannot go so far as to provide an explanation for its long-term popularity.

Respondents in one discussion group of over-sixties fell immediately into reminiscence about the war years after collectively viewing an episode of *Dad's Army*. What, on one level, may be nostalgia in recollections of 'spam' and 'air raid warnings', however, quickly turned to talk of 'our' bulldog spirit and, above all, a sense of a community pulling together. The marked emphasis on watching with father and family viewing revealed across age groups right down to young people today, whose only possible direct connection to the Second World War would be through ageing grandparents, indicates perhaps a sense of longing for family-social connections which today's fragmented society scarcely allows. Where watching *Dad's Army* together affords access to the past to a generation which has no sense of history – and certainly no memory of a serious conflict which might threaten directly its security (the Falklands and Iraq wars taking place at a geographical distance) – pleasurable surprises may be found in the historical depths beneath postmodern surfaces. Where neither viewer has had direct connections with the war (the respondent who remarked that 'it's set in an age when neither of us was alive . . . hence we both laugh at the same jokes'), pleasure lies primarily in a more general familial sharing. *Dad's Army*, itself a metaphor of a conflicted but (just about) coherent family, facilitates an enactment of bonding between family members, and thus it both represents and embodies, in the shared viewing experience, a utopian vision of the harmonious collective. Emotionally, this appears to be powerful enough to mask over the fissures which rational analysis would reveal to be a sham.

To return, in conclusion, to the opening of this essay, Mainwaring's own utopian vision is somewhat at odds with the first characteristic of Sir Ernest Baker's *The Character of England* (1947), namely social cohesion based on established hierarchy. Though Mainwaring's dream of a classless society implies a principle of social cohesion, it is precisely not based on a hierarchy of status. Such a new, egalitarian-meritocratic society promised after the Second World War has not exactly been fulfilled. Indeed, any broad-fronted approach to socially egalitarian reform through structural change has all but disappeared, with young people under pan-capitalism being encouraged to fulfil their dreams through individualist consumerism rather than pulling together in common cause. At best, a hierarchy of established social class has merely been displaced (and only partially at that) with a hierarchy based on material wealth and celebrity. And thus, the dichotomy noted in *Dad's Army* at the outset between a liberal-conservative affirmation of the status quo and a more radical vision of social reform remains unresolved, indeed it is held in place by the apparent resolution of *Dad's Army*'s comic form in the episodes' happy endings.

The sustained popularity of *Dad's Army* in traditional terms may be taken as a mark of a popular text holding a utopian vision of a better world achieved through collective means, or it may be taken to epitomise an inherent 'Englishness', too stoical, too good-humoured but, ultimately, too subservient to effect radical social change. Perhaps its capacity to be read from different angles – or even from two different perspectives almost simultaneously – adumbrates what is taken to be 'Englishness', a sense of values beyond the purely commercial ('faith in good form') a non-aggressive self-assertion ('reluctance to be regimented', 'amateurism') which somehow cannot be disentangled from the Establishment ('chronic consciousness of class').

On the evidence gleaned in preparing this essay, it does appear that *Dad's Army* brings out the familial and the liberal-conservative dimensions of British history noted above. At worst, it appeals to a xenophobia arising from an insular culture ('deep-rooted distrust of outsiders'). The experience of contemporary life in a socially fragmented Britain, a member of the European Union, under a right-leaning 'New Labour' government which has taken 'us' with the Americans into a highly questionable war with Iraq, may be different, but it seems that *Dad's Army* brings out not so much nostalgia as a myth of Old England. It is difficult to refrain from concluding that if people keep up this myth in the face of so much countermanding evidence of contemporary England then they really do 'like it up 'em!'.

But that, of course, would be a po-faced view: Stupid boy!

Notes

1 Lyric written by Jimmy Perry, see McCann 2002: 71.
2 See *Don't Panic: The Dad's Army Story* (BBC1 2000).
3 A brief episode guide is provided in McCann 2002: 231–248, and fuller details in Webber 2001.
4 For details of viewing figures see McCann 2001: 120 and 276, n. 41 and 48ff.
5 *The Army Game* (BBC 1957) and its spin-off *Bootsie and Snudge* (BBC1960–63) predate *Dad's Army* but they deal with National Service and were not set during wartime.
6 Some 768 (including fifty civilians) were killed in the course of Home Guard activities and 5,750 injured according to *The Real Dad's Army* (C4 2001).
7 There was awareness in the Establishment both of the questionable track record of the men at Osterley and that many self-appointed and self-directed Home Guard platoons saw themselves as above the law. It was not until Churchill took command of the war effort and established his secret Auxiliary Home Guard that greater central control and discipline more broadly was achieved (see *The Real Dad's Army*, C4 2001).
8 See *The Real Dad's Army* (C4 2001).
9 Paul Fox was appointed controller of BBC1 in 1967.

10 Though it is almost impossible now to imagine actors other than those cast playing the roles, John Pertwee was the original choice to play Mainwaring and a young David Jason was being considered for Corporal Jones.

11 'Stupid boy' was coined by Perry's father as a comment on young Jimmy's behaviour (see Perry 2003).

12 The narrative device of the 'Mum's Army' episode is a drive to recruit women to support the Walmington-on-Sea platoon in which Captain Mainwaring encourages the men to present women known to them for selection.

References:

Barthes, R. (1972), *Mythologies*, London: Paladin/Collins.

Creeber, G. (ed.) (2001), *The Television Genre Book*, London: British Film Institute.

Feuer, J. (1986), 'Narrative form in American network television', in C. MacCabe (ed.), *High Theory/Low Culture*, Manchester: Manchester University Press.

McCann, G. (2002), *Dad's Army: The Story of a Classic Television Show*, London: Fourth Estate/Harper Collins.

Perry, J. (2003), *A Stupid Boy*, London: Arrow Books/Random House.

Rapping, E. (1992), *The Movie of the Week*, Minneapolis: University of Minnesota Press.

Richards, J. (1977), '*Dad's Army* and the politics of nostalgia', in *Films and British National Identity*, Manchester: Manchester University Press.

Webber, R. (2001), *The Complete A–Z of Dad's Army*, London: Orion.

Further reading:

Jancovich, M., Lucy Faire and Sarah Stubbings (eds) (2003), *The Place of the Audience*, London: British Film Institute.

Marc, D. (1989), *Comic Visions: Television Comedy and American Culture*, Oxford: Blackwell.

Neale, S., and F. Krutnik (1990), *Popular Film and Television Comedy*, London: Routledge.

Perry, J. and D. Croft (1975), *Dad's Army* (five scripts), London: Hamish Hamilton.

Pertwee, B. (1989), *Dad's Army: The Making of a TV Legend*, London: David & Charles.

Part II

Quality and the 'other' drama

Editors' introduction

Academic studies of television have attempted to address the question of quality in a range of ways, and this introduction can only provide an overview of that debate (see Brunsdon 1997, Mulgan 1990 for example). Quality is not only a matter of contested definition as an academic term, but also relates problematically to the notion of 'good' television. While academic work has largely eschewed the making of distinctions that value one programme or genre over another, informal discourse about television and television drama in particular very often consists in identifying a 'good' programme (or channel, or viewing experience). Bignell (2004: 2) offered the brief definition that quality 'is an informal category that often separates plays and art films, adaptations and authored serials from the rest, from "popular" television'. While this comment opens up a number of further questions, it draws attention to the ways in which assigning the designation 'quality' involves assigning cultural importance to programmes or genres that have attained cultural value. As the sociologist Pierre Bourdieu (1984) argued, the discrimination of quality functions as a marker of taste and discernment in a cultural hierarchy that encompasses both the object to which quality is attributed and also the person making the judgement. Within the television industry, quality refers to lavishness of budgets, the skill of programme makers and performers, and the prestige accruing to programmes because of their audience profile and seriousness of purpose. But within the academic discipline of Television Studies, quality has a broader meaning that also focuses attention on popular television that might be regarded by insiders as merely commercial and generic work that has little aspiration to cultural or artistic value.

As we pointed out in the introduction to this book, the attention to popular television drama might be concerned to relate programmes to the 'literate' components shared with canonical literature or written drama such as 'narrative, sequential, abstract, univocal, "consistent"' aesthetic features (Fiske and Hartley 1978: 125). This seeks to appropriate the characteristics that connote quality in forms outside of television and attach them to a broad range of popular television texts. But since television drama's modes of address also draw on the 'dramatic, episodic, concrete, social, dialectical' forms of popular performance or informal talk, Fiske and Hartley saw television as the inheritor and mediator of organic popular culture and thus connected with the needs, enthusiasms and experiences of its audiences. Since Television Studies has valued the inherent vitality of audiences as active interpreters of meaning, the analysis of television drama as both a quality and popular form opens up a means of linking the aesthetics of television drama texts to the lived dialectics of sense-making and taste-making.

The analysis of drama programmes has been concerned with identifying the grounds for valuing one programme over another as aesthetically challenging, conducive to social change, or the product of authorial creativity. Informed by the interest in supplementing the close study of audio-visual texts with a recognition of television drama as a popular mode that works with and against generic expectations and recognises the pleasures offered to its audiences, work on the question of quality has broadened the range of programming it addresses, towards programmes that had been little regarded because of their apparently formulaic and generic narrative patterns and their consumption by audiences whose tastes and discrimination had been undervalued.

This section contains four essays that engage in different ways with this complex of debates around authorship, aesthetic and textual complexity or experimentation, and address to popular audiences. Peter Billingham discusses the Channel 4 drama series *Queer As Folk* (C4 1999–2000), focusing on its status as an authored intervention in debates about the representation of homosexuality, and specifically the social position of gay men in the community of Manchester's city-centre 'gay village'. As Billingham shows, the programme drew on Channel 4's institutional remit to address new configurations of audience, to represent hitherto under represented social groups and to debate the terms in which gay sexuality and its subcultural expressions could be given a place in prime time. By exploiting the specific cultural geography of Manchester's Canal Street, which Billingham terms its 'geo-ideological' meanings as a place of licensed pleasures, the programme established patterns of relationships between characters that concretised and mediated questions of assimilation of gay identity and the tensions and contradictions around sexuality as a conduit for identity-formation. Place, personhood, class and wealth were each represented as material circumstances that bear on the dramatic representation of gay identity. At various points in his essay, Billingham draws attention to the ways in which the status of the drama as a 'quality' authored series ran up against the limits of this kind of 'progressive' intervention. The withdrawal of the programme's sponsor, regulators' investigations of complaints from interest groups about its sexual explicitness, and the question of who its audience may have been and how the programme may have addressed that audience, are considered. While *Queer As Folk* remains a landmark television drama in the ventilation of questions of sexuality and representation, attention to the text itself is insufficient without an understanding of the conditions that brought it to the screen and affected its reception.

Mark Bould's essay on the 'cult' adventure drama *The Prisoner* (ITC 1967–68) demonstrates that the series inhabits some similar contradictions. Bould unpacks the complex question of the series's authorship, and the inadequacy of attributing its meanings to its creator, star performer or production team, for example. The series works with and against generic expectations deriving from its relationships with the spy adventure drama that came to prominence in television and also in film and other media in the 1960s. If *The Prisoner* evades the closure and stability of the spy adventure, there is a temptation to call on transhistorical interpretations that frame it as an allegory about a universal human nature. Bould demonstrates that this reduction of the fantastic mode to allegory will not work either, and argues that the series foregrounds its own play with interpretative schemas and thus ensures its longevity as a text of fascination and temptation for audiences. Using detailed discussion of the programme's aesthetic strategies and structural games, Bould brings *The Prisoner* into dialogue with theoretical work on modernity and subjectivity that places such hesitations and contingencies of meaning at the centre of a theory of subjectivity. Although *The Prisoner* has been the subject of extensive critical debate among fans and academic theorists alike, Bould shows that the programme in a sense anticipates this debate and enfolds its multiple positions within its own television realisation. Thus the series both fails to match some of the criteria of quality (such as coherence, well-formed narrative or engagement with issues of public political concern) yet carves out a place for itself as an instantiation of sophisticated questions of aesthetics, textuality and representation.

Máire Messenger Davies combines three of the predominant approaches to quality in her essay on *The Demon Headmaster* (BBC 1995–96, 1997, 1998). She explains its claims for authorial seriousness of purpose and relationship to its literary antecedents, noting the programme's engagement with questions of children's place in society, tensions between liberty and constraint, and its representations of technology and power. She argues that *The Demon Headmaster* makes a significant contribution to the project of exploring and defining questions of ethics and justice in social organisation, in part by claiming children's culture as a space of experimentation, resistance and subversion. But she also places the programme in the context of the ongoing concerns within the broadcasting industry, regulatory discourses and public debates about television's responsibility to child audiences and the struggle to retain 'quality' drama for children (as both a high-budget and a high-concept form) in the contemporary television landscape. This attention to institutions and production contexts reorients questions of quality in relation to the material circumstances of television as an industry. Furthermore, her research into child audiences for *The Demon Headmaster* gives a valuable insight into how children themselves recognised quality in the programme, showing that children can be not simply an absent constituency appealed to in adults' arguments about quality but also an active voice in the discrimination of the pleasures and political stakes of television for children.

The final essay in this section connects with the questions of institutional understandings of quality, authorship and audience that have been developed by the other contributors. Jonathan Bignell's essay shows how, in the early years of the science-fiction drama series *Doctor Who* (BBC 1963-96), negotiations around quality guided the planning and production of the programme, and informed the understanding of audience feedback about it. Adopting a specific focus on the Doctor's notorious opponents, the Daleks, Bignell shows how their realisation drew on a tradition of science fiction in film, television and other media that distanced them from notions of quality, but also on a concern to offer both realist representations of scientific subjects and historical narratives that gave the programme seriousness of purpose. *Doctor Who*'s producers also drew on newly developed television technologies and emphasised moments of visual revelation, displaying a concern for the medium's aesthetic specificity within the episodic serial form and suggesting a reflexivity about means of representation that argues in favour of quality. However, as thrilling entertainment for a predominantly child audience the Dalek stories in *Doctor Who* were perpetually negotiating with their own success as popular merchandising opportunities and attractions for large and socially diverse audiences. Bignell's essay demonstrates the shifting meanings of quality in this context, and its relationships with aesthetic forms, institutional constraints and relations with the audience.

References

Bignell, J. (2004), *An Introduction to Television Studies*, London: Routledge.

Bourdieu, P. (1984), *Distinction: A Social Critique of the Judgement of Taste*, London: Routledge.

Brunsdon, C. (1997), *Screen Tastes: Soap Operas to Satellite Dishes*, London: Routledge.

Fiske, J. and J. Hartley (1978), *Reading Television*, London: Methuen.

Mulgan, G. (ed.) (1990), *The Questions of Quality*, London: BFI.

4

Space for 'quality': negotiating with the Daleks

Jonathan Bignell

This essay connects a study of the commissioning and production processes of the well-known science-fiction drama series *Doctor Who* with the larger theoretical question of the understandings of 'quality' guiding its production and reception. The serial most fully discussed is 'The Daleks' (BBC 1963), which ensured *Doctor Who*'s survival by attracting significant audiences with a futuristic science fiction adventure.[1] As James Chapman has noted (2002: 3–4), the evaluation and justification of quality in British television drama has focused on its social realist tradition or on its relationship with literature. Chapman also argues that the association of quality with authorship has reduced attention to the popular genre series devised and authored by teams of contributors. Because programme format establishes continuing characters and situations, repetition and predictability seem also to separate series television from the criteria of quality. My discussion of the development and pre-production stages in the creation of 'The Daleks' focuses on the dynamic negotiations around quality among key personnel in the BBC Drama Group in 1963, and the ways that audience research highlighted questions of quality and legitimated production decisions in the early years of *Doctor Who*'s broadcast. Drawing on archival research from BBC Written Archives Centre,[2] this analysis differs from existing studies by focusing on the production process rather than the programme text, and on the culture of production and reception. The essay shows how the assumptions of the production team, the aesthetics of the programme text, the audiences for programmes, and the publicity discourses and merchandising contexts surrounding a programme lead to different understandings of 'quality' and negotiations with and between these understandings.

The culture of production

Science fiction had a cinematic heritage primarily in US film serials of the 1930s and 1940s, such as *Flash Gordon* (1936) and *Buck Rogers* (1939), whose form and low cultural standing reflected their origins in syndicated comic strips. US television science fiction drew on this sometimes explicitly (as in *Buck Rogers*, 1950–51) or by following its conventions (as in *Space Patrol*, 1950–55). The television anthology series *The Twilight Zone* (1959–64) and *The Outer Limits* (1963–65) were aimed at adult viewers, and drew their writers and their tone from published US science-fiction novels and short stories. In the UK, the BBC's early dramas in the genre drew on British and European (as well as some US) novels and short stories by established names. The first television science-fiction programme was the BBC's adaptation of *R. U. R.* by Karel Čapek (1938), then a 1949 adaptation of H. G. Wells's *The Time Machine*, a live single play from the Alexandra Palace studios. Nigel Kneale's six-part original serial *The Quatermass Experiment* (1953) was a BBC success, and its sequels both gave impetus to science-fiction drama as a distinctive quality form and also suggested that BBC might compete with ITV in adult science-fiction drama. As head of drama at ABC Sydney Newman had in 1959 commissioned the live seven-part children's serial *Pathfinders in Space*, by Eric Paice and Malcolm Hulke. This fast-moving space exploration story, featuring Professor Wedgewood and his children, was based on scientific fact, and its success led to the studio-recorded sequels *Pathfinders to Mars* and *Pathfinders to Venus* (1961) with more elaborate filmed effects and models. In 1960 Newman placed *Target Luna* in a Sunday afternoon slot, featuring a young boy in a space adventure drama. These and other ITV programmes attracted younger audiences with science fiction, while BBC children's programming was headed by low-budget costume adaptations in the classic serial format. His success in drama for adults and children gave Newman considerable power when he moved from ABC to become BBC Head of Drama in 1962, the same year that ABC's adult-targeted science-fiction anthology *Out of This World* began. Newman divided the Script Department into Plays, Series and Serials divisions, and among other initiatives he suggested that Serials should create a science-fiction serial for a family audience on early Saturday evenings, to rival the Children's Department's classic novel adaptations. Relationships with literary sources, a basis in scientific fact and speculation, and a concern that the writing should match the quality of serials for adults, guided the planning.

Two Drama Group staff, John Braybon and Alice Frick, produced a report for Donald Wilson, Head of Serial Drama (Television) in July 1962 (BBC WAC T5/647/1). Following Serials' experience in adaptation, it investigated science-fiction short stories that fulfilled four requirements. They did not include 'Bug-Eyed Monsters', because these were perceived to derive from the US cinematic heritage of adventure serials. The central characters could not be robots since human performers would be too obviously inside them. No large and elaborate science-fiction settings were possible since these would be expensive and also too obviously fabricated. Substantial characterisation and logical storylines were required. Braybon and Frick favoured two science-fiction sub-genres, involving either telepaths or time travel, and argued that the new series could be 'the *Z Cars* of science fiction'. Not only could the programme become as popular as BBC's prime-time police drama, but also a robust production system could be established in which numerous freelance writers could contribute to a stable format where quality could be reliably assured.

Children aged eight to fourteen, and adults watching with them, were the target audience, and production staff distanced the programme from science fiction's generic associations with US and low-quality programmes. Donald Wilson's notes dated 30 July 1963 on a preliminary promotion meeting (BBC WAC T5/647/1) stated: 'The serial cannot accurately be described as either space travel or science fiction . . . as the stories themselves spring from the reactions of the characters to the environment and periods in which they find themselves'. *Doctor Who* was designed to draw on realist conventions of representation partly to appear educational and improving, containing factual and historical information in storylines set around historical events such as the Roman invasion of Britain, and exploring the scientific possibilities of time travel, spatial dimension and planetary exploration. Chapman (2002: 136) notes in relation to *Doctor Who*: 'one of the hallmarks of British science-fiction, especially that produced by the BBC, is that it tends to use a realistic, at times almost documentary-like style to present unlikely events'. Dennis Spooner (script editor) noted in October 1964 in a letter to a viewer that *Doctor Who* storylines avoided the sixteenth to nineteenth centuries since BBC classic serials were usually set then (BBC WAC T5/649/1): this accommodation emphasises *Doctor Who*'s similarity to and difference from adapted serial drama, and demonstrates the connection between the two forms as different approaches to the concept of quality. But *Doctor Who* was unpopular with the Children's Department because Drama Group controlled it, and Newman was regarded as an interloper from ITV, promoted over existing BBC staff, who had brought many former ABC colleagues with him. Newman's pet project also used resources which necessarily detracted from other possible output.

A small circle of writers and production staff circulated between BBC, the ITV companies and ITC in this period, dominating the popular drama output in science fiction, action and fantasy. David Whitaker, the first script editor on *Doctor Who*, sought experienced television serial and series writers. For example, he initially commissioned ABC's contributing writers Dennis Spooner, John Lucarotti and Bill Strutton, and Malcolm Hulke, who wrote the *Pathfinders* serials. Terry Nation was approached, having been recommended by his friend Spooner.[3] He had written for ABC's *Out of This World*, but Nation initially turned down the offer of writing for children. Because he became unexpectedly unemployed, Nation accepted the commission to write the serial later titled 'The Daleks' in July 1963 (BBC WAC T48/445). Whitaker was pleased with the script, while Wilson's more conventionally Reithian outlook made him dislike the relatively simplistic Manichaeanism and monster adventure in 'The Daleks'. Whitaker added a defensive note to his Copyright Brief recording Nation's commission: 'Terry Nation has written a considerable amount of drama for ITV . . . His writing has improved in quality and he has been writing film scripts. He has given us a detailed and highly fancied storyline'. Wilson was persuaded to accept 'The Daleks' because it was the only futuristic serial ready for production, and a futuristic offering was required after Anthony Coburn's 'Tribe of Gum' (retitled '100,000 BC') began *Doctor Who* in 1963, with John Lucarotti's historical 'Journey to Cathay' as the third story. Unpromising audience research reports on the first serial arrived during production of 'The Daleks', but an initial decision to cancel *Doctor Who* was postponed, by which time the response to 'The Daleks' had ensured the programme's survival. Whitaker was pleased with Nation's efficiency, but Nation's reward for quality and reliability was to be a decades-long series of requests for Dalek serials and other science-fiction adventure as *Doctor Who* moved increasingly to stimulate and satisfy audience preferences for futuristic adventures rather than alternating these with historical stories.

The context of the devising and production of *Doctor Who* required 'The Daleks' to connect both with the highly conventionalised popular science fiction associated with US paperback publishing, films and comics, and also with the intellectual pretensions of the genre's literary forms. 'The Daleks' draws on Wells's *The Time Machine* and George Pal's

1960 film adaptation (Bignell 1999). In episode one, Nation's original storyline described the TARDIS travellers' impressions of the Dalek city:

> The buildings are more modern than those they know on Earth, glass being widely used in design . . . The floors and roadways are made from metal. There are no steps anywhere, only sloping ramps. Dr Who is quite excited. They make their headquarters in what appears to be a public building. Dr Who directs each of them to go in a different direction and find, if they can, books, or whatever replaced books. Dr Who hopes to learn something of the history of the planet. (quoted in Brunt and Pixley 1998: 21)

The search for books parallels the investigation of an ancient library in *The Time Machine*, and the subsequent encounters with the warlike metal-shelled Dalek and effete Thal races echoes Wells's traveller's meeting with the carnivorous Morlocks, operating industrial machines, and their passive Eloi prey. In Pal's film (but not in Wells's novel), the time traveller provokes the Eloi to fight their oppressors, and in 'The Daleks' the Doctor (William Hartnell) similarly goads the Thals to attack the Dalek city. E. M. Forster's *The Machine Stops* may also have suggested 'The Daleks''s contrasts between forest and city, for example. But literary borrowings coexist with Nation's description of the Daleks in the storyline (BBC WAC T5/647/1) as hideous, legless machine-like creatures with no human features, a lens on a flexible shaft replacing eyes, and arms with mechanical grips and strange weapons. The Daleks were intended to be uncannily monstrous, drawing on science fiction's popular forms, especially in visual media. The producer, Verity Lambert, described the story simply as an 'adventure in a world stricken by an atomic explosion' in promotional material dated 30 July 1963 (BBC WAC T5/647/1). While 'The Daleks' offered its audience motifs and narrative structures that linked it to literary science fiction and adaptations of 'classic' works in the genre, it was also conceived as an opportunity for specifically televisual revelation of alien and thrilling creatures and physical action, in the tradition of low-budget US cinema and popular publishing.

The revelatory aesthetic

Television scholarship has defined the medium as one in which a distracted domestic viewer glances at relatively simple image compositions with low density of visual information, where images are emphasised and anchored by sound and music. This has militated against detailed work on television's audio-visual aesthetic (see Caughie 2000), but as Catherine Johnson (2002) has argued, television science fiction and fantasy can refuse the restriction of television to dialogue-driven intimate drama. Images of science-fiction settings, creatures and technologies, as well as punctual narrative moments which foreground spectacular effects, are aesthetic components that address and retain viewers through distinctive forms. 'The Daleks' makes use of the intimacy available to multi-character, multi-camera performance 'as if live' in the restricted space of the television studio, but also provides opportunities for spectacle, thus connecting the serial with both conventional television naturalism and cinematic science fiction. Building fan audiences and developing a 'cult' aesthetic in niche programmes were not very significant in the 'era of scarcity' (Ellis 2000: 39–60) when two channels provided a restricted diet of programming for mass audiences. But the emergence of a culture of 'cult' programmes, repeated viewing, programme-related merchandise and exploitation of franchised formats in science-fiction and fantasy television was significantly dependent on the visual and aural aesthetic developed in the specifically televisual form of the episodic serial.

Television science fiction could fall between the two stools of competition with cinema in visual effects, and the challenges to conventions of realism and naturalistic characterisation that novelistic science fiction could offer. This is especially true of studio-shot drama such as *Doctor Who*, and the acclaimed television producer Tony Garnett wrote, looking back on his own experiences in the 1960s:

> Studio-based drama was a bastard child of two forms: the theatre (continuous performance) and cinema (various length of lens affording different points of view and sizes of image) . . . it seemed to me to have all the disadvantages and none of the advantages of its parents . . . five or six cameras were deployed around the studio trying to catch the action whilst the whole thing was being simultaneously edited. This resulted in a form of cinema on the run. (Garnett 2000: 16)

The orthodox critical view of television science fiction has stressed its inadequacy in these terms. Discussing the relationship between literary science fiction and other media, Kingsley Amis (1969: 100) wrote in 1961: 'In the visual media the effects have got to be lavish: it is no use trying to produce a convincing BEM [bug-eyed monster] by fiddling around with slow-motion process shots of newts.' Studies of science-fiction cinema (e.g. Scholes and Rabkin 1977) sometimes make claims for its intellectual credentials, but emphasise the awe induced by visual spectacle and its relationship with the horror genre, and rarely credit television science fiction with any significance in aesthetic terms.

Television cannot win this debate because of the assumptions about the aesthetic possibilities of its technology, its status as a mass broadcast medium and its viewers. In general, writers of literary science fiction have a disparaging attitude to television material, regarding it as aimed at a child audience and therefore conceptually underdeveloped. Indeed, the disparagement of television (and cinema) texts and fan communities is a rhetorical mechanism for sustaining the hard-won intellectual prestige gradually achieved for literary science fiction. *Doctor Who*'s production team aimed for the visual emphasis that cinema was reputed to do better than television, yet also the conceptual focus that literature was thought to offer. They approached science-fiction writers in September 1964 to script *Doctor Who*, because of their literary skills but also for financial reasons (BBC WAC T5/647/1). If an author would accept £400 for a storyline, this compared well with the £750 he or she would earn in royalties on a novel selling ten thousand copies at 15 shillings each. An experienced television adaptor could be paid £1,450 for six episode scripts, saving £125 on the usual fee paid to screenwriters. Writing and writers were a central feature of *Doctor Who*'s claims for quality, and the production team's approaches to them combined respect for literary seriousness with hard-headed strategies to reduce costs.

The twin aims of the programme were not only to continue the Department's ethos of 'quality' writing in terms of character, dramatic logic and thematic complexity but also to use the visual and aural resources available from recently-invented videotape recording processes, camera effects, electronic sound and inserted film effects and models. This innovative production system utilised the minimum number of film inserts or post-production processes since most of the effects were created on set at low cost. When *Doctor Who* entered production, Mervyn Pinfield occupied the role of Associate Producer, as technical adviser. Pinfield had trained new directors and production assistants and had worked with the Langham Group, led by Anthony Pellissier at the Langham Studios, on experimental aesthetic forms using inlay, overlay and split-screen. His experiments with video feedback generated the cloud-like streams in *Doctor Who*'s title sequence. Whitaker, the script editor, gave potential writers a six-page briefing document (BBC WAC T5/647/1) which specified the maximum and minimum number of episodes, episode length, an all-year run and the requirement for a storyline climax both at the end of each episode and half-way through (so overseas buyers could insert commercials). Although the document described *Doctor Who* as 'primarily a series of stories concerning people rather than studio effects', the need for climactic moments and the availability of Pinfield as 'the arbiter on technical and factual detail' was designed to allow moments of visual spectacle and technical experiment.

Though clunky by today's standards, mise-en-scène was a significant priority at the time. 'The Daleks' used five days of models and special-effects filming at the BBC's Ealing studios (BBC WAC T5/648/1), and its seven episode scripts were each performed and recorded in a single day. A grant of £3,278 had been given for the construction of the TARDIS, to be paid back in weekly instalments, and 'The Daleks" budget per episode of £2,500 included the significant proportions of £200 a week for externally contracted scenery, and £500 a week for studio sets and outside filming. But estimates increased, for example to up to £8,000 for special props (including the Daleks themselves). As a result, Donald Baverstock (Chief of Programmes BBC1) wrote to Donald Wilson on 18 October 1963 cancelling *Doctor Who* after the first four-episode serial and requesting plans for a new children's series. But 'The Daleks' was already in production, and arresting visual moments were crucial to its reception.

The full or partial visual revelation of the Daleks was acknowledged by the writers, script editor and directors as a crucial structural motif. In the original storyline, Barbara (Jacqueline Hill) is suddenly attacked at the end of episode 1 when a panel opens behind her and 'a pair of grotesque arms move out to encircle her' (quoted in Brunt and Pixley 1998: 21). The Daleks were first fully visible in the second episode, and at the end of the fourth episode the claw of an organic creature, removed from its metal casing and protruding from under a blanket, suggested what the creatures inside the machines might be. In this and all later Dalek stories, minor threats led up to the appearance of a Dalek, usually at the end of episode one. The Daleks' presence was later advertised in serial titles, such as 'Planet of the Daleks' (1973), 'Death to the Daleks' (1974), or 'Genesis of the Daleks' (1975). The foreknowledge of their appearance both generates anticipation, and also reduces surprise when they appear, so the dramatic build-up to that moment had to be increasingly carefully prepared.

Dalek serials, especially those by Nation, are formulaic, but their repetitions make intertextual references to previous storylines, and their naturalistic performance style, and punctuation by spectacle amid familiar narrative arcs and intimately known characters were part of their appeal. In an interview in the BBC video *More than 30 Years in the TARDIS* (1994), Barry Letts (*Doctor Who* producer 1969–74) comments: 'To a cer-

tain extent we set out to frighten the viewer.' In the same video, Tom Baker
(who played the Doctor from 1974 to 1981) refers to the family audience
that the programme was intended for, and the range of viewer reactions
that are commonly held to occur: 'The smallest child terrified behind the
sofa or under a cushion; and the next one up laughing at him; and the
elder one saying, "Shush, I want to listen . . ."; and the parents saying,
"Isn't this enjoyable?"' Chapman refers (2002: 5) to the work of Umberto
Eco (1990) on the narrative structures in popular television series, where
Eco argues that formula produces pleasure through a recurrent narrative
pattern. The expected pattern rewards predictive activity, producing a
second kind of pleasure, and repetition and conformity to viewer expectations result in potentially larger and more satisfied audiences. Audiences accepted and revelled in the limited verisimilitude available to
Doctor Who, which was sometimes counterpointed by moments of visual
pleasure and surprise like those in 'The Daleks'. The emergence of a Dalek
from the waters of the Thames, surrounded by a devastated but recognisable London cityscape in 'The Dalek Invasion of Earth' (1964), for example, used the realism of location filming to emphasise the pleasure of an
expected revelatory moment by displacing it from the studio's associations with artifice and spatially restricted intimacy.

'The Daleks' foregrounds vision in numerous ways. The climactic
moment when Barbara is approached by a Dalek is shot through a circular cowl representing the Dalek's point of view, and other sequences also
use point of view to align the audience with the Daleks. The plot of 'The
Chase' (1965), in which the Doctor and his companions are pursued
through space and time by the Daleks, is initiated when the Doctor sees
them on his Space-Time Visualiser, something like a giant television set
which he tunes also to images of Elizabeth I, Shakespeare, Abraham Lin-
coln and Francis Bacon. The first episode of 'The Keys of Marinus' (1964)
features a conversation about colour television (introduced by BBC2 in
1967) in which the Doctor says to his Earth companions, 'I was working
on that on your planet – you remember the first time we met. My colour
rays weren't mixing properly. I went along to the British Broadcasting
Corporation but they were infernally secretive.' A reflexive awareness that
Doctor Who was television, despite its allusions to and background in literature, cinema and other media, was crucial to its play with contrasts
between the alien and the familiar, the exotic and the domestic, and
between spectacle and character-based, dialogue-driven scripts. The relative bareness of the programme's monochrome images, production
values and narrative complexity were the ground against which visual

pleasure and the effect generated by its monsters, action sequences and special effects stood out strongly.

A memo from Baverstock to Newman dated 31 December 1963 (BBC WAC T5/647/1) hoped that in the ten more episodes Baverstock allowed *Doctor Who* in 1964 'you will brighten up the logic and inventiveness of the scripts' and attempt to 'reduce the amount of slow prosaic dialogue and to centre the dramatic movements much more on historical and scientific hokum'. The mixture of educational material with 'hokum' (adventure drama) was established as the driver of the series's success, and a rapid displacement towards popular generic drama involving the moments of spectacle and revelation discussed above led to changes in *Doctor Who's* production system. As their success became evident, Dalek stories were allowed to break BBC production norms. In 1966 a memo from Shaun Sutton (Head of Serials) to producers, directors and production assistants in his department reminded them not to allow more than five breaks in their studio recording day because of consequent overruns and overtime costs (BBC WAC T5/782/3). But he acknowledged that the Daleks required more breaks because their operators experienced such discomfort, and technical problems tended to occur. The second Dalek story, 'The Keys of Marinus' was allowed a large number of sets and props: alien planet and pyramid sets, midget submarines and the elaborate Conscience Machine prop. Even so, cost control led to the use of low-key lighting and black drapes instead of a set in some scenes, and stock film footage to open out the studio setting rather than location work. Some Dalek serials had more than the usual number of episodes both because they were popular with audiences and also because they minimised costs by spreading them over a longer run, and even the twelve-episode extended Dalek serial in their mid-1960s heyday retained the low-cost production system with minimal uses of film and restricted production values. But this seemed to encourage audience enthusiasm for the programme as specifically televisual; as both domestic and homely but also realistically fantastic and absorbing.

Dalek-mania

Daleks were immediately successful, as audience research reports indicated, and quality was measured in part by their appeal to large audiences and viewers' comments on the quality of the serials. In 1963 the average Reaction Index (a measure of appreciation) for television drama was 62, and the average for children's programmes 64 (BBC WAC T5/647/1).

Audience research information on 'The Daleks' serial showed a lowest
Reaction Index of 59 (episode one) and highest of 65 (episode seven), and
a lowest audience share of 13 per cent (episode two) and highest share of
21 per cent (episodes six and seven) (BBC WAC T5/648/1). The serial's
episodes achieved an average audience of nine million, comparable to
both the Drama Group's family and adult-oriented programmes, and to
Children's Department output. Newman (*Radio Times* 1983: unpagi-
nated) described the target audience: 'I wanted to bridge the gap on a Saturday between the afternoon's sports coverage, which attracted a huge
adult audience, and *Juke Box Jury*, which had a very large teenage following. It was never intended to be simply a children's programme, but
something that would appeal to people who were in a rather child-like
frame of mind!' The original main characters were designed for broad
appeal. In a memo of 29 March 1963 to Wilson (BBC WAC T5/647/1),
staff writer Cecil Webber argued that they could not be children because
child viewers disliked characters younger than themselves. They could
not be girls because boys would not watch. An older woman should be
included to catch older woman viewers, and men who had been watching
Saturday sports television could identify with an older man. So the
characters should be a handsome young man, a handsome well-dressed
heroine aged about thirty, and an older man with some character twist.
This was the basic pattern for the main cast when the series began, with
the significant addition of the Doctor's teenage grand daughter Susan
(Carole Ann Ford), included as a figure of identification and aspiration
for young children.

By the 1970s, more sophisticated audience research information was
being gathered to estimate the address of BBC programmes to different
age, sex and class sectors in the audience. This information is not available for the first 1960s Dalek serials, but a sense of the composition of the
Doctor Who audience and the programme's penetration (the percentage
of the available audience tuning in) can be gained from a BBC Audience
Research Report of 14 March 1977 which gives detailed breakdowns for
weeks 1–8 of that year (BBC WAC T51/369/1). 59 per cent of children
aged five to fourteen chose to watch *Doctor Who*, and 17 per cent of
adults. The report broke the audience down by social class, into upper-
middle-class viewers of whom 21 per cent tuned in to the programme,
lower-middle-class viewers of whom 25 per cent watched it, and working-class viewers of whom 23 per cent watched. These statistics show that
the audience was equally weighted across social classes, and, although
upper-middle-class viewers comprised only 4 per cent of the audience as

a whole, compared to 33 per cent lower-middle-class and 64 per cent working-class viewers, the programme was gaining between a fifth and a quarter of the viewers watching television early on Saturday evening in each class group. This was a 'quality audience' comprising significant shares of each social class. It is sometimes assumed that science-fiction audiences are predominantly young men, but *Doctor Who* was seen by family groups watching together, thus producing a roughly equal divide between male and female viewers. In total, 23 per cent of the viewers were boys and 18 per cent were girls, 29 per cent were men and 30 per cent were women. It would be hasty to assume that these figures were the same in 1963 as they were in 1977, but it seems likely that Newman and his colleagues' desire to attract boys, girls, men, women and especially family groups was successful.

Statistical information does not reveal, however, how individual viewers evaluated and understood the attractions and pleasures of the Daleks. But information about individual viewers' responses to the Daleks can be gleaned from BBC audience research, though this is necessarily indicative rather than representative. For an Audience Research Report dated 22 July 1965 on episode six of 'The Chase' (BBC WAC T5/1243/1), a 'Housewife' reported that her children 'sit fixed before the television as though hypnotised', a grandmother recounted: 'I don't like it but if my grandchildren are here it gives me a peaceful half hour or so as they sit enthralled', and a 'Salesman' reported, 'I wouldn't miss it for anything and nor would the children'. A sizeable majority of adults thought *Doctor Who* was ridiculous, the story disjointed and fantastical, but nevertheless found it compelling. An Audience Research Report dated 11 January 1966, on episode three of 'The Daleks' Master Plan' (1965) (BBC WAC T5/1247/1), contained a rare comment from a child, when a schoolboy commented, 'I love Dr. Who but enjoy the futuristic episodes, especially those with the Daleks, much more than the historical ones. This adventure is simply super.' The Daleks were crucial to increased audiences for BBC's Saturday schedule, the highest-rating evening of the week, and from BBC executives' and schedulers' point of view this raised the status of the programme.

Audience research reports were supplemented by monitoring press coverage of programmes. Publicity effort for *Doctor Who* centred on the beginnings of new serials where new alien creatures or new actors playing the Doctor or his companions were introduced, or at significant times of year, especially Christmas when merchandising sales were expected. BBC had four Daleks stored at Ealing Studios by Christmas 1964, and had an arrangement with BBC Publicity department to lend these out to officially-organised children's Christmas parties or exhibitions, particularly those benefiting charities. Almost universally positive press coverage resulted from these initiatives, press releases and stunts. From 1963 to 1965, the BBC dealt with viewers' letters about the Daleks, which were the main subject of correspondence about *Doctor Who* (BBC WAC T5/649/1). The production team received requests for photographs of the cast and the Daleks, and do-it-yourself instructions on how to build a Dalek as shown on *Blue Peter*, for example. Most of the letters were from enthusiastic children, though a few adults wrote to point out factual inaccuracies, to complain about violent or potentially disturbing scenes, or make suggestions for future storylines. Again, viewers' letters are not representative of the reactions of the whole audience, but the focus of the overwhelming majority of letters on Daleks at this time demonstrates the significance of the visual revelations of the creatures within the narrative, as described above, and also the prominence of the Daleks (and *Doctor Who* in general) as BBC 'brands' which had enormous public profile and attraction.

Along with merchandise, spin-off and supplementary texts in various media supported the attractions of *Doctor Who* and especially the Daleks, both stimulating and satisfying Dalek-mania. Whitaker scripted the 1964 theatre play *Curse of the Daleks* and the Dalek comic strip in *TV Century 21* comic (1965–66). The strip finished when the Daleks located Earth, thus framing 'The Dalek Invasion of Earth' on television. Whitaker wrote two *Doctor Who* novels and the first *Doctor Who* annual, co-wrote the first Dalek cinema film and wrote the dialogue for the second (both were based on television storylines). By 1966 Dalek-mania had waned, leaving the BBC and outsiders to question their continued power to gain audiences. Nation ceased working on BBC programmes in 1966 as his work for ITC increased. He tried to obtain BBC backing for a filmed Dalek series deriving from *Doctor Who*, but the BBC turned it down, as did the US network NBC (Brunt and Pixley 2000: 178–179). However, Nation and other writers scripted Dalek appearances and Dalek-centred serials for *Doctor Who* across the 1960s, 1970s and 1980s. Daleks featured extensively in other BBC programmes, partly as a BBC brand, and partly as a means of signalling a set of science-fiction conventions in programmes which negotiated their place in the genre or in parodic counterpoint with it.

In the 1960s, programmes were rarely repeated and retail videotape did not exist. In this context, the persistence of viewers' memories of the Daleks demonstrates how important visual revelation, viewer involvement with them and the enfolding of revelatory moments in different viewing contexts were. Patrick Mulkern's description and discussion of 'The Dalek Invasion of Earth' contains occasional reminiscences contributed by readers of *Doctor Who Magazine*. Esther Flyte of Kendal reported: 'My earliest memory of *Doctor Who* is my terror at the sight of the Dalek's head coming out of the water [The Thames, at the end of episode one]. Its eye bobbing up and down, and its other arms, one of which my brother told me was a weapon' (quoted in Mulkern 1988: 19). The memory is one of uncanniness and terror, as the monstrous Dalek appears in a familiar setting. Flyte was watching with her brother, and commentary and explanation were significant to young viewers' experiences. This communal viewing situation was also significant to James Robertson of Swansea's memory of the same serial:

> The return of the Daleks was looked forward to with great excitement by me, and my friends. I can remember everyone cutting out pictures from the paper and *The Radio Times* and playing Daleks after school. Then on that Saturday afternoon, about five of us went round to my friend's house and we all watched in silence as the episode was shown . . . the ending when the Dalek appeared out of the Thames had us all cheering. (quoted in Mulkern 1988: 19–20)

The collective context of viewing was reinforced by collective play and gathering supporting materials that supported the affects of the story. Here, perhaps because of the male audience group, silent attentive viewing and celebration of the Daleks' sudden appearance is remembered rather than the fear and a requirement for talk that Flyte recalled. But the persistence of memories of the Daleks in these different situations testifies to another kind of quality, measured by the enduring effect of television and its embedding in processes of identity-formation.

Audience has to be constituted by the text, in the sense that positions for interpretation are laid out for the television audience, and 'The Daleks' addressed different audience constituencies. Its science-fiction storyline included aspects of the Gothic's depiction of the monstrous, but also adopts television naturalism: it features genetic inheritance, evolution, free will and choice constrained by circumstance and psychology, social conditions and laws which inform experience and action, symbolism and microcosmic models of complex wholes, plausible environments, narrative logic and cause–effect structures (on genre and mode in *Doctor Who* see Tulloch and Alvarado 1983: 99–143). As Matt Hills (2002) has argued of fantasy programmes (such as *The Avengers* (ABC 1961–69), for example), *Doctor Who*'s mysterious fictional world and the lack of conventional closure in individual episodes or in series as a whole leaves room for sustained involvement, repeated viewing and intense attention. The mixed genres and modes of 'The Daleks' provide an internally consistent surface narrative which is simultaneously metaphorical and can be read by some audience members as a commentary on aspects of their knowledge and experience.

The success of 'The Daleks' led to commissions for Nation to write more Dalek serials and secured his position at the BBC, and he became known rather disrespectfully as 'the Dalek man'. He gained first refusal in Dalek serial commissions but found it hard to escape his connection with them, although over 130 merchandising spin-off products based on the Daleks made him wealthy. Popular television drama is made possible by the capitalist system that underwrites copyright ownership and generates merchandising income, and Dalek-related merchandise itself responded to the longings for abundance, community and pleasure that entertainment partially satisfies (see Dyer 1977). But, paradoxically, the Daleks are an emblem of dystopian imperialism, racism and ecological disaster that reverses the utopian premises inherited in science fiction from the emerging social sciences of the nineteenth century. The perceived quality of the Dalek serials is also a function of their reversal of television entertainment ideologies and their simultaneous imbrication in them.

British public service broadcasting has aimed to provide educative or improving programmes, and to offer a range of different programme types at different levels of accessibility. *Doctor Who* claimed these qualities, through its historical and scientific content, and its address to mixed family audiences of different age groups, sexes and social classes. The specific uses of newly developed television technologies, aesthetic forms reflexively thematising vision, point of view and television transmission were added to episodic broadcast narrative and realist and naturalist dramatic conventions. These varying forms appeared in storylines that adopted conventions from cinema, and literary and 'pulp' science-fiction publishing. This heady mixture produced a complex of interwoven and sometimes contradictory negotiations about quality among production staff, audiences and critics. Understandings of quality in these different contexts demonstrate a hesitation between considering it as a property of the text, its production systems and values, its positioning of the audience and the audience's composition, and the modes of watching, remembering and discussing television.

Notes

1 'The Daleks' (w. Terry Nation, d. Christopher Barry and Richard Martin, prod. Verity Lambert, des. Raymond Cusick, seven episodes, BBC, tx. weekly, 21 December 1963 – 1 February 1964). The Doctor, his granddaughter and their two adult companions arrive on the planet Skaro, where the Daleks (encased in protective metal shells) and the pacifist Thals have survived a neutron war. The TARDIS crew side with the Thals and assist them in defeating the Daleks after a series of skirmishes, capture in the Dalek city and a perilous journey through irradiated wasteland. The term 'serial' refers to one storyline transmitted in several episodes. Several such serials formed one season of the series.
2 Archive sources are indicated by the abbreviation BBC WAC followed by the file number concerned. I gratefully acknowledge the assistance of Archive staff, and the support of the Arts and Humanities Research Board during research conducted on this material.
3 See Bignell and O'Day (2004) for further details and analysis of Nation's contributions to *Doctor Who* and other programmes, and their production and reception contexts.

References

Amis, K. (1969), *New Maps of Hell* [1961], London: New English Library.
BBC WAC T5/647/1 *Doctor Who* General A.
BBC WAC T5/648/1 *Doctor Who* General B
BBC WAC T5/649/1 *Doctor Who* viewers' letters.
BBC WAC T5/782/3 Drama Memos July–December, 1966.
BBC WAC T5/1243/1 *Doctor Who* 'The Chase'.
BBC WAC T5/1247/1 *Doctor Who* 'The Daleks' Master Plan'.
BBC WAC T48/445 TV Script Unit: Terry Nation.
BBC WAC T51/369/1 *The Lively Arts*: Whose Doctor Who?
Bignell, J. (1999), 'Another time, another space: modernity, subjectivity and *The Time Machine*', in D. Cartmell, I. Q. Hunter, H. Kaye and I. Whelehan (eds), *Alien Identities: Exploring Differences in Film and Fiction*, London: Pluto, 87–103.
Bignell, J., and A. O'Day (2004), *Terry Nation*, Manchester: Manchester University Press.
Brunt, D. and A. Pixley (1998), *The Doctor Who Chronicles: Season One*, London: Doctor Who Appreciation Society.
Brunt, D., and A. Pixley (2000), *The Doctor Who Chronicles: Season Four*, London: Doctor Who Appreciation Society.
Caughie, J. (2000), *Television Drama: Realism, Modernism, and British Culture*, Oxford: Oxford University Press.

Chapman, J. (2002), *Saints & Avengers: British Adventure Series of the 1960s*, London: I. B. Tauris.

Dyer, R. (1977), 'Entertainment and utopia', *Movie* 24, 2–13.

Eco, U. (1990), *The Limits of Interpretation*, Bloomington: Indiana University Press.

Ellis, J. (2000), *Seeing Things: Television in the Age of Uncertainty*, London: I. B. Tauris.

Garnett, T. (2000), 'Contexts', in J. Bignell, S. Lacey and M. Macmurraugh-Kavanagh (eds), *British Television Drama: Past, Present and Future*, Basingstoke: Palgrave Macmillan.

Hills, M. (2002), *Fan Cultures*, London: Routledge.

Johnson, C. (2002), 'Histories of telefantasy: the representation of the fantastic and the aesthetics of television', unpublished PhD thesis, University of Warwick.

Mulkern, P. (1988), 'The Dalek Invasion of Earth', *Doctor Who Magazine* 141, 18–22.

Radio Times (1983), *Doctor Who* 20th Anniversary Special, 19–26 November.

Radio Times (1973), 'Two of the Daleks live in my front drive' (interview with Terry Nation by unnamed journalist), *Doctor Who* 10th anniversary special (undated), 38.

Scholes, R. and E. Rabkin (1977), *Science Fiction: History, Science, Vision*, New York: Oxford University Press.

Tulloch, J., and M. Alvarado (1983), *Doctor Who: The Unfolding Text*, Basingstoke: Macmillan.

Further reading

Bentham, J. (1986), *Doctor Who, The Early Years*, London: W. H. Allen.

Bignell, J. (2002), 'Writing the child in media theory', *Yearbook of English Studies* 32, 127–139.

Bignell, J., S. Lacey and M. Macmurraugh-Kavanagh (eds) (2000), *British Television Drama: Past, Present and Future*, Basingstoke: Palgrave Macmillan.

Corner, J. (ed.) (1991), *Popular Television in Britain*, Studies in Cultural History, London: BFI.

Fiske, J. (1983), 'Dr Who: ideology and the reading of a popular narrative text', *Australian Journal of Screen Theory*, 13/14, 69–100.

Gillatt, G. (1998), *Doctor Who – From A To Z*, London: BBC Books.

Howe, D., M. Stammers and S. J. Walker (1993), *Doctor Who – The Sixties*, London: Virgin.

Tulloch, J. and H. Jenkins (1995), *Science Fiction Audiences: Watching Doctor Who and Star Trek*, London: Routledge.

5

This is the modern world: *The Prisoner,* authorship and allegory

Mark Bould

In 1954, Lew Grade formed the Independent Television Corporation (ITC) in order to bid for one of the new British commercial television franchises, but the Independent Broadcasting Authority (IBA) considered ITC's board, comprised of cinema- and theatre-chain owners, too strong: 'They accused us of having a monopoly on entertainment in Great Britain, and suggested that we should supply programmes to the companies that were eventually given the franchises' (Grade 1987: 158). Afterwards, Grade was approached by an American producer who wanted to make a series about Robin Hood, starring Richard Greene. ITC's subsequent *The Adventures of Robin Hood* (1955–59) was bought by the American CBS network and ran for 165 episodes; it was followed by other period adventure series, such as *The Buccaneers* (1956–57), and the contemporary crime/spy drama *The Invisible Man* (1958–59). And then came *Danger Man*: thirty-nine half-hour episodes in 1960–61, and forty-five hour-long episodes between 1964 and 1967 which CBS bought and retitled *Secret Agent*. Featuring the globetrotting adventures of John Drake (Patrick McGoohan), a more cerebral than libidinal secret agent, it was a massive hit. In 1965, 'Grade announced that the sale of three of his series to the American networks – *Danger Man* to CBS, *The Saint* to NBC and *The Baron* to ABC – would net a total of $10 million' (Chapman 2002: 10).

Danger Man made McGoohan a star, the 'highest-paid actor on British television' (Gregory 2002: 28), but it was suddenly abandoned after shooting the first two colour episodes, ostensibly because McGoohan was bored, 'convinced that *Danger Man* no longer had a great deal to offer'. Instead, he presented Grade, who 'was keen to continue . . . but even more so to keep McGoohan as house star' (Carrazé and Oswald 1995: 210), with a proposal for a series to be called *The Prisoner*, including – depending on which source one reads – a treatment, storylines, notes, diagrams, location photographs, a script and a budget. Confronted with 'details of the new concept as well as projections and budgets', Grade asked McGoohan 'to describe the project in his own words' and, after listening to the pitch, 'Grade struck a deal there and then' (Davies 2002: 23), saying 'it's so crazy, it might work. When can you start?' (White and Ali 1988: 120). According to McGoohan, 'From the very moment that he said "go" and shook my hand, he never interfered with anything I did' (Davies 2002: 23). McGoohan's production company, Everyman Films Ltd, was contracted to produce thirteen episodes, and committed to produce more if the series was successful.

The opening credit sequence outlined the premise. An unnamed secret agent (Patrick McGoohan) resigns. He is gassed, abducted. He wakes up in the Village – an architectural mélange, a place of blazers, boaters, brass bands and brollies, with a polyglot population who may or may not be fellow prisoners. Renamed Number 6, he is held against his will while Number 2 (played by various actors) tries to find out why he resigned. Each week, Number 6 attempts to escape, or to overcome some scheme to break his will, or to discover the identity of Number 1. Eventually, he triumphs, sort of, and is permitted to leave. Sort of.

As namelessness, the erasure of names and the use of characteristics rather than proper names suggests, *The Prisoner* (1967–68) stands outside the critically dominant realist traditions of television drama and attracts allegorical interpretation. Indeed, popular criticism of the series has produced many such readings, but it has also followed the pattern of academic television drama criticism in proposing McGoohan as the authorial creator of the drama's meanings. John Caughie, arguing that television drama is 'central to an understanding of what happened to British modernism in the second half of the twentieth century' (2000: 6), concentrates on 'serious drama' – the single play tradition of Play for Today and The Wednesday Play, of figures such as Dennis Potter, Ken Loach, Troy Kennedy Martin, Tony Garnett and David Mercer. It is unsurprising therefore that he overlooks *The Prisoner*. However, he does address the transformation of 'the single play into the art, or "quality" film [and] the multi-part serial', the latter of which evolved in the 1980s and 1990s into a variety of 'paranoid narrative'. In *Edge of Darkness* (BBC 1985), *The Monocled Mutineer* (BBC 1986) and *GBH* (C4 1991), 'the extension of time allows the slow erosion of order and the invasion of everyday normality by irrationality and unreason', transforming 'realism

into the surreal' (2000: 205). It is here that the omission of *The Prisoner* –
with its paranoid, irrational and surreal narrative(s), its negotiations
between series and serial formats and between television and film, and
the vexed nature of its authorship – is most striking.

Having it both ways: the modern and the postmodern

This essay will note *The Prisoner*'s precocious concern with such staples
of postmodern criticism as simulation, consumption and identity,
address questions of authorship and genre, and consider how and the
extent to which *The Prisoner* can be seen as allegorical. It will suggest that
The Prisoner cannot be reduced to a single meaning, but that its allegorical tendencies are simultaneously part of a calculated, self-conscious lure
and provocation and evidence of the postmodern's dialectical sublation
of the modern (or, more accurately, the modern's continued sublation of
the premodern).

The chapter will begin, however, not with *The Prisoner* but with
'Wanna Buy a Television Series', an episode of another ITC series, *Jason
King* (1971–72), which opens in Geneva, where a woman is undergoing
plastic surgery. Next, in London, a man is released from prison. He jets to
Switzerland to witness her unveiling: she now resembles the woman
whose picture he carries. The title sequence follows. Jason King, the
dandy crime-writer cum reluctant crime-fighter from *Department S*
(1969–70), pounds away at his typewriter, while shots of him in action
and posed with various 'dolly-birds' are inset in the upper right corner of
the screen.

Cut to New York, and then to King, played with absolute relish by Peter
Wyngarde. Resplendent in lilac shirt and tie and tight dark waistcoat, with
a cigarette and glass of whisky in one hand and a script in the other, he is
pitching a series featuring Mark Caine, the hero of his novels, to Harry
Carmel (David Bauer), a dyspeptic, pill-popping United States Television
Corporation executive obsessed with viewing figures and rival networks.
The pre-title teaser sequence is actually from the first *Mark Caine* episode
as outlined by King (Carmel would rather have the show described to him
than read a script). As the scene cuts between Carmel's office and shots of
Caine, King describes his protagonist: 'Six feet and a half inches of steel.
Not tall by today's standards but so slim and well-proportioned that he
gives the appearance of a lithe athlete. He has dark curly hair, streaked by
the sun, and a moustache . . . oh, by the way, I still haven't thought who
should play him.' Caine, of course, is also played by Wyngarde.

Henceforth, the episode, an entertaining critique of television's commercial demands, cuts between the diegesis (the primary narrative level where King tries to tell the story to Carmel) and the hypodiegesis (a secondary narrative level composed of footage of the story King is trying to tell). Carmel repeatedly interrupts, beginning with the advice that 'in television you have to punch into the story'. When King protests about the lack of 'motivation and characterisation', Carmel concedes that it is necessary 'in your novels . . ., yeah, sure, but in television, I've got all those other channels to worry about – one wrong move and we've lost an audience'. When King describes a scene containing a woman who is 'just there for dressing, sex appeal', Carmel demands that King should 'get her clothes off!'; and in the hypodiegesis her dress is replaced by a bikini. Carmel's interjections are all of this nature. He complains that there has not yet been a fight; when one is inserted, he exclaims, 'Now, that's television, that's exciting'. Uncertain which will attract the most viewers, he introduces a sidekick who switches between being white, black and oriental. The action relocates abruptly from Monte Carlo to Greece, because 'TV audiences like a change of scenery – details are unimportant'. He replaces King's final low-key gunfight with a longer, more exciting exchange of fire. Such changes, he insists, will help to make *Mark Caine* special, adding that 'the Networks like to give the audience choice'. King contemplates Carmel's television sets – tuned to different networks, each shows a hospital drama – with eloquent disdain.

The primary effect of the interplay of diegesis and hypodiegesis, climaxing when Carmel's ringing telephone distracts Caine, is to permit *Jason King* to have its cake and eat it. King repeatedly distances himself from the more formulaic, spectacular, violent and libidinal elements which Carmel wishes to inject into *Mark Caine*, thus establishing his felt, evident and arch superiority to such things; and *Jason King*'s self-conscious metalepsis – its violation of the hierarchy of narrative levels – makes similar assertions about its difference from such standard fare. However, just as there is little difference between King and Caine, so there is little to distinguish *Jason King* from *Mark Caine*, and despite attributing all the vulgar elements to the debasing influence of US networks, *Jason King* itself was shot on 16mm film, 'a production economy measure that militated against it being bought by American television' (Chapman 2002: 213).

Such narrative playfulness, typically described as 'postmodern', has become a staple of television drama from *Moonlighting* (ABC 1985–89) and *Cop Rock* (ABC 1990) to *Buffy the Vampire Slayer* (Fox 1997–2003) and *Family Guy* (Fox 1999–2002), engendering a tendency to 'celebrate television as the child of postmodernity, the place where postmodernism finds its logic and its quintessential cultural form' (Caughie 2000: 17). However, Caughie continues, it is 'important to insist that postmodernity is not an achieved condition but a process of becoming, and it is a process which is marked by uneven development'. This is best understood from the perspective offered by Carl Freedman, who rejects attempts to distinguish modernism from postmodernism on formal or aesthetic grounds, arguing that they can be understood only within their general historical situation. Classical modernism corresponds to the collapse of entrepreneurial capitalism and the birth of monopoly capitalism, and is characterised by a particularly intense struggle between modern and premodern forms. The postmodern emerges after the Second World War, alongside the multinationalisation of capital, and is better understood as the period of pure modernity, when battles with premodern forms are no longer so prevalent and 'capitalist modernization is so thoroughly triumphant that, owing to the lack of contrast on which visibility depends, it becomes somewhat difficult to see' (Freedman 2000: 188). To capture this distinction, Freedman compares the isolated, impoverished, scandalous modernists with the cosy relationship between postmodernism and capital:

> The half-starving Montparnasse painter producing modernist masterworks for an indifferent or hostile world, though by now a cultural stereotype, was originally a real enough figure. The postmodernist successor is likely to be adequately fed and even to be receiving lucrative commissions from banks and high-tech firms interested in decorating the walls of their corporate headquarters (Freedman 2000: 185–86).

Jason King, caught between these positions, tends toward the latter. Financially successful, he is none-the-less presented as a talent fighting for his (admittedly delicious) voice to be heard, but, rather than struggling against the vulgarity of a medium and organisations indifferent to his artistry, he seeks an accommodation with capital, eventually taking his script to another network.

As I have argued elsewhere (Bould 2003), visual science fiction provides a privileged site for observing the conflict between premodern and modern forms. For example, the towering skyscrapers and abstract machinery of *Metropolis* (1926) suggest the triumph of reason but there also is an irrational premodern residue of messianic religiosity and hysteria about female sexuality; and in *Frankenstein* (1931) fabulous electrical equipment hums and sparks and sputters in a run-down Gothic turret. Similarly, *The Prisoner* depicts a post-austerity Britain, modern and affluent, but weighed down by history and tradition. Number 6 drives a Lotus 7, but drives it past the Houses of Parliament, an institution which could be seen as modern and democratic were it not for its backward-looking architecture and the archaic privilege of the upper house. Number 6's London apartment is decorated with antiques and colonialist paraphernalia, while his luggage includes photographs of exotic locations, betokening the growth of international consumer tourism. His boss drinks tea from bone china while machines do the filing. Beneath the (faked) Italianate architecture of the Village lie tunnels and chambers austerely 'modernist' in the manner of a Ken-Adam-designed James Bond set or the Daleks' home planet, Skaro. Despite often seeming to be trapped in an imaginary England of an earlier decade, symbolised by the previously cutting-edge technology of the penny-farthing bicycle, the Villagers travel in Mini Moke cars and communicate by cordless phones.

In the title sequence, there is a point-of-view shot of sleek office blocks seeming to swirl around before the viewer. This not only signifies Number 6's fading consciousness but also suggests the instability and groundlessness that Vivian Sobchack identifies with the city in 1990s science-fiction movies. Lacking 'both logically secure and spatially stable premises for its – and our – existence', its 'inhabitants suffer from giddiness or vertigo and, rootless, they "free fall" in both space and time' (1999: 138). They are 'increasingly dislocated in space – and, dislocated, their very identities shift and become displaced and ungrounded' (140). This groundlessness and dislocation relates to the rejection of modernism's utopian project and the turn away from historicism described by Fredric Jameson (1991). In *The Prisoner*, modernist utopianism (reconfigured as totalitarianism) continues, signified by the spaces occupied by the Village's controllers, whereas the kitsch Village exemplifies Guy Debord's sense that 'Everything that was directly lived has moved away into a representation' (1983: thesis 1). This is exacerbated not only by the continual uncertainty as to which Villagers are guards-passing-for-prisoners but also by the frequency with which the Village is seen on screens within the screen and by a growing sense that, like Jean Baudrillard's Disneyland (1983: 25), it 'is presented as imaginary in order to make us believe that the rest is real'. The series's circular narrative(s), discussed below, also represent a disengagement from history which disavows a necessary or probable future while simultaneously problematising the past and questions of origin.

Allegory and authorship

Although the above account of the creation and commissioning of *The Prisoner* is, like that of *Mark Caine*, a familiar enough story of accommodations with capital, Chris Gregory notes that the 'cult of *The Prisoner* is inevitably also a "cult of McGoohan", which positions its creator as a transcendent artistic "genius"' (2002: 197). Several elements of the origin story contribute to this: the original pitch; the never-asked question of who compiled the material in McGoohan's briefcase, and the implication that it was him; the handshake with Grade; the suggestive name of Everyman Films. Add to this the parallels and confusions between Number 6 and McGoohan, and McGoohan's various roles in the production, as well as his increasingly perfectionist (megalomaniacal?) involvement (interference?) at all stages of production, his split with story editor George Markstein (who shares some credit for originating the series), his infrequent and reluctant interviews and a hagiographical tendency in popular discussions of the series, and the image of McGoohan as 'author' is unsurprising. Even Gregory, who distances himself from the cultists' position, states that McGoohan was 'given a unique chance in the television context to take "authorial" control over the series and turn it into a vehicle for his own very personal vision' (2002: 2). He draws out a parallel between Number 6 and McGoohan – 'Just as the story depicts allegorically the struggles of the Individual against a superficially "caring" but actually viciously repressive society, so McGoohan's role in the production process pits him as a creative individual against the entire weight of the established corporate production process of series TV' (32) – and then reiterates his claim that 'Uniquely for a television series, the text (or "texts") of *The Prisoner* can be ascribed to one over-riding authorial voice' (33). Gregory is clearly working in a tradition of romantic or modernist criticism, ascribing 'value to difference . . . creativity and originality . . . the individual talent speaking with a unique voice from within a tradition' (Caughie 2000: 22), but, as Caughie notes, much of television's pleasure derives from 'repetition, recognition, and familiarity' (23). Consequently, both this image of authorship and the privileging of difference as the source of value are problematic, particularly with a series whose episodes 'do not really relate to one another syntactically' but are 'linked *syntagmatically*, each one rearranging the different ideas implicit in the basic premise' (Britton and Barker 2003: 116).

The question of McGoohan's authorship is further complicated by his description of the series as 'an allegorical conundrum for people to interpret for themselves' (quoted in Carrazé and Oswald 1995: 6). Strictly speaking, an allegory cannot be a conundrum because there should be a direct correspondence between its poetic or narrative elements and the ideas for which they stand. Its latent meaning should be as manifest as its manifest meaning. This kind of correspondence does, at first, seem to occur in the final episode, 'Fall Out'. Empanelled observers sit behind signs reading 'welfare', 'pacifists', 'activists', 'nationalists', 'youngsters', and it is explicitly stated that Number 48 (Alexis Kanner) represents youthful-rebellion-for-the-sake-of-it, that Number 2 (Leo McKern) represents biting-the-hand-that-feeds and that Number 6 represents the individual. However, apart from the signs behind which they sit, the observers are indistinguishable from one another; although they might occupy poten-tially allegorical positions, that potential is never activated. Similarly, the identification of Number 48, Number 2 and Number 6 as allegorical fig-ures is made by another character, and therefore the extent to which these designations explain or reconfigure the previous episodes is debatable. Indeed, Gregory's unexamined invocation of allegory seems merely to reiterate a commonplace in popular criticism of the series which is every bit as dubious as the structural homology he describes between the respective positions of Number 6 and McGoohan. His discussion of the series founders on this failure to properly consider the nature of allegory, or the extent to which repetitions and rearrangements might create the appearance of allegory, or something structurally homologous to alle-gory, without creating an allegory. Furthermore, this tendency to describe *The Prisoner* as allegorical betrays an anxiety about its authorship while retaining the sense that the series has a particular meaning. McGoohan *does* imply that he knows what that meaning is – 'If one gives answers to a conundrum, it is no longer a conundrum' (quoted in Carrazé and Oswald 1995: 6) – but, as Brian McHale (1989: 82) notes, in a different context, 'Allegorical reading is possible here, perhaps even tempting, but it is not in any sense *necessary*: the literal level . . . seems perfectly self-con-tained, quite able to do without an allegorical level'.

Since the 1950s there has been a reformulation of literary allegory into allegory that knows itself to be undone by incredulity towards metanar-ratives. Just as the postmodern 'field of stylistic and discursive hetero-geneity without a norm' has resulted in the replacement of personal style with pastiche, so 'the absence of any great collective project' (Jameson 1991: 17) has replaced allegory with what McHale (1989: 82) calls the 'postmodernist allegories' of writers such as William Burroughs, Thomas Pynchon, John Barth, Donald Barthelme and Robert Coover – to whose works, I contend, *The Prisoner* should be added. Roughly contemporary, they all exhibit a hesitation between the literal and the allegorical as the ontological levels in their fictional structures collide with each other. McHale traces this kind of allegory back to James Joyce, Samuel Beckett and Franz Kafka, whose texts (like Herman Hesse's novel *The Glass Bead Game* (1943), from which McGoohan derived the 'Joseph Serf' pseudonym under which he wrote and/or directed several *Prisoner* episodes) 'seem to promise allegorical meaning, soliciting an allegorical interpretation from the reader, yet withholding any indication of *specific* allegorical content', and in which 'Everything is *potentially* allegorical, but nothing is *actually* an allegory' (1989: 141). Such overdetermined allegories 'have *too many* interpretations, more than can possibly be integrated into a univocal reading', resulting in an 'indeterminacy' which induces 'an ontological oscillation' (142) in which literal and allegorical levels become chaotically intertwined.

However, properly postmodernist allegories seem to prefer 'relatively transparent, univocal, allegorical narratives', typically involving a confrontation between 'Apollonian and Dionysian principles, rational order vs. mindless pleasure' (McHale 1989: 142); but this is mere appearance. Such binaries become radically unstable – in postmodernist allegories, the 'Manichaean allegory is in fact only another lure, an invitation to the unwary reader to interpret in terms of a univocal allegorical meaning' (141). (The dangers of such interpretations are highlighted by the jammers in 'It's Your Funeral', who openly plot fake plots, and more pointedly by the conspiracy Number 6 fakes in 'Hammer into Anvil' so as to destroy the paranoid Number 2 (Patrick Cargill), manipulating him into initiating his own replacement.) Consequently, claims that *The Prisoner* 'reflects a timeless struggle between the Individual and society, and between eternally warring dualistic forces within the Individual' (Gregory 2002: 213–214) not only are ahistorical bourgeois mystifications but also fundamentally misrepresent the series, ironing out its contradictions, its excesses and evasions of meaning. With postmodernist allegory, the reader must recognise 'the inconsistencies and incoherences of the allegory' and the dissolution of 'determinate meaning . . . into indeterminacy' (McHale 1989: 144). This typically occurs when opposed forces are revealed to possess 'the characteristics that ought to belong, according to the logic of the allegory, to the other', when the apparent 'polar opposition proves to be a complex and paradoxical interpenetration' (144). This can be seen in the 'metronomic whimsy' (Disch 1980: 19) of the Village and in the Manichaean conflict of the Cold War milieu (in 'The Chimes

of Big Ben', Number 6, unable to determine which side runs the Village, is
assured by Number 2 (Leo McKern) that East and West are identical).
Additionally, Number 6, despite his rebelliousness, is more Apollonian
than Dionysian. Sober and prudish, he opposes those who run the Village
so as to restore order to a world whose absurdity is exemplified by the
revolving surveillance seesaw, the diegetic and extradiegetic recurrence of
nursery rhymes and his Pinteresque exchanges with Number 2 in 'Once
Upon a Time'.

Furthermore, *The Prisoner* belongs to a particular offshoot of the
secular *Bildungsroman*. In this narrative tradition, curious ontological
blurrings recur between protagonist-as-individual and protagonist-as-
example and between protagonist and author: the 'hero is simultaneously
– and not wholly convincingly – "humanly" representative and yet atom-
ically individual, an investment of the authors' core personal values and
yet an example for all the readers insofar as they are all supposed to be
individuals, only individuals, and nothing but individuals' (Suvin 2003:
56). In this particular offshoot, beginning with Yevgeny Zamyatin's *We*
(1924) and continuing through dystopian science fiction to *The Matrix*
(1999) and its sequels, the positivised individual protagonist and his
female sidekick tackle the negativised collectivity of the centralised state
(or, latterly, the global electronic-capital-information order) with some
blend of political and erotic subversion – except in Aldous Huxley's *Brave
New World* (1932) and *The Prisoner* where sex is part of the negativised
collectivity. As with many of these fictions, *The Prisoner* is rather unconvincing as a celebration of the individual *contra* society. Firstly, this interpretation assumes an untroubled notion of the individual subject, as if it
were 'the consciousness of men that determines their existence' rather
than 'their social existence that determines their consciousness' (Marx
1987: 263). In *The Prisoner*, such transcendent subjectivity is undermined
in those episodes in which a brainwashed Number 6 uncovers or recovers
his 'true' identity because of the material evidence of his body: in 'A., B.
and C.' needlemarks on his arm reveal that he has been drugged; in 'The
Schizoid Man', a bruised thumbnail enables him to prove to himself that
he is himself. Secondly, the opposition of individual and society as universal categories depends upon the series only ever depicting society as a
bureaucratic, hierarchical hive-mind, and on evoking 'community' and
'mutuality' merely to portray them as their opposites. Finally, most obviously, Number 6 – the idealised individual – is not particularly admirable.
A misogynistic, manipulative bully, he is as calculating in his relationships as the Village bosses. For example, in 'Checkmate', Number 6

discovers which Villagers are guards by observing whether or not they act with unconscious arrogance – but one of his co-conspirators decides that the unconsciously arrogant Number 6 must be a guard and so betrays him.

Narrative at play

In addition to the tension between levels of meaning in its postmodernist allegory, *The Prisoner*, like *Jason King*, confuses ontological levels through metaleptic game-playing. For example, after the title sequence of 'A., B. and C', Number 2 (Colin Gordon) watches the title sequence (minus titles) projected on a screen as if it were Number 6's memory of his resignation, thus intruding material from a higher ontological level into the primary diegesis, from the paratext into the text, from 'the metalanguage relative to the object-language of the text' (McHale 1989: 111) into the object-language of the text. 'The Girl Who Was Death' offers a more complex example. Colonel Hawke-English (uncredited) is assassinated while playing cricket by the mysterious Sonia (Justine Lord), who replaces the ball with a bomb. Number 6, inexplicably not in the Village, continues the Colonel's efforts to locate Dr Schnipps (Kenneth Griffith), who intends to destroy London. After various attempts on his life, Number 6 finds and destroys Schnipps's rocket. Throughout, this lengthy comic pursuit has been interrupted by shots of a page being turned in a children's book, and each new illustration is roughly matched by the next establishing shot. This atypical episode is revealed to be a bedtime story Number 6 has been telling to the Village children, while Number 2 (Kenneth Griffith) watches from his sanctum. The introduction of the diegetic world repositions what has hitherto appeared to be the diegesis as a hypodiegesis; but, as the episode closes, this neat reordering of diegeses is disrupted as Number 6 looks directly into the surveillance camera in the nursery (and thus directly out of Number 2's screen *and* out of the television screen) and says with ironic savour, 'Goodnight, children. Everywhere.' Whose words are these, and to whom are they addressed? Is it Number 6 or McGoohan-as-Number-6 who speaks, or both? Does he address Number 2 or the viewer, or both? This kind of transdiegetical address often recurs courtesy of McGoohan's mannered acting and idiosyncratic diction. For example, the opening sequence of 'The Schizoid Man' ends with Number 6 bidding farewell to Alison (Jane Merrow) with what appears to be calculated indifference. Is Number 6, aware that he is under constant surveillance, self-consciously performing for the cameras? Is this effect a product,

intentional or not, of McGoohan's performance? Or is it a combination
or negotiation of these possibilities?

Further ontological confusions arise from the circularity of the narrative. Despite critical attempts to impose a story arc, *The Prisoner*'s
episodes generally function like those of the classic British sitcom (discrete blocks with no memory of previous episodes, or consequences in
following ones), furthering an overall sense of entrapment. This is most
pronounced in the episodes in which Number 6 escapes, or seems to
escape, from the Village. In 'Many Happy Returns', he finds the Village
deserted, constructs a boat, returns to London and returns to his apartment, now occupied by Mrs Butterworth (Georgina Cookson). It is the
day before his birthday. He returns to his office and persuades his former
superiors to help locate and destroy the Village. Flying over it, Number 6's
pilot says 'Be seeing you!' – a Village expression, betokening inevitable
return – and ejects him. Returned to the village, he returns to his house.
In walks Mrs Butterworth, the new Number 2, with a birthday cake to
wish him 'many happy returns'. This episode is remarkable not only for
its self-conscious circularity but also for its emphasis on motion and
movement.

Caughie contrasts cinema – which spent thirty years 'with the image
and no speech', developing 'a narrative based on a highly elaborated visual
rhetoric and spectacle' which continued 'even after sound' – with broadcasting – which spent 'thirty years with speech and no image', becoming
'a medium of speech, carrying a respect for the written word forward into
its dramas' even after television (2000: 18). (Not inaccurate, this contention ignores television drama's frequent aspiration to the cinematic,
beginning with work by figures such as Rudolph Cartier and Nigel
Kneale.) Charles Chilton, discussing his radio series *Journey Into Space*
(1953–55), recalls: 'Our listening figures succeeding so well against those
of television did not please everybody. One TV producer considered our
success a fluke. He challenged me to write an episode . . . that could not
be played equally well on television. My response was episode eight,
which takes place in total darkness' ('Journey Into Space . . . Again'). In
contrast, after the title sequence and for over half of its running time,
'Many Happy Returns', contains no dialogue but for an indistinct radio
transmission and two very brief unsubtitled exchanges in German and
Romany. Instead, Number 6 roams the Village, fells trees, constructs a
raft, sails, fights, swims, climbs, hikes and runs. Despite all this action, the
sense of his entrapment remains. Following the preceding six episodes,
including his previous 'escape' in 'The Chimes of Big Ben', it is difficult for

the viewer to conceive of all this activity achieving anything, and it is almost with a sense of relief that he is returned to the Village. As with Harold Steptoe (Harry H. Corbett) or Reginald Perrin (Leonard Rossiter), Number 6's desire to escape his circumstances must be thwarted.

The pattern of discrete episodes and narrative amnesia is finally broken with the straightforward continuation of the narrative in the final two episodes, which also toy with closure: Number 1's identity is revealed (but makes no obvious sense); the Village is destroyed; Number 6, Number 48, Number 2 (Leo McKern) and the butler (Angelo Muscat) escape – but, back in London, Number 6's apartment door now opens automatically, like the door of his house in the Village, and, in the closing credits, McGoohan is identified only as 'the prisoner'. There is a sound of thunder like that which plays over the first shot of the first episode and of the usual title sequence, and the final two shots of the episode (and of the series) are identical to the second and third shots of the first episode and of the usual title sequence. *The Prisoner* can therefore be seen, like Joyce's *Finnegans Wake* (1939), as 'a text with its tail in its mouth, the unfinished sentence on its last page resuming on its first page, and so "continuing indefinitely"' (McHale 1989: 111). However, these two shots also open the title sequence. Therefore, to the extent that the series can be seen as ouroborous-like, it can also be seen as spiralling from one ontological level to another, like Barth's 'Bellerophoniad' (1972), in which the final sentence suddenly breaks off: 'It's no *Bellerophoniad*. It's a' (308). This sentence is not completed by the story's opening sentence but by the book's title: 'It's no *Bellerophoniad*. It's a *Chimera*.' The difference is that

> strictly speaking, the title does not belong to the text; it *names* the text, and therefore occupies the level of metalanguage relative to the object language of the text itself. Thus the incomplete closing sentence of *Chimera* does not shape the text into a circle, but a spiral, returning it to its beginning while at the same time ascending to a higher level, that of metalanguage' (McHale 1989: 111)

Piers D. Britton and Simon J. Barker argue that narrative is defined by 'teleological unity' and design by 'suggestive plurality': where mainstream screen narratives follow a causal chain from equilibrium to disequilibrium to fresh equilibrium, 'design is inevitably multidimensional and never monolithic in its significance' (2003: 16). Circles and spheres are central to *The Prisoner*'s production design – as in the penny-farthing bicycle (seen in Number 2's sanctum, on Villagers' badges and in the closing titles) and the balloon-like Rovers. The shape is emphatically repeated in light-fittings, parabolic dishes, devices for reading thumbprints, tables, the Villagers' horizontally striped jerseys, and aerial shots of opened umbrellas. In 'Arrival', a square hole irises into a circular one so a round peg can fit into it, and 'Checkmate' opens with an iris out from the Village. The two main rooms from which the Village is run are circular, and their floors consist of concentric circles. The circularity of the control room is emphasised by the rotation of the surveillance seesaw and the spherical device circling the ceiling. Number 2's sanctum features several round holes in the floor through which chairs, including his Aarnio ball chair, rise.

Britton and Barker suggest that this 'globe motif reaches saturation level' (2003: 112) with the climax of 'Fall Out'. The final confrontation between Number 6 and Number 1 'takes place inside a rocket, which is, of course, circular in cross-section' and the hooded Number 1 'is behind a circular table entirely covered by terrestrial globes, and as he turns to greet Number 6, he holds out a crystal ball, which *The Prisoner* smashes to the ground' (112). They connect this global motif to the notion of the global village, an idea borne out by the episode's use of the Beatles' 'All You Need Is Love' – a track they performed in the first global satellite television link-up in 1967 – and by the end credit sequence of the press preview version of 'The Chimes of Big Ben' – in which the spinning wheels of the penny-farthing give way to a shot of the Earth adrift in the galaxy; the Earth rushes into the foreground and is replaced by the word 'POP'.

This imagery should also be seen as an aspect of *The Prisoner*'s concern with surveillance, perception and illusion, as eye imagery. Number 2's sanctum is often shown from such an angle that its concentric circles become lenticular. Statues with surveillance cameras for eyes rotate. Number 2's chair in the council chamber is surmounted by an eye. Number 6's bedroom is usually seen through a keyhole arch. The Rovers resemble giant eyeballs, a similarity emphasised in 'Once Upon a Time' when one nests in Number 2's ball chair before a monitor screen. In 'Fall Out', Number 1's rocket has a giant '1' painted on the side – it resembles an 'I' and is next to a lidded, circular eye-like opening – and his gown is decorated with a similar '1'; on the soundtrack, when Number 6 unmasks Number 1, McGoohan's voice repeats 'I, I, I, I, I' over and again; and a Rover deflates to the sound of Carmen Miranda singing the repeated 'I' of 'O Yi Yi Yi Yi (I Like-A You Very Much)'. In this final episode, both circles and individuals become 'eyes'.

But if this is allegory, it is not allegory in the sense typically intended in criticism of the series. Similarities might be noted and connections made, but they do not lead anywhere other than to homogenising assertions and desperate puns. As its polysemous design suggests, *The Prisoner* proliferates meanings, exfoliates possibilities. This potentially endless circulation of signifiers and the multiple virtual trajectories that the would-be interpreter might map through them – trajectories which ultimately circle back on themselves – is paralleled in popular and academic criticism of the series. Debates cycle and recycle around the twin gravitational pulls of McGoohan-as-*auteur* and series-as-allegory – like the signposting eventually introduced into the Westin Bonaventure Hotel's disorienting lobby, like Number's 6's assertion that he is not a number but a free man, they constitute 'pitiful and revealing, rather desperate, attempt[s] to restore the coordinates of an older space' (Jameson 1991: 45). Such tensions are indicative of the postmodern's dialectical sublation of the modern (or the modern's continued sublation of the premodern). This process is evident in *The Prisoner*'s nostalgia for a transcendent meaning (the moral certainty of allegory, Number 6's quest for meaning) and a transcendent subject (the imagined single author, Number 6's desperate reassertion of a unique subjectivity – not a number, a free man), even as the series's fascination with commodities and its various destabilisations of meaning and identity (the refusal, or failure, to allegorise, the 'premature' dislocations, displacements and groundlessness Sobchack identifies with 1990s science fiction movies) pull the series in the other direction.

Elsewhere, drawing on psychoanalytic constructions of paranoia, I have argued for a Marxist conceptualisation of the fantastic 'as constrained and informed by the mode of subjectivity of modern capitalism, and as modelling that mode of subjectivity in textual microcosm with a peculiarly neurotic precision' (Bould 2002: 83). Central to this argument is a combination of Louis Althusser's model of the ideologically interpellated subject with the more complex notions of causality and determination proposed by non-linear dynamics (chaos theory) which suggests a fuzzily determined paranoid subject, shuttling between and trying to reconcile multiple simultaneous determinants and, moment-by-moment, barely holding together a constantly emergent self. Connecting the fantastic and the subject is a sense that 'fantasy's paranoia is an expression of the fact that the *only possible mode of life* for the modern subject is one of everyday paranoid artifice' (Bould 2002: 83; see also Miéville 2002). On both narrative and formal levels, and for both characters and viewers, *The Prisoner* draws upon and evokes the paranoid centripetal drive of the sub-

ject-emergent-in-construction and that subject's self-constituting paranoid drive to construct meanings. The dialectical interplay of *The Prisoner*'s contingent failures of coherence and its calculated, self-conscious
incoherence simultaneously refuses mapping and teases us into thinking
we might be cartographers. And this, I contend, is the source of its success
and longevity – it is not an allegory, and to the extent that it avoids allegory, avoids meaning a particular something, it remains a conundrum: a
conundrum that flirts with meaning, that flirts with us and flatters.

References

Barth, J. (1977), *Chimera*, London: Quartet.

Baudrillard, J. (1983), *Simulations*, trans. P. Foss, J. Johnston and P. Patton, New
    York: Semiotext(e).

Bould, M. (2002), 'The dreadful credibility of absurd things: a tendency in fantasy
    theory', *Historical Materialism: Research in Critical Marxist Theory*, 10:4, 51–88.

Bould, M. (2003), 'Film and television', in E. James and F. Mendlesohn (eds), *The
    Cambridge Companion to Science Fiction*, Cambridge: Cambridge University
    Press.

Britton, P. D., and S. J. Barker (2003), *Reading Between Designs: Visual Imagery
    and the Generation of Meaning in The Avengers, The Prisoner, and Doctor Who*,
    Austin: University of Texas Press.

Carrazé, A., and H. Oswald (1995), *The Prisoner: A Televisionary Masterpiece*,
    trans. C. Donougher, London: Virgin.

Caughie, J. (2000), *Television Drama: Realism, Modernism, and British Culture*,
    Oxford: Oxford University Press.

Chapman, J. (2002), *Saints and Avengers: British Adventure Series of the 1960s*,
    London: I. B. Tauris.

Davies, S. P. (2002), *The Prisoner Handbook*, London: Boxtree.

Debord, G. (1983), *The Society of the Spectacle*, Detroit, MI: Black & Red.

Disch, T. M. (1980), *The Prisoner*, London: New English Library.

Freedman, C. (2000), *Critical Theory and Science Fiction*, Hanover: Wesleyan Uni-
    versity Press/University Press of New England.

Grade, L. (1987), *Still Dancing: My Story*, London: Collins.

Gregory, C. (2002), *Be Seeing You: Decoding 'The Prisoner'*, Luton: University of
    Luton Press.

Jameson, F. (1991), *Postmodernism or, The Cultural Logic of Late Capitalism*,
    London: Verso.

'Journey Into Space . . . Again', on *Journey Into Space: The Return from Mars* audio
    cassette. BBC Worldwide, 2000.

McHale, B. (1989), *Postmodernist Fiction*, London: Routledge.

Marx, K. (1987), 'Preface to a contribution to the critique of political economy',
    in K. Marx and F. Engels, *Collected Works*, vol. 29, London: Lawrence & Wishart.

Miéville, C. (2002), 'Editorial introduction', *Historical Materialism: Research in Critical Marxist Theory*, 10:4, 39–49.
Sobchack, V. (1999), 'Cities on the edge of time: the urban science-fiction film' in A. Kuhn (ed.), *Alien Zone II: The Spaces of Science-Fiction Cinema*, London: Verso.
Suvin, D. (2003), 'Reflections on what remains of Zamyatin's *We* after the change of leviathans: must collectivism be against people?', in M. S. Barr (ed.), *Envisioning the Future: Science Fiction and the Next Millennium*, Middletown: Wesleyan University Press.
White, M., and J. Ali (1988), *The Official Prisoner Companion*, London: Sidgwick and Jackson.

Further reading

Bloom, C. (1996), *Cult Fiction: Popular Reading and Pulp Theory*, Basingstoke: Macmillan.
Freeman, N. (1999), 'See Europe with ITC: stock footage and the construction of geographical identity', in D. Cartmell, I. Q. Hunter, H. Kaye and I. Whelehan (eds), *Alien Identities: Exploring Difference in Film and Fiction*, London: Pluto.
Hunt, L. (1998), *British Low Culture: From Safari Suits to Sexploitation*, London: Routledge.
Le Carré, J. (1994), *The Spy Who Came in from the Cold*, London: Coronet [first published 1963].
Stewart, G. (1985), 'The "videology" of science fiction', in G. E. Slusser and E. S. Rabkin (eds), *Shadows of the Magic Lamp: Fantasy and Science Fiction in Film*, Carbondale and Edwardsville: Southern Illinois University Press.
Stewart, G. (1999), *Between Film and Screen: Modernism's Photo Synthesis*, Chicago: University of Chicago Press.

6

Can kinky sex be politically correct?
Queer As Folk and the geo-ideological inscription of gay sexuality

Peter Billingham

In this essay I explore the ways in which, within a geo-ideological analysis of the controversial Channel 4 drama series *Queer As Folk*, one may view fundamental issues regarding the politics of the representation of gay sexuality. My use of a popular cultural colloquialism, 'kinky sex', is deliberately, ironically provocative. Within that term are potent subtextual signifiers of erotic otherness and exotic marginalised positions: the 'kink' is simultaneously 'bent' (a diminutive pejorative of homosexuals) whilst, as a deviation from a restrictive normative mean, conveying a sense of alternative pleasure(s). From a dominant reactionary, heterosexual viewing position, homosexuality in and of itself may be viewed as a profoundly disturbing 'kink' or deviation of sexual imagination, conduct and practice. However, I shall also be examining the extent to which the explicit, unrestrained depiction of homosexual activities with an uncensored connotation of libidinous pleasure was also a signifier of profound ideological disturbance within sections of the gay community. Indeed the problematic nature of what constitutes the ideological space and location of a/the 'gay community' is central to my discussion and analysis. That geo-ideological descriptor has evolved from a form of liberal political activism over the last three and a half decades that has sought to achieve legislated inclusion for homosexuals and lesbians within the United States, Britain and Western Europe. It is in that sense of a politicised pressure group, consolidating and seeking recognition as a rational, consensual, democratic ideological representation of homosexuality as a sexual activity and homosexuals as individual citizens, that one might identify the gay community's ideological position as complicit with the rhetoric and aims of 'political correctness'.

Queer As Folk had its first broadcast in 1999–2000 on Channel 4 television, screened in eight hour-long episodes. The series was made by the

Manchester-based independent company Red Production, the producer and executive producer was Nicola Shindler and the series's creator and co-producer was Russell T. Davies. The directors were Charles McDougall and Sarah Harding. The series starred Aidan Gillen as Stuart Jones, Craig Kelly as Vince Tyler and Charlie Hunnam as Nathan Maloney. Situated in Manchester's 'gay village', centred on Canal Street, the opening episode of the first series managed to outrage the reactionary tabloid press and even served to unsettle some liberal media commentators, both gay and straight. The principal reason for the outcry was the explicit portrayal in the first episode of gay sexual intercourse between Stuart, a man nearing thirty years of age, and Nathan, a fifteen-year-old (legally under-age) boy whom he has picked up that evening. The outrage was such that the producer of a popular lager, Becks Brewery, which had sponsored the series (seeking 'hip' credentials amongst the young, beautiful and wage-earning) withdrew its sponsorship after the first episode, clearly making a calculated value judgement in more senses than one in terms of the fashion credos of gay and lesbian sexuality and the 'pink pound'. In this essay, all quoted references to dialogue from the series come from my own detailed transcriptions and viewing notes. Nevertheless, for readers who would like to consult the scripts, they were published after the first screening of the series (Davies 1999a). At the time of writing (April 2004) there is still relatively little published material available on the series. My own book (Billingham 2000) contains an extended chapter that was the first academic discussion of the series to be published, and the Further Reading section at the end of this essay suggests work on related topics that readers interested in the wider themes of alternative sexualities and their representation within the media may find stimulating and helpful. They represent only a small sample of texts available in a rapidly growing discipline area.

Provocation

In the opening credits for the first episode in the series, and for each sub-sequent episode, there is a coloured montage of shifting crimson and scarlet serving as a backdrop for a similarly shifting network of glittering golden lights, a kind of sequinned spermatozoa. In symbiotic tandem with this rich, camp visual aesthetic is a pounding, rhythmic musical signature theme, which is percussive and punctuated by a celebratory whoop of anticipated pleasure. A voice-over begins to speak and opens the narrative. We are introduced as if 'face-to-face' to the three principal characters that serve as the main ideological and narrative framework of the series. These are Stuart – twenty-nine, handsome and wealthy; Vince – twenty-nine, white working-class, life-long friend to Stuart and assistant manager in a suburban supermarket; and Nathan – fifteen, attractive, from a suburban lower-middle-class family and still at school. An ironic sense of the constructedness and relativity of both identity and sexuality very much characterises the postmodern nature of the series and its narrative strategies. Across the eight episodes – constituting a major six-episode first series and a two-episode sequel and finale – there is an ideological counterpoint between the questioning of and the search for a notion of fixity and coherence within gay and lesbian relationships. This narrative line is most evidently and consistently expressed by the character of Cameron Roberts (played by Peter O'Brien), an older successful Australian businessman – briefly Vince's lover – exercised in direct conflict with what he views as Stuart's damagingly irresponsible and manipulative hedonism. The series takes the viewer on a non-stop helter-skelter ride of characters, relationships, love affairs and sexual excess, and challenges and exposes both reactionary homophobic prejudice and what are considered as the disingenuous – even dishonest – constraints of liberal political correctness.

It is my contention that the fictitious representation of Canal Street in Manchester as a geo-ideological site of provocation to both reactionary heterosexual and liberal, politically correct viewing positions creates a site of ideological disruption – a running street battle in which the radical 'queering' of representational strategies confronts those attitudes like a queen high on vodka-caffeine drinks who not only dares to speak love's name but also screams out its mobile phone number. The publicly aired and angry debate between those gay men who viewed the series as dangerously reinforcing homophobic stereotypes of homosexuals and homosexual activity, against those – most especially Russell T. Davies, the series's author – who advocated that a policy of representing the truth of the gay scene was the sole priority, informs and underlies the entire series. It is significant that this struggle about the 'correctness' and efficacy of two diverse political strategies was enacted and fought simultaneously with the formally political, parliamentary debate concerning Clause 28 and the equalisation of laws of consent regarding adult sexual behaviour. The Broadcasting Standards Commission censured Channel 4 in upholding a formal complaint that had been made by the National Viewers and Listeners Association (NVALA). The judgement against the broadcaster was solely on the grounds of the 'explicit sex scenes' between Stuart and

Nathan that 'exceeded acceptable boundaries'. In reply Channel 4 had argued in response to this judgement against them that the illegality of the relationship between the adult man and the boy was as valid a subject for television drama as any other illegal act such as murder or theft. It is worthwhile mentioning that the letter from the NVALA (founded by the late Mary Whitehouse – the paradigm of meridian reactionary values) to the Independent Television Commission (24 February 1999) alleged that 'this programme is calculated to influence public opinion at a time when the age of homosexual consent is being debated in Parliament', The confrontational position of *Queer As Folk*, if calculated to provocatively disrupt both right-wing homophobic and centrist accommodating viewing positions on homosexuality, had clearly fulfilled its aim.

I conceived the critical concept of the 'geo-ideological' whilst researching and preparing material for my earlier, full-length study of contemporary television drama (Billingham 2000). It arose partly out of my engagement with Foucault's concept of the 'heterotopia' and also my growing realisation and conviction of the fundamental sense in which our perception of the geographical-as-location inevitably carries within it a prevailing sense of the ideological signing of that location. I believe that, as the primary medium of mass communication within popular culture, television – and especially television drama – is a prime initiator and channel of the complex process of geo-ideological inscription. Clearly, there are important issues attendant upon this concept related to the extent to which members of a constituent group or subculture either effectively define the limits and boundaries of that geo-ideological spatial formation or are willing or resistant participants within that process. I also want to propose my concept and understanding of the viewing position that constitutes my own ideological, interpretative – in that sense, subjective – viewing position. In doing so I should state that I am a white man in my middle age who grew up in a close-knit, east-Midlands working-class family and environment. I am now, through education, profession and income, middle-class. I am heterosexual but with an ideological and empathetic commitment to advocacy that promotes the value of bisexuality. My political position is radical socialist, post-Marxist and cultural materialist. I believe that the ideological context and marking of viewing for an audience is inevitably subject to considerations of class, sub-class and the complex relationship of cultural or subcultural infrastructures of identification and expression. I am not proposing a crude stratification of autonomous, constitutive audience bases marked by either economic income or socio-geographic demography. Nevertheless,

what I do want to propose in my discussion of *Queer As Folk* is a belief
that the production, encoding and broadcasting of most television drama
as a complex cultural product is expressed in my concept of the viewing
public as a site of marketed homogeneity determined by dominant eco-
nomic-cultural interests. Within the economic (global, multinational)
and cultural (postmodern) conditions of late capitalism, the construction of the allegedly privileged consumer is but one primary aspect of
other similar myths such as that of 'the public'. Not surprisingly, this construct of the public is inherently – even 'naturally' – a centre-right, Blairite
home-owning bourgeoisie.

The premeditated decision to position and locate constructs and discourses of gay and queer sexuality in a location with such a profound
iconic status as a place of the disruptive exhibition of pleasure and excess
constitutes a 'queering' of reactionary and liberal, gay or straight viewing
positions, and was in a sense an act of war. Not class war perhaps, but a
war waged with a vivid sense of a sumptuous visual aesthetic and fought
with a self-knowing sense of class: a 'classy war'. Russell T. Davies identified what he viewed as the 'enemy' in angry reaction to the criticism he
and the programme had received from within the gay community. In the
June 1999 issue of the British gay magazine *Attitude* he stated:

> When this all began in November 1997, no one told me there was an agenda.
> Because there must be an agenda – every gay politician, spokeswoman and
> militant has shouted at me for not following it . . . Right now, I'd love to see
> it, this set of rules, as unwritten as the British Constitution and as rigid,
> dictating what, how and why a gay writer must write. The creation of the
> series was entirely personal . . . And that's where the trouble started . . . I
> knew I had to invent specific lives rather than portray the entire so-called
> community. So where did I look? The clubs . . . Some of the men and
> women who claim to speak on our behalf would rather this night-life did
> not exist . . . It's more than political correctness, it's far, far worse. It's those
> old and powerful ghosts, the unholy trinity: Self-loathing, Fear and Shame.
> (Davies 1999b: 34)

The first Molotov – rather than vodka and martini – cocktail to be
thrown at this 'unholy trinity' exploded within fifteen minutes of the
opening episode of the first series. Significantly, in terms of the politics of
representation, and especially that of the naked male body, the incident
that put the match to the petrol was a scene showing Stuart Alan Jones
having sex in his apartment with Nathan, a young gay virgin he's picked
up on Canal Street. This scene of explicit sexual love between an older
man and an under-age adolescent provoked more complaints from the

viewing public than any other programme previously broadcast on British television. *The Guardian* reported on 22 June 1999 that

> More than 160 people complained to the Independent Television Commission, mostly about the first episode which showed a 15 year old boy being introduced to gay sex by a promiscuous 29-year-old. In the ITC's history, only Martin Scorcese's hugely controversial feature film 'The Last Temptation of Christ' . . . prompted more complaints from viewers.

The shock impact of this scene was deliberate and intentional in terms of communicating the serial adventurism of the character of Stuart as a signifier of unrestrained, eroticised masculine virility. In this important sense he is a potently mythic figure, perpetuating and redefining the nineteenth-century icon of the 'Byronic hero' and like Byron epitomising a shifting sign of bisexuality as excess. However, it is equally important to recognise the material basis of this character's geo-ideological domain. There is a clear relationship between his Byronic adventures and conquests within the meta-geo-ideological location of Canal Street and the economic, material conditions that facilitate and fund those exploits. The construction of Stuart as this kind of character is predicated upon an economic and material base. The power relations of Foucauldian sexual politics are replicated and facilitated by the economic relations and purchasing power of Stuart as a phallocentric protagonist. The scene that expresses this analysis most clearly is where Stuart goes on to the Internet to find a casual sexual partner for an evening's pleasure. Potently, in addition to Stuart's definition in the reductionist terms of a saleable commodity as a recipient of sexual gratification, Stuart's computer screen reveals another commodity image, a disembodied, reified, 'classic' male torso. This commodified phantom of cyberspace is defined by a generic term that conveys him as a means of guaranteed functional outcome: 'Goodfuck'. When 'Goodfuck' materialises as a northern, white, middle-aged working-class man in the entrance to Stuart's expensive, warehouse conversion apartment, he objects to Stuart introducing him to Nathan by his Internet epithet. With quiet but steely self-respect, he reproves Stuart with, 'Colin. My name's Colin.' Throughout the series, there is an assumption that Stuart's wealth – as evidenced in his canal-side penthouse and four-wheel-drive jeep – is a given material condition. Whilst the viewer sees him on one occasion in episode one in a work location – a high-quality, big-account advertising agency – where, with knowing irony, the agency presentation that morning is a homoerotically charged campaign for denim jeans, and where Stuart seduces a young married

male colleague in the company toilets – there is never any explicit indication of his professional role or income. Nevertheless, there is significance
in his means of employment being in a sub-geo-ideological location
where wealth and profits are generated through the manipulation and
marketing of the seductive surface of consumer capitalism's fetishised
products.

Stuart and his micro-geo-ideological territory are signified through
the motifs of fetishised economic surplus and sexual excess. When it
looks as if Stuart is not, on reflection, going to have sex with Colin, Stuart
rebuffs his erstwhile, ageing rent-boy with the remark 'I never promised
you anything'. This might be construed as his leitmotif throughout the
series. Indeed, as Cameron, Vince's short-lived committed partner says
accusingly to Stuart in the context of the power struggle between the two
men for Vince: 'It's sex. Everything's sex with you. There's no such thing
as Vince. He doesn't exist on his own. You don't let him.'

Confrontation and assimilation

The conflict between Vincent and Cameron is the most persuasive evidence of the ideologically strategic battle that I outlined in my opening to
this essay between a liberal, consensual assimilation and outright – 'Out-
rage-ed' – queer subversion. Vince is initially very reluctant to respond to
Cameron's advances towards him and it is, ironically, Stuart who eventually acts as the catalyst for his friend to agree to a dinner date with
Cameron at an exclusive restaurant. This setting, with its quiet, under-
stated elegance, is in direct and sharp relief to the brash colour and music
of Canal Street's bars, clubs and pubs. Cameron is Australian, older and
defined not only as a geographical outsider but also as someone who
inhabits a different geo-ideological territory to Stuart in particular.
Cameron distances himself from the gay scene. In a later scene, he
remarks to Vince, 'The problem is it all starts to look the same. Same men,
standing in the same clubs.' The tensions between Stuart and Cameron
continue to grow with each man seeking to exclude the other from the
object of desire. Significantly of course, whereas Cameron seeks and
offers Vince long-term commitment and a stable sexual and emotional
relationship, Stuart will only ever remain a problematic and domineering
voyeur in relation to Vince.

Stuart organises and holds a party for Vince's rite-of-passage thirtieth
birthday at his penthouse flat. The party serves as a micro-geo-ideological location for the next and penultimate stage in the struggle for Vince.

The two gifts bought by Cameron and Stuart respectively for Vince are powerful emblems of their desires and relationships for and with Vince. Stuart deliberately spoils what is intended as a surprise gift from Cameron to Vince of a Mini car. Simultaneously Stuart has sought to upstage Cameron's generous gift by purchasing the original K9 remote-controlled robotic dog from the classic cult series *Doctor Who*. It is significant that these two gifts represent both the differing intentions of their givers but also their givers' views of Vince in relation to themselves. He remains the perpetual touchstone for their own expression of subjectivity, at the same time as each of them tries to mould Vince's subjectivity in his interests.

Another crucial incident in the exploration of the tensions between confrontational and assimilationist strategies comes in the penultimate episode of the second series relating to a secondary character called Alexander. Alexander is constructed in such a way that he embodies the stereotypical attributes of camp, 'feminised' homosexuality. He endures a continuous and profoundly painful experience of homophobic rejection by his parents. As this sub-plot develops, Alexander's father is rushed into hospital, critically ill. Alexander, the wounds of rejection and alienation running deep, resolves not to visit his dying father. However, his mother urges him to come to the hospital and, with the active supporting presence of Vince and Stuart, he reluctantly concedes. It transpires that the only reason that the mother – Mrs Perry – requires him there is to sign a disclaimer barring Alexander from any of the father's wealth or possessions in the context of his imminent death. Alexander proceeds to sign it, despite Vince urging him not to, questioning the document's legality. For Alexander, the signing of the document is simultaneously a ritualistic 'signing' of himself as the victim of his parents' excoriating, bourgeois disdain and a judgement upon himself as a young, unapologetically gay man. Significantly, in terms of the wider metanarratives of the series, this episode also serves as the engine that will drive an inexorable energy of retribution upon the Perrys' familial destruction of their son. As Mrs Perry is about to leave the hospital, Stuart confronts in her in the sterile anonymity of a hospital corridor and effects an iconic moment of the series, one with almost Tarantino-esque, postmodern *film noir* irony. Stuart enacts a kind of savage dumb-show routine of calculating intimidation and violence, whose tone I have tried to capture in this description:

> Violence in the air. Very slowly, he brings his arm up, straight, pointing at her head. All his strength, everything he is, concentrated in that arm. Two

fingers out. His hand is a gun. She's transfixed. Scared of him. The gun
pointing. Stuart's stare, taking aim. Her terror. Then he just relaxes, opens
his hand and brings it down. And he smiles.

With Mrs Perry left stunned and frightened, Vince reproves Stuart's
actions by saying, 'There's no point making it worse'. However, when a
little later in the episode Alexander makes a serious but unsuccessful suicide attempt in the aftermath of his signing off from his former life, it
serves as the final catalyst for Stuart's anger and enactment of revenge.
This proves a climatic moment both in the relationship between Stuart
and Vince but also as a signifying embodiment of the deep tensions
between queered direct action and liberal gay accommodation-as-accept-
ance. The power dynamics inherent within the Stuart–Vince relationship
are superbly realised in the following short dialogue extract from the
moment when Stuart invites Vince to accompany him on his planned retribution on behalf of Alexander:

> STUART: Does she deserve it?
> VINCE: You'll make it worse.
> STUART: Does she deserve it?
> (Silence)
> VINCE: You can't.
> STUART: Watch me.
> (Vince makes his decision. Colder, cutting himself off)
> VINCE: Yeah. You'd like that. Spent years watching you.
> (Vince turns and goes)
> STUART: Coward.
> (Vince keeps walking, breaks into a run. The camera stays with Stuart. A
>   wild grin, almost glad that Vince has gone; now he can do anything. He
>   shouts after him)
> STUART: Coward!

This profound tension between these two characters epitomises, in the
most heightened and even theatrical way, the ideological tension between
a politicised queer sensibility and a quasi-assimilationist gay position. In
a scene of almost literally breathtaking cinematic bravura, Stuart deto-
nates a bomb underneath Mrs Perry's car parked outside her home in
suburban Altrincham – a geo-ideological sub-site of straight bourgeois
respectability. That surface of ideological stability and permanence is literally and metaphorically exploded in the visual aesthetics of the massive
fireball that engulfs the car and illuminates, with savage, celebratory
queered light, the shadowed hypocrisy of the curtained cul-de-sac.
Having successfully completed his Aeschylean act of revenge, the Armani-

suited Fury that is Stuart walks calmly back to his jeep that he has parked nearby. Paradoxically, his baby son Alfred is strapped in the back seat awaiting his father's return. This juxtaposition of the suburban and the domestic located against an act of terror designed to shake bourgeois homophobia to its foundations is potent. In one important sense, the positioning of the pre-speech infant in the context and moment of violent adult terrorism is perhaps an anticipation of his future allegiances.

When, in the aftermath of that episode, Vince questions why Stuart had to resort to such violent action, he asks Stuart why he hadn't just told Mrs Perry to 'fuck off', Stuart replies with: 'It's not enough any more'. Stuart's assertion that 'It's not enough any more' is expressed as a power-ful expression of unflinching and direct opposition to the varied posi-tions and strategies of homophobia. Equally however, its enactment by and through Stuart is once more a signifier of the material base upon which he is enabled to take such actions. Vince conveys this in defending his decision not to have been a partner in that act of violence: 'There's people relying on me. Mum, and that house, I end up paying the mortgage every other month, that lot don't earn tuppence. I can't start . . . (Pause) You're on your own.' Stuart's premeditatedly, cruelly dismis-sive response unequivocally collates Vince's need to avoid criminal activities and stay in work with a savage critique of Vince's sexuality: 'You're just straight, Vince. You're a straight man who fucks men, that's all.'

Within the series's metadiscourses and disruptions of the binary con-structs of straight and bent, queer and gay, male and female, Stuart's words cut through and expose the liminal interfaces between the ideo-logical construction and enactment of those concepts. Herein lies a potentially crucial paradox within the construction of Stuart – most especially evident in the dynamics of his relationship with Vince: that is, the strong sense in which Stuart is positioned and performed as playing a 'masculinised' role in relation to a 'feminised' Vince. This is expressed with humour and latent camp pathos in the scene early in the first episode of the first series where the two characters are standing, inter-twined, on the hospital roof above a Manchester skyline in the early hours. The pulsating array of distant lights across the city at night evokes associations of the spermatozoa visuals of the opening credits. Stuart is trying to come to terms with his new role as 'father' following the birth of Alfred, his surrogate son. As he and Vince stand together on the rooftop edge, they re-enact – the perfect postmodern ironic motif – the cruciform coupling of Kate Winslet and Leonardo Di Caprio on the bow of the *Titanic*. Vince complains that 'I'm always Kate Winslet' and indeed, in some complex mutual ritual between the two men, he is always defined as the 'feminised' submissive recipient of Stuart's actual and mythic gaze and desire: a phallic, penetrative ownership of Vince as subject. The tensions and issues concerning the extent to which these roles are mutually self-chosen and enacted or whether they are imposed runs as a powerful dialectic throughout the series. This paradigm of reactionary, heterosexual, socially gendered roles exists simultaneously and paradoxically with the signing of Stuart as an agent-provocateur queering the geo-ideological formation(s) of the series. Also and quite deliberately paradoxical is the fact that, for all of the character's libidinous exhibitionism, Stuart has not 'come out' of the closet of denial and secrecy within his own family. When he is finally provoked into an admission of his sexuality through the attempted blackmail by a young nephew, Stuart does so through a speech of barely controlled power and anger:

> I'm queer, I'm gay. I'm homosexual. I'm a poof. I'm a bum-boy batty-boy backside-artist bugger, I'm bent, I am that arse bandit, I lift those shirts, I'm a fudge-packing shit-stabbing uphill gardener, I dance at the other end of the ballroom, I dine in the downstairs restaurant, I'm Moses and the parting of the Red Cheeks, I fuck and I'm fucked, I suck and I'm sucked, I rim them and wank them and every single man's had the shag of his life, and I am not – [*pause*] – a pervert. If there's one twisted bastard in this family, it's that little blackmailer, so congratulations, Thomas, I've just officially outed you.

In what is effectively a litany of the pejorative, discriminatory language traditionally used to oppress and denigrate homosexual men, Stuart – in a guerrilla operation – covertly transforms and inverts their power into a celebration of himself as a queer man. This is the diametric opposite of an alternative strategy of seeking quiet accommodation within the dominant heterosexual geo-ideological location of either homophobic prejudice or polite liberal accommodation of the different other. Stuart is simultaneously and paradoxically a performative sign of reactionary masculinised dominance in his relationship to Vince whilst serving as the principal channel for the provocative queering of the series's geo-ideological territories.

The other major moment in the series that challenges the fixed marking and delineation of sexual and gendered boundaries is the encounter between Nathan and the character of Christian Hobbs. Hobbs is the school bully whose gang frightens and intimidates those other boys who are perceived in any sense as different or deficient. However, Nathan is sexually attracted to his erstwhile tormentor and, successfully, seeks an opportunity to have sex with him. Nathan follows Christian down to the school changing rooms where his 'enemy' is mopping up the changing-room floor as a punishment for some earlier misbehaviour. Nathan offers to help him in this menial task as a means of facilitating a sexual pass at Christian. The two teenage boys sit and take a rest from their chore and Hobbs begins to recount an episode of alleged sexual bravado with a teenage girl. As he relives his sexual frustration at being masturbated by the girl but without being brought to climax, Nathan masturbates his sexually aroused classmate, achieving what the – perhaps imagined – girl neglected to do. This episode communicates a powerfully disruptive questioning of the parameters of ideologically constructed naming of sexual activity and its participants. Within the subversive queering of an institutionalised geo-ideological location – the school changing room – this encounter radically reveals the shifting nature of the power relations between the two characters. In doing so, the naming of the sexual activity is exposed as conditional and subject to renaming. Hobbs is constructed as the very epitome of binary, reactionary, aggressively controlling straight masculinity. Nevertheless, within a location of eroticised concealment, concomitant with the awareness of the possible public discovery of secret pleasure, Hobbs surrenders himself to Nathan's sexual intervention. This crucially defining moment in the power dynamics of their relationship is finally consummated for Nathan when, later, he sees Christian and a girlfriend at one of the gay pubs in Canal Street and regards them as interlopers. Nathan then proceeds to exercise a potent act of revenge and retribution against his tormentor who has led continuous homophobic attacks upon Nathan at school. It is significant that Nathan's ultimate opportunity to effect a decisive counterattack is when Hobbs enters into the geo-ideological territory of Canal Street where his homophobic prejudices are marginalised and resisted in a location defined as a gay/queer centre. It's 'Karaoke Night' and Nathan forgoes the opportunity for yet another Gloria Gaynor rendition and instead publicly 'outs' his oppressor using the pub's amplified sound system:

> Cos that boy over there. Blue shirt, white T-shirt, dark hair, with the blonde girl, him . . . His name's Christian Hobbs, d'you know what he does? He finds a boy, and if that boy's a bit quiet, if he's a bit different, Christian Hobbs kicks his head in. He kicks them and he calls them queer. That boy there. He beats us up 'cos we're queer.

Inevitably, Hobbs is shaken, exposed and embarrassed and his girlfriend storms off without him. Nathan concludes his open-microphone assault when he shouts across to him: 'Plenty more I could have said, Christian. And that's a favour.'

Reception and the question of effect

In 1999, *Queer As Folk* had its United States premiere at the International Lesbian and Gay Film Festival. The response was phenomenally positive with audiences cheering wildly at each screened episode. Within Britain when it was first broadcast in the same year, one representative of those gay men who were not supportive of its style and subject matter was the high-profile, 1980s transgressive-dressing singer Boy George. Writing in the *Sunday Express* (a bastion of right-wing 'Little England' racist, sexist and homophobic values) and by now a highly respected Ibiza DJ, Boy George angrily criticised the series for what he viewed as a dangerously gratuitous depiction of explicit and serial gay sexual behaviour. What is also interesting in terms of the social and cultural context in which the series was originally broadcast was that audience research revealed that the series's largest single demographic viewing group was made up of young women between the ages of eighteen and thirty. Furthermore, whilst the series sustained quietly solid and respectable viewing figures of just over four million viewers, these figures did not describe or represent a significantly large national audience. The relatively small – if respectable – size of the British viewing audience and the fact that the largest viewing group was young women is very significant and directly relevant to the wider issue of the transgressive impact of the series. If *Queer As Folk* was engaged in a battle for hearts and minds, was it more actually and prob-ably a local war, civil unrest challenging and exposing the supposed homogeneity of a gay culture and gay community seeking only ultimate accommodation through the successful passing of more equitable legis-lation regarding the homosexual age of sexual consent? From an assimi-lationist perspective and viewing position, subsequent policy decisions by the British government have been decisive and symbolic. Same-sex civil ceremonies and contracts are to be introduced for gay and lesbian cou-ples along with the simultaneous introduction of promised legislation which will provide gay and lesbian couples with rights to inherit property and pensions, rights that were previously denied to non-heterosexual partners. Furthermore, the long campaign to see the overturning of Clause 28 was finally successful when it was repealed from the statute book in 2003. There is no evidence available on the sexual orientation or lifestyle choices of those young women who regularly tuned in to the eight-episode series. One can only therefore speculate on the basis on which their viewing positions engaged with the series, its characters and its themes. A significant proportion of the commercials preceding and following each episode, and the commercials in the advertising break half-way through, were for products intended for female consumers, and principally included tampons, feminine hygiene products and cosmetic accessories. I have a latent, residual optimism for pluralistic social change and I would conjecture that a significant proportion of young women may have viewed *Queer As Folk* as a potentially liberating, open-ended, playful and empowering enactment of sexual pleasure and tolerance of the 'other'.

Inscribed within *Queer As Folk*'s production values, character construction and dialectical interplay of themes of gay community, identity and representation lies a confrontational, postmodern queer discourse that proclaims: 'We're queer, we're here and we're not going away.' Also, the programme signifies the irresistible rise in the social and cultural visibility of gay sexuality in urban geo-ideological sites such as Manchester's Canal Street. Significantly, especially in relation to the material conditions and context in which Stuart's character is constructed and signed, that vibrant, self-confident visibility has been accompanied – and driven by – a growing commercial exploitation of cultural and economic consumption in terms of fashion, music and recreational sub-sites such as the bars and clubs of Canal Street. Herein lies a powerful ideological paradox and contradiction. The geo-ideological site in and through which a more politically radicalised, confrontational queering of location and representation is enacted is, in economic material conditions, an epitome of postmodern consumer capitalism.

In conclusion, once the shock value of the explosion of the unrestrained, libidinous, gay male body had settled as sequined dust, the series nevertheless left in its wake some provocative questions about the construction and representation of sexual identity and sexuality. These questions will quite properly resist polite rationalisation or even hip postmodern cool disdain. With its potential at least for confrontational disruption, the struggle to resist both the reactionary and politically correct resolution of those questions might also signify the possibility of sexual politics transmuting into a new, post-Marxist oppositional formation. Before you, dear reader, dismiss such outrageous optimism, please remember and be advised: There's nowt as queer as f**k.

References

Billingham, P. (2000), *Sensing the City through Television*, Exeter: Intellect.

Davies, R. T. (1999a), *Queer As Folk – The Scripts*, London: Channel 4 Books/ Macmillan.

Davies, R. T. (1999b), 'Queer as fuck', *Attitude*, June, 34.

Gibson, J. (1999), 'Gay programme upsets viewers', *Guardian*, Media section, 22 June.

Further reading

Dines, G., and J. M. Humez (eds) (1995), *Gender, Race and Class in Media*, London: Sage.

Garber, M. (1997), *Vice Versa: Bisexuality and the Eroticism of Everyday Life*, London: Hamish Hamilton.

Medhurst, A., and S. Munt (eds) (1997), *Lesbian and Gay Studies – A Critical Introduction*, London: Cassell.

Solomon, A. (1997), *Re-Dressing the Canon – Essays on Theatre and Gender*, London: Routledge.

Wandor, M. (1987), *Look Back in Gender – Sexuality and the Family in Post-War British Drama*, London: Methuen.

7

'Just that kids' thing': the politics of 'Crazyspace', children's television and the case of *The Demon Headmaster*

Máire Messenger Davies

We can use Crazyspace for that. No-one's going to spot it so long as we keep the messages sounding like nonsense. (Gillian Cross, *The Demon Headmaster Takes Over* (1997: 107))

Much of the ideology in and around children's books is hidden. (Peter Hunt, *Criticism, Theory and Children's Literature* (1991: 142))

In a scene in the third of the *Demon Headmaster* television series broadcast on Children's BBC in 1998, the mysterious 'Demon Headmaster' is once again attempting to achieve world domination by disrupting and then taking over all communications systems, using his special hypnotic powers. Standing in his way, as so often in children's fiction, is nothing but a group of children – thirteen-year-old, scientifically gifted orphan Dinah Hunter, her adoptive brothers Lloyd and Harvey and their friends, all for some reason immune to the Demon Headmaster's powers. The computer screens in the Internet café where the children are working suddenly crash. But one is still functioning, with a young girl 'hunched over it', and Gillian Cross's novel of the series describes the subsequent action in this way:

The man at the next table came back, looking disgusted. 'She's not on the Net' he said to the woman next to him. 'Just that kids' thing – Crazyspace or whatever it's called.'

'Typical.' Crossly the woman picked up her briefcase. 'We can't do our work – but kids can chat as much as they like.' She stamped out and most of the other adults followed . . . [Dinah] got up and walked across to the girl . . .

'The server's packed up'. Dinah waved a hand at the blank screens. 'How come you're still on line?'

'I'm not on the Internet,' Kate said. 'This is a separate network for kids to chat. Supposed to be *safer* than surfing the Net.' She pulled a funny face, and laughed . . .
'So you can still chat? To people all over the place?'
'Only children.'
'Children will do fine.' Dinah pulled up a chair and sat down. 'Can you show us how to get in?' (Cross 1997: 60–61)

This scene flags up some issues in the debate about the politics and ideology of children's television, which I want to develop in this essay (for further discussions of this debate see also Bazalgette and Buckingham 1995; Buckingham, Davies, Jones and Kelley 1999; Buckingham 2000b and 2002). Firstly, as the scene suggests, children's media can be defined as 'a Crazyspace' of which adults are scornful, and are therefore likely to ignore; such a space can thus be construed as a place of refuge. Secondly, 'Crazyspaces' can be utilised to disseminate messages of resistance and liberation, again because adults are not paying any attention to them. And finally, as Kate in this scene laughingly points out: adult attempts to make children '*safer*' by closing down access to communications media may well backfire in that children will use the means still open to them – the supposedly apolitical 'Crazyspaces' of children's entertainment – to seek political knowledge and to challenge the status quo. The scene suggests, as do the books and the television series from which they come, that there might be such a thing as 'children's culture' which is quite significantly different from, and may be in opposition to, adult culture. In this it is at odds with much in contemporary sociological childhood studies (see for example James and Prout 1997; James, Jenks and Prout 1998), a field which, as the kids in the Internet café might expect, has not paid very much attention to children's media and culture so far.

The idea that children's media can be politically subversive is not new. Alison Lurie in *Don't Tell the Grownups* (1990), subtitled *Subversive Children's Literature*, pointed out that many children's literary classics, such as *Wind in the Willows, Little Women, The House at Pooh Corner, The Secret Garden* and *Alice in Wonderland*, were not the secure havens of conservative heritage respectability that many people think they are: they all, in their different ways, challenged adult authority and the prevailing social order, and showed children, and other powerless groups, as potential agents of this subversion. Lurie was talking about books – and children's literature, of course, is regularly discussed within the mainstream of academic literary and ideological criticism. Peter Hunt even claims: 'Critics create the intellectual climate which produces the [children's literary] text' (Hunt 1991: 143). But children's *television*, despite serving similar pleasurable narrative functions for children as children's books, and even despite the fact that much of it, like *The Demon Headmaster*, is based on children's books, doesn't have critics, in the sense that Hunt was talking about, to produce an 'intellectual climate' for it. Hunt quotes critics such as Patrick Shannon, Robert Leeson, Nicholas Tucker and Terry Eagleton. Such figures do not exist in the debate about children's television, although David Buckingham of the Institute of Education and Cary Bazalgette of the BFI and some contributors to the present volume have been doing their best to remedy this situation (see Bazalgette and Buckingham 1995 and Buckingham 2002). Peter Hunt and Robert Leeson also write children's fiction themselves, thus closing the circle of 'intellectual climate' and the act of storytelling. In contrast, the producers and writers of children's television are not academic critics, neither do any of the main academic television critics write children's drama. Producers can be very suspicious of academic criticism. Anna Home, head of Children's BBC at the time *The Demon Headmaster* was broadcast, was asked to comment on the story's themes of 'people gaining control over other people, and threats to individual freedom'; she replied somewhat impatiently: 'Yes, but I don't think that anybody [in television] sits down and analyses it like that' (Davies and O'Malley 1996: 138).

If it is true that there is no 'intellectual climate' to 'produce the texts', what can be the origins of the 'climate', intellectual or otherwise, that produces children's television drama? In writing this essay, as well as giving my own interpretations of the *Demon Headmaster* series, I draw on interviews I carried out with its producers and their colleagues in children's television in the 1990s. Producers are a major source of information about the making of television drama because, by virtue of its collaborative and technological nature, it can never be fully defined through one sole authorial voice, as with literature. I also use quotations from Gillian Cross's *Demon Headmaster* books, many of which are common to the television screenplays. This aids precise citation, and also gives readers the opportunity to follow them up – something which is much more difficult to do with screenplays and videos. *The Demon Headmaster* is currently not available on video or DVD whereas the books are all in print. I also quote interviews with children, carried out as part of a BBC-funded study on children and television drama (Davies 2001; Davies, O'Malley and Corbett 1997; Davies and O'Malley 1996). All of these voices, I suggest, share in the production of 'the intellectual climate' for children's television – although some might disagree that this is what they are doing.

The corrupting world of kidvid

Many would disclaim any intellectual component at all to 'the climate' of children's television. For some scholars, children's television is anti-intellectual: part of the global broadcasting industry and, as such, suspect both as a capitalist commodification of childhood (Kline 1993) and as a corrupting source of the destruction of childhood precisely because it is *not* literature (Postman 1982). 'Kidvid' is seen as a place of, in Buckingham's words (2002: 10), 'anarchy and game playing'; where to be 'wacky' and 'cool' is absolutely necessary to appeal to 'kids'. Any systematic attempt to characterise the quality of children's television often comes from broadcasting institutions with their own axes to grind. In his introduction to *Small Screens* (2002), Buckingham contrasts the different constructions of children's television produced by the BBC in its 1998 promotional film, *Future Generations*, and the satirical spoof on this film produced by the commercial channel, Nickelodeon, also self-promotingly. On the one hand, the BBC, attempting to promote the licence fee as the primary source of 'quality' children's television, used a child in a 1950s prep-school uniform walking through the sets of 1960s and 1970s pre-school television programmes – a supposed reassuringly old-fashioned appeal to public service nostalgia. On the other hand, Nickelodeon championed the cause of cable subscription through its 'wicked cartoons', 'brilliant live shows' and 'fantastic comedy' – a primarily commercial American landscape.

In this essay I want to suggest that the BBC drama series *The Demon Headmaster* (1995–96, 1997, 1998) managed to combine the contrasting terrains of 'quality' children's television drama – book-based, literate and filmic – with the more commercial requirements of 'wacky kidvid' to produce a very radical piece of television. Furthermore – and true to Cross's Internet café scene – one of the most radical things about it was that hardly anyone at the BBC, or indeed anywhere else, seems to have recognised it as such. But – again, as the Internet café scene would predict – there is quite a lot of evidence that children did. I suggest that this relationship with its audience – a large, diverse, multicultural audience – makes children's television generally, and this drama series in particular, politically interesting: it is a crazyspace where children can meet, and in which adults are not interested. So things can happen there that might merit scrutiny.

The story of *The Demon Headmaster*

The three series of *The Demon Headmaster*, broadcast between 1995 and 1998, based on the books by Gillian Cross (1982, 1995, 1997) and adapted for television by Helen Cresswell, portrayed the struggle of gifted Dinah, her adoptive brothers, Lloyd and Harvey and their friends – a group called SPLAT (The Society for the Protection of our Lives Against Them) – against the power-crazed would-be world dictator, The Demon Headmaster (a man with no name) and his brainwashed cohorts of prefects, laboratory assistants, fellow-teachers, university researchers, parents and other duped adults. The first and most popular series was set in a school with disturbingly orderly children. Dinah sets out to find out why:

> Dinah knew . . . that there was something wrong about the school with its well-behaved children all doing the right thing at the right moment, but she could not understand what it was . . . and she hated not understanding things. . . . Everyone in the room was scribbling busily and she was suddenly sure that they had all just written 'the magnitude of the sun is –29.6' . . . Thirty little robots, all obediently writing down the same things, things that had been put into their heads for them. (Cross 1982: 52–56)

Simply as 'a thumping good story' as Anna Home (the Head of Children's BBC) described it, the series had potential for popularity, with all the narrative requirements of such a story: a mystery, a familiar setting (school) strangely defamiliarised, a Cinderella figure (orphaned outcast heroine with special gifts, initially rejected by siblings), a kids' gang like Blyton's Famous Five (children saving the world in the face of adult myopia) and special-effects 'scariness', with themes and incidents reminiscent of classic film and television science fiction – many of our child interviewees compared the series to *The X-Files* (Fox 1993–2002).

Within these narrative frames, and following well-established traditions set by them, *The Demon Headmaster* addressed a number of difficult contemporary political, scientific and ideological themes: freedom versus order, the encroachment of cybertechnology into diverse areas of life, the civil liberties implications of technological surveillance, the morality of genetic modification. Profound philosophical issues were touched on, including the nature of truth, the meanings of 'nature', the abuse of science and the extent of individual free will. The basic premise of *The Demon Headmaster*, particularly the first series set in a school, was of particular relevance to children in 1990s Britain: the series touched on 'formal' versus 'progressive' teaching methods, discipline versus dissent, the responsibilities of the family, the nature and necessity of childhood itself and the anarchic power of children's entertainment. Given all this deep background and its philosophical implications, it might be predicted that such a series would be a big turn-off for the 'wacky', short-attention-span 'kidvid' audience of tabloid mythology in the 1990s. In fact, *The Demon Headmaster* was the top-rated children's programme in 1995–96, with an unprecedented audience share of 70 percent of nine-to-twelve-year-olds. The 1995–96 series even entered the top ten of *all* programmes watched by children that year – something which is very difficult for a children's programme to do. It is the top adult shows such as *EastEnders* (BBC 1985–) which usually attract the largest numbers of child viewers, but in the week ending 3 November 1995 *EastEnders* was at number nine in the top ten for children and *The Demon Headmaster* was at number seven. As Dinah might have said, something very unusual was going on here.

The changing world of children's television drama

The Demon Headmaster was aired at a time when children's broadcasting was undergoing many changes as British broadcasting became increasingly deregulated after the 1990 Broadcasting Act, and American commercial children's channels, such as Nickelodeon, Disney, Fox Kids and the Cartoon Network, became available to challenge the BBC (see Davies and Corbett 1997; Blumler 1992). These were developments of which children themselves were aware, as my colleagues and I found in a study on children and television drama carried out with over 1,300 six-to-thirteen-year-olds in England and Wales on behalf of the BBC (see Davies 2001). This study was commissioned in 1995 and completed in 1997 – a period when the BBC, still under John Birt's Director Generalship, was questioning its own role in a number of ways. Robin McCron and Stephen Whittle of the Policy and Practice department (no longer in existence) required us to 'find out what children thought of television drama'. We carried out a survey of nearly 1,400 six-to-thirteen-year-olds in nineteen schools in different parts of England and Wales, and conducted qualitative discussion tasks with smaller groups of children in sixteen of these schools, including a number of discussions of *The Demon Headmaster*. We also interviewed children's drama producers in both the BBC and the commercial sector – many on the point of losing their jobs, including, ironically, both the producer and the director respectively of CBBC's biggest ever ratings hit, *The Demon Headmaster*, Richard Callanan and Roger Singleton-Turner.

As this shakeout might suggest, British children's television was under some unfriendly pressure at this time. Part of our study's literature review was an analysis of press coverage of children's media in 1996 and this revealed a strong discourse of scepticism about the supposed necessity for separate children's provision as a public service. According to such writers as Cosmo Landesman in Rupert Murdoch's *Sunday Times* (11 June 1995) children were mainly watching adult programmes, and they were more sophisticated nowadays, and spending more time on the Internet, so why the need for a protected area of provision for them? It is necessary to consider the ratings success of *The Demon Headmaster* within the context of this debate, because, if these claims about the declining audience for traditional children's 'quality' programming such as home-grown drama were true, then it ought to have been a resounding flop. It was the exact opposite.

The changing world of children's television drama

In an interview with me in March 1996 Anna Home explained the changing environment in which drama programmes were being commissioned and produced, especially within the publicly funded BBC: 'Over the last few years the whole area of the afternoon period leading up to the six o'clock news has become much more of a battleground and much more competitive in terms of building the early evening audience The BBC in general is much more aware and concerned about ratings than it used to be.' These pressures also affected the kinds of drama that it seemed sensible for Home to commission; an example of the ways in which children's television drama, far from the luxury of being influenced by academic 'intellectual climates', had to conform to commercial constraints arising from global changes, not only in the broadcasting industry but also in the publishing industry:

> We used to do a very large number of adaptations of children's novels, we
> now do fewer . . . Modern children's novels, partly because of publishers'
> requirements, tend to be shorter than their counterparts in the 1960s . . . Six
> episodes is the minimum in terms of economics and building the audience
> . . . *The Demon Headmaster* is a very good example of that. It is based on
> two books by Gillian Cross . . . I don't really want to say they are great
> children's literature, though they are certainly good children's literature.

In Anna Home's comments there is clearly a 'quality' discourse – about 'good' versus 'great' children's literature – but she suggests that one of the

primary justifications for broadcasting *The Demon Headmaster* was pragmatic: that two short books could be turned into six episodes and could
be produced fairly economically. Home does not discuss the *televised*
adaptation of *The Demon Headmaster* as potentially 'great television.' As
so often, television drama is measured against quality criteria drawn from
literature, and to some extent found wanting.

The quality of *The Demon Headmaster*

Anna Home's distinction between 'good' and 'great' children's literature is
probably justified in describing *The Demon Headmaster* books. They are
an easy, lively read with page-turning plots; however they are not in the
same league as, say, Philip Pullman's *His Dark Materials* (1995–2000). I
hope that Gillian Cross will not be insulted if I say that, in their television
versions, they do become something much more powerful and even
potentially 'great'. The advantage of television dramatisation is that it
gives verisimilitude to what on the page can sound unconvincing – a particular problem with children's books which have to use relatively simple
language. For instance, for obvious reasons, in *The Demon Headmaster*
books the science is only briefly sketched in. In the television series, with
generous amounts of location shooting, we see real schools, laboratories,
university campuses and libraries, in which plants grow rapidly under
infra-red lights, in which there are dramatic computer simulations of
DNA modification and in which a lizard can turn terrifyingly into a girl,
all through the use of special effects. These settings are peopled by skilled
professional adult actors giving credibility to words which, on the page,
might not mean very much to child readers. As Roger Singleton-Turner
pointed out in an interview with me in March 1996, the casting of Terence Hardiman as the Demon Headmaster was particularly inspired.
Similarly, the casting of accomplished child actors and their skilled direction gives credibility to the basic narrative unlikelihood of a group of kids
being able to overthrow an adult dictator: 'I was fortunate to find good
actors, good children who seemed to work well together and I was very
fortunate that Terence Hardiman seemed to be such a wonderful Demon
Headmaster.'

Singleton-Turner has written about the craft of writing and directing
for and with children (1994, 1999), and has been responsible for training
others in the industry to work with children. When I interviewed him, we
looked at an episode of *The Demon Headmaster* together and he pointed
out some of the techniques he used to enhance the narrative, such as put-

ting the camera at child height (a technique he had developed in *Grange Hill* (BBC 1975–)) to convey adult threat. He liked to use 'the arty shot of the week' from time to time, for instance an expressionist-type high shot of rows of white-coated children all obediently working on computers in the Demon Headmaster's computer lab, and he and his crew enjoyed making allusions to other directors – to Hitchcock in their use of sound, and also to the creators of *Doctor Who* (BBC 1963–), especially in the opening credits. Singleton-Turner had a variety of techniques to make the best use of his child actors, for instance in making the 'hypnotised' children act like zombies, while at the same time showing that the leading character, Dinah, well played in the first series by ten-year-old Frances Amey who matured into a teenager in the three years she battled with the Demon Head, wasn't quite as much of a zombie as the others. In these ways, as Singleton-Turner pointed out, children's television drama becomes a form of painless education in media literacy; child viewers are introduced to filmic and televisual techniques for enhancing suspense and indicating motivation, as well as codes specific to particular genres such as science fiction, to which they can become very attuned (see Davies 1997).

Several of our other interviewees referred to *The Demon Headmaster*, then doing so surprisingly well in the ratings, as a paradigmatic example of 'good children's television drama'. Steven Andrew, now head of children's programming at ITV, then producing *Grange Hill* for the BBC, explained this to Kate O'Malley in March 1996 in terms of its narrative quality: '[It] is such a simple story, well told . . . it seems to me, that if you can hit them with the right type of drama, then they will watch it.' But what is 'the right type of drama'? Anna Home's criteria, stated in the interview quoted above, were:

> Is it strong, has it got good identifiable characters, is it exciting, is it fun? . . . *The Demon Headmaster* has also got a thumping great plot, a good and evil plot, and enough sci-fi effects to make it [exciting] . . . it really was a great success . . . absolutely middle of the road, middle-class traditional children's books. And there's a lot of people saying you should be doing more wacky, funky things based on computer games, and they [children] don't want it.

The paradox of entertainment

One paradox in the success of *The Demon Headmaster* was that it could actually be read as a *defence* of 'wacky, funky things based on computer games'. In what Home characterised as the story's 'battle between good

and evil', a battle between totalitarianism and intellectual and civic liberty, it was the 'wacky, funky things' in 'Crazyspace' which were enlisted
on the side of good. In contrast, it was the formal educational institutions
– in the first series a school, in the second series a research station and in
the third series a university – which quickly fell prey to the Headmaster's
hypnotic seductions and were all-too-easily enlisted on the side of evil. In
the first series, during a silly game show modelled on *Tiswas* (ITV
1974–82), the Head was deluged in 'gunge' by one of Dinah's friends
before he could hypnotise the nation's television viewers. In the second
series, a more straightforward adventure along the lines of Blytonian
kids-against-the smugglers, Dinah and her helpers sabotaged the Head's
research station where he was seeking to modify DNA to 'speed up evolution' and so abolish childhood. In the third series, all 'normal' communications including phone, Internet, television, radio and print media
were put out of action by the Head, and tabloidised to provide only anodyne information. The Head's supporters all wore little hand-shaped
badges with networked two-way cameras in them. Dinah and her friends
used the children's chatroom, Crazyspace, to feed nonsense messages into
the badges and thus sabotage the Head's attempt to take over Hyperbrain,
a computer containing all the world's knowledge. This was their battle
cry: 'Give them nonsense overload. Netspeak junk till they explode.' The
denouement had Dinah, wired up to the Brain, defending herself by
drawing on an earlier piece of subversive nonsense: 'Twas brillig and the
slithy toves / Did gyre and gimble in the wabe.' 'For the Hyperbrain it was
the last straw . . . the computer screen went blank and the Headmaster
crumpled and fell to the ground' (Cross 1997: 156). The children's world
of 'wackiness' had overthrown the dictator, and rescued the duped adult
world of formal education from his power.

Totalitarianism; education; childhood

> A pity that there should be children at all. Childhood is such a waste of time.
> So pointless, so useless. Imagine a world where childhood could be
> bypassed, could be telescoped into a mere fraction of the human lifespan.
> What a beautifully efficient way of saving time. A world peopled by adults
> . . . but not ordinary adults, not the kind of fools you see all about you wast-
> ing time on pointless pursuits . . . Order. That's what the world needs. Beau-
> tiful, perfect order. (*The Demon Headmaster*, series two, episode two, BBC
> 1997, written by Helen Cresswell, adapted from the books by Gillian Cross,
> directed by Roger Singleton-Turner)

In the 1990s, British children, along with British children's television, were getting rather a bad press. Educational standards were declared to be in danger, and standardised testing was becoming universal in primary schools, under the critical (one might almost say hypnotic) eyes of Ofsted and its chief inspector, Chris Woodhead. A series of overhauls of the exam system, both GCSE and A Level, was under way. In 1993, one of the most appalling crimes ever committed against a child – James Bulger – was committed by two other children, which led to an outpouring of self-examination about what the nation was doing, or failing to do, to its children. Part of this examination was a Gulbenkian Foundation report, *Children and Violence*, which recommended, among other things, a dilution of parents' 'right' to use corporal punishment on their children (see Barker and Petley 1997). This resulted in angry newspaper headlines such as the *Daily Express*'s on 10 November 1995, 'Fury at call to ban smacking', and a *Sun* editorial chiding the 'busybodies' and their 'trendy claptrap'. Regular stories appeared in the press about children who were out of control, and there were calls for curfews to protect citizens from them. A number of academic works inspired by these issues appeared (Buckingham 1995; Barker and Petley 1997; Springhall 1998). Further, the sociological revision of childhood suggesting that childhood was either 'dead' or a culturally constructed invention of the Romantic era and irrelevant to a multi cultural world was also well under way (James and Prout 1997). The universal declaration of the Rights of the Child had been published in 1989, but the idea that there could be such a thing as the universality of childhood, as a natural state with a generally-accepted set of rights, had been challenged by academics such as Christopher Jenks, who claimed in 1982: 'Childhood is not a natural phenomenon and cannot properly be understood as such. The social transformation from child to adult does not follow directly from physical growth. . . . Childhood is to be understood as a social construct' (Jenks 1982: 12).

The educational establishment – schools, universities, research – was, it seemed, turning its back on the idea that childhood should be a time of natural freedom, playfulness and, of course, innocence. Children themselves were a problem and they needed to be controlled. *The Demon Headmaster* series was a loud counter-blast to all this. It turned on the critics of children and childhood and pointed out the link between their formal, rote-learning methods of education and totalitarianism. It demonstrated a connection between harsh adult discipline and political repression. And it asserted repeatedly that adults should listen to children, who may see such ideological issues more clearly. When, in the first series, Dinah realised that the Head was force-feeding facts into his pupils without their conscious knowledge, she pointed out: 'We're not learning to *think*. We're just learning to repeat things like robots. It looks good but it's no use at all.' When her adoptive brothers tried to suggest that she was exaggerating the political threat from the Demon Headmaster's ability to hypnotise children, she replied: 'He's got a whole school full of children who will do precisely what he wants. He must feel very powerful . . . Think of it. He's got a whole army of people – people like me – who'll do and say exactly what he wants. Why should he stop there? Sooner or later he's going to want to do something with his army' (Cross 1982: 86).

The outcome of all three series, with the Head's attempts to achieve totalitarian control being overthrown not just by a group of children but also by 'childish things' – by SPLAT and gunge and game shows and nonsense rhymes – must have appeared to the nation's children in 1996 as a spirited defence of their right to be seen as a group with some moral and political value to society, rather than as a group which threatened it. *The Demon Headmaster* defended childhood (and children) as a necessary state of being, different from adulthood, which is required to preserve essential human freedoms. Abolish childhood, says the Demon Headmaster gleefully, and the way is paved for him to dominate the world. Childhood, in *The Demon Headmaster* stories, is not a problem for the adult world to solve; the problem is the other way around, with children rescuing adults from themselves. And, most subversive of all, this message was doubly underlined because it appeared on television, in 'crazyspace'. The show combined the skilled techniques of 'quality' children's television drama, with 'wacky, funkiness' and showed such values as having political usefulness.

Audience reactions

> It's that these children are alone and nobody else will believe them. (Girl, twelve, inner-city primary school, Cardiff, November 1996)

In our research for the BBC we were interested to find out whether child audiences were picking up any of this. We already knew that the series had been a big ratings hit with the general audience – which seemed to us suggestive. We also knew that, in a piece of BBC audience research on the programme, before it aired, it had been equally popular with both boys and girls aged nine to twelve years, something that is very difficult to achieve. Alan Horrox, formerly head of children's programming at Thames Television, now head of Tetra Productions (producers of *Mike and Angelo* (Thames 1998–2000) and *The Tomorrow People* (Thames 1973–79)), pointed out in an interview I conducted in May 1996:

> Over the last twenty or thirty years one of the clichés [in children's televi-
> sion] was that boys will watch boys' programmes and won't watch girls'
> programmes . . . If you want a winner make it a boys' programme because
> girls will watch it . . . In this market you need 40 per cent share. What is very
> difficult to do is to create a central character who is characteristically female.

One clear reason for *The Demon Headmaster*'s ratings success was that it overcame this problem. Its main protagonist was a 'characteristically female' girl, but in the BBC's preliminary study both boys and girls liked the show and thought it was 'for them': fifty-three out of fifty-five chil-dren agreed that it would appeal to 'both boys and girls'; only one thought it was 'for boys only' and one 'for girls only'.

In our discussion tasks with children in primary schools we were inter-ested in probing a number of issues, but in particular three of these ide-ological themes. The first was the differences between reality and fantasy – an issue which, as Hodge and Tripp (1985) have pointed out, is always linked to questions of political power and who decides which version of events should be accepted. Secondly, we were interested in children's views on the programme's representations of childhood, and its thesis that childhood was necessary as a defence against totalitarianism. Thirdly, we were interested in their general comments on the quality of the programme. In the following passage transcribed from a discussion with me in December 1996, a group of mixed-age primary children in a rural Durham primary school talked about the credibility of someone like a headmaster wanting to kill a child, Dinah. As this exchange demon-strates, they fully understood that his motive was political and that he wanted to kill her because she stood in his way to power:

> GIRL 1: Miss, why did the Demon Headmaster want to kill Dinah?
> BOY 2: Because she knew about him.
> GIRL 2: Because she knew what he was going to do.
> INTERVIEWER [to Girl 3]: Why do *you* think he wanted to kill Dinah?
> GIRL 3: Because she always screwed up his plans.
> GIRL 2: She was the one person that knew about them.

The ideological component of the story that produced particularly vehe-ment support was its defence of childhood:

> INTERVIEWER: Can I ask you what you thought about him saying that
> childhood wasn't necessary?
> GIRL 1: I think that's not very real because he was a child once.

GIRL 2: That wouldn't be very clever because you couldn't exactly go to
    school when you're an adult . . .
INT.: We agree that he might want to rule the world, but we don't agree with
    him about getting rid of childhood?
[Chorus of 'No, No'.]
INT.: Because childhood is necessary to do what?
GIRL 1: It would be impossible to get rid of childhood.
BOY 1: It's necessary to start your life. It gives you things like –
GIRL 2: Freedom.
BOY 2: You'd have to get rid of every child in the world as well.
[Everybody: yeah, yeah.]
BOY 1: With every child it would be impossible.
GIRL 1: You'd have to get rid of everybody on the other side of the world.
INT.: So we think it would be a bad idea?
GIRL 1: A totally bad idea.

Pursuing issues of credibility and likelihood, plus the abuse of power,
they then discussed not just the realism, or otherwise, of turning a person
into a lizard but what was more important to them in their discussion, the
motivation of such a person:

BOY 1: He combined the DNA of Dinah Hunter with the DNA of a lizard
    and then the giant egg hatched and it came out half lizard half person.
INT.: So you don't think that could happen?
[Chorus of 'No, no.']
GIRL 2/BOY 2: Not if you were a really, really good scientist.
GIRL 1: Miss, even if you really hated somebody, you wouldn't have enough
    aggression to turn somebody into a lizard . . .
INT.: So who do you think is going to win? The goodies or the baddies?
[Chorus: The good.]
GIRL 1: The good always win.
BOY 1: I'd like to see a programme where the bad guy wins; just once.

The triumph of the Demon Headmaster? The future of public service children's television

At the time of writing (early 2004) the latest British broadcasting legislation has been going through Parliament. This is still more deregulatory
than the 1990 Act, and, unlike the 1990 Act, protected status for children's
(as distinct from educational) programming has been dropped. It has
been impossible for pressure groups, including former and current workers in children's television and groups such as the Voice of the Listener
and Viewer, to modify this legislation to make children's broadcasting a

special case, like news and documentary. There has never been much understanding on the part of politicians of what children's television actually does, or why it might be important – as the scene in the Internet café, with which this essay began, would predict. Anna Home described the situation in 1996, and since then the voices speaking on behalf of 'quality' television drama for children have been even fewer:

> I went and talked to a group of MPs and members of the House of Lords. They'd heard of *Blue Peter*, just about, but apart from that . . . The other question that's being asked is: is it really necessary to spend so much money on providing a service for children when actually they watch so much adult television, and if you just gave the young ones something, and threw in a bit of animation, wouldn't that be enough? . . . My answer to that is that it is a complete denial of the fact that children have a culture which is very specific . . . If organisations like the BBC and other public service broadcasters don't actually hang on to some kind of home-made children's programming, then what is going to become of that? . . . They need to know about the world in which they live, from their point of view, they need to know about their own books, their own customs, their own cultural background, their own history. [If they don't] you just lose the past, apart from anything else.

With children's culture, both literature and now television, there is always – as here – a discourse of a lost 'Golden Age', as Humphrey Carpenter (1985) has pointed out. This partly derives from adults' nostalgia for their own childhoods, and the stories of their own childhoods, as well as from talented professionals such as Anna Home viewing with frustration the failure of policy-makers to appreciate the value of their work. As such it can be seen as special pleading and not 'relevant' to modern children. But such nostalgia, and the resulting desire to pass on valued experiences to the next generation of children, is one of the primary ways in which culture is transmitted over time; it need not inevitably be seen as cause for embarrassment.

Even so, nostalgia can blind adults – as in the case of the MPs who knew only about *Blue Peter* (BBC 1958–) – to interesting things that might be going on at the moment, despite the problematic nature of hegemonic global capitalism. I do not get as much chance to watch children's television as I used to, which creates a tendency to pessimism. But in 2003 there was another fine CBBC serialisation (co-produced by BBC and Strand Productions) dealing with contemporary political themes, *The Face at the Window*. Once again, the reliable narrative format of a group of brave and foolhardy children taking on the adult world was the basic premise: in this case, three prosperous middle-class children somewhere in the Home

Counties hid a child from a Balkan country who had witnessed a mas-
sacre and was being hunted down by the murderers, posing as charity
workers. True to format, the adults were taken in by the plausibility of the
charity workers – but the children saw the truth. As with *The Demon
Headmaster*, production values of script, setting, performance, casting
and post-production were high. There was even some comic relief when
the little boy sometimes proved rather difficult to help, owing to various
cultural misunderstandings.

The series acknowledged such cultural differences between children,
but, like *The Demon Headmaster*, also proposed a universal value: that,
when it comes to challenging tyranny and abuse, childhood and the
moral solidarity of children, as distinct from the myopic confusion, if not
downright brutality, of adults, can cut across differences and conflicts and
can be one of our main defences against political injustice. This need not
be a falsely sentimental, Rousseau-esque point of view. Painful realism is
admissible too. The ending of *Face at the Window* was not a happy one,
and uncomfortable for a child audience seeking resolution. When the
Balkan child was finally handed over to trustworthy adult authorities, his
identity had to be changed and his English child friends realised that they
could never see him again, nor would he ever be able to acknowledge
them. Such is the world created by demon headmasters. This series
seemed to me a worthy successor to *The Demon Headmaster*. It was a
warning to us Golden Age types not to see every change in the 'crazyspaces' of children's culture as a sign of the death of childhood or of the
downfall of civilisation – as Dinah and her friends might point out to us,
it may well be quite the opposite.

References

Barker, M., and J. Petley (eds) (1997), *Ill Effects: The Media Violence Debate*,
   London: Routledge.
Bazalgette, C., and D. Buckingham (eds) (1995), *In Front of the Children: Screen
   Entertainment and Young Audiences*, London: BFI.
Blumler, J. G. (1992), *The Future of Children's Television in Britain: An Enquiry for
   the Broadcasting Standards Council*, London: BSC.
Buckingham, D. (1995), *Moving Images*, Manchester: Manchester University Press.
Buckingham, D. (2000a), *The Making of Citizens: Young People, News and Politics*,
   London: Routledge.
Buckingham, D. (2000b), *After the Death of Childhood*, Cambridge: Polity.
Buckingham, D. (ed.) (2002), *Small Screens*, Leicester: Continuum.
Buckingham, D., H. Davies, K. Jones and P. Kelley (1999), *Children's Television in*

Britain, London: BFI.

Carpenter, H. (1985), *Secret Gardens: A Study of the Golden Age of Children's Literature*, London: George Allen and Unwin.

Cross, G. (1982), *The Demon Headmaster*, Oxford: Oxford University Press.

Cross, G. (1995), *The Demon Headmaster* and *The Prime Minister's Brain*, London: Puffin/Penguin.

Cross, G. (1997), *The Demon Headmaster Takes Over*, Oxford: Oxford University Press.

Davies, M. M. (1997), *Fake, Fact and Fantasy: Children's Interpretations of Television Reality*, Mahwah, NJ: Laurence Erlbaum Associates.

Davies, M. M. (2001), *'Dear BBC': Children, Television Storytelling and the Public Sphere*, Cambridge: Cambridge University Press.

Davies, M. M., and B. Corbett (1997), *Children's Television in Britain, 1992–1996: An Enquiry for the Broadcasting Standards Commission*, London: BSC.

Davies, M. M. and K. O'Malley (1996), *Children and Television Drama: A Review of the Literature*, unpublished report to the BBC.

Davies, M. M., K. O'Malley and B. Corbett (1997), *Children and Television Drama: An Empirical Study with Children aged 5–13 years in England and Wales*, unpublished report to the BBC.

Hodge, R., and D. Tripp (1985), *Children and Television: A Semiotic Approach*, Cambridge: Polity.

Hunt, P. (1991), *Criticism, Theory and Children's Literature*, Oxford: Blackwell.

James, A., and A. Prout (1997), *Constructing and Reconstructing Childhood: Contemporary Issues in the Sociological Study of Childhood*, London: Falmer.

James, A., C. Jenks and A. Prout (1998), *Theorizing Childhood*, London: Falmer.

Jenks, C. (ed.) (1982), *Constituting the Child – The Sociology of Childhood: Essential Readings*, London: Batsford.

Kline, S. (1993), *Out of the Garden: Toys and Children's Culture in an Age of TV Marketing*, London: Verso.

Landesman, C. (1995), 'With an all-too-knowing look: children are sophisticated viewers', *Sunday Times*, 11 June.

Lurie, A. (1990), *Don't Tell the Grownups: Subversive Children's Literature*, London: Bloomsbury.

Postman, N. (1982), *The Disappearance of Childhood*, London: W. H. Allen, reprinted 1994.

Singleton-Turner, R. (1999), *Children Acting on Television*, London: A. & C. Black.

Singleton-Turner, R. (1994), *Television and Children*, London: BBC.

Springhall, J. (1998), *Youth, Popular Culture and Moral Panics: Penny Gaffs to Gangsta Rap, 1830–1996*, New York: St Martin's Press.

Part III

Revisiting the familiar

Editors' introduction

The essays in this part cover a variety of formats, genres and concerns, which at first sight may appear unconnected: social realism (Lez Cooke on Paul Abbot's *Clocking Off* (BBC 2000–3)); spectatorship and genre (Helen Wheatley on the female viewer and adaptations of Gothic novels for television); connections between British theatre and popular or canonical television drama (Stephen Lacey on Joan Littlewood's Theatre Workshop and sitcoms of the 1960s and 70s, Brecht and conceptions of the popular); and institutional programme policies at the BBC (Steve Blandford on programming in the national and regional Drama Departments in the 1990s). However, there are connections between these essays that lie below their ostensible subject matter, especially the ways in which they return to, and re-examine, familiar programmes, policies, genres and categories (critical and programme). 'Familiar' in this context means 'visible' in Television Studies – that is, having a currency within the field, and an importance to it. In this way, all four essays fulfil one of the main intentions of the collection, which is to test the rigidity of some of the fixed points of contemporary critical argument.

A great deal of television drama has been discussed in relation to ideas of social realism; this is as true of popular drama series and soaps (*Coronation Street* (1960–) and *EastEnders* (1985–)) as it is of the more experimental and politically challenging one-off plays and films associated with the BBC anthology series, The Wednesday Play (1964–70) and Play for Today (1970–84). Paul Abbot's award-winning and popular drama series *Clocking Off* is, as Cooke argues (and the series's makers acknowledge), clearly social realist in its orientation, looking towards both the personal, domestic and everyday narratives of the working class and the more issue-based, filmed drama of some of the most high-profile

Wednesday Plays. Yet to see it as such involves a rethinking of the category itself. Both Lacey and Cooke address this issue in different ways. Cooke argues that *Clocking Off*'s social realism was familiar in the sense that it provided an account of the social experience of (predominantly) working-class people through their immediate relationships and problems viewed within their community or class or work contexts. However, in order to do this in a way that recognised the social experience, political concerns and viewing competences and expectations of contemporary audiences, the series refocused both the specific narrative conventions and the recognisable 'look' associated with dominant traditions of social realism. The result, as Cooke notes, was an innovative drama that brought social realism into the twenty-first century and offered an alternative to the low-budget, fractured 'flexi-narratives' of much series or serial drama.

Viewing social realism from a different angle, Lacey argues that it is not simply a series of conventions but is frequently a political and cultural 'project' that owes a lot to postwar British theatre, in its naturalist and 'non-naturalist' forms, for its shape and trajectory. From this perspective, the (largely) filmed dramas of Ken Loach and Tony Garnett for The Wednesday Play (*Up the Junction* (BBC 1965) and *Cathy Come Home* (BBC 1966) in particular) owed their use of techniques drawn from documentary and current affairs to a conscious strategy to create a 'Brechtian' television, one significant point of reference for which was contemporary theatre practice.

Although the term 'social realism' is not used by Blandford in his discussion of BBC commissioning and programming policies in the 1990s, his essay is supportive of the efforts to create a culturally specific, popular and contemporary drama in the nation or regions – a drama that shares much of the same territory as contemporary social realism. It might be expected that the Drama Departments of Wales, Scotland and Northern Ireland would produce drama that was grounded in the precise cultural identities of contemporary regions or nations in a context where the idea of a 'British' identity is being called to account; the question might be why there was not more of it, and one answer given here lies in the struggle between the BBC power-base in London and its satellite Departments – a struggle that enacts an older, familiar battle between the centre and the periphery within British institutions, and between the specific identities of a diverse, modern region or nation and a more homogenised 'national' (i.e. acceptable to the English) culture.

Both Cooke and Wheatley continue this collection's concern with audiences, but do so in different ways. Cooke's argument précised above

views the audience for *Clocking* Off from the point of view of the programme makers, who, in seeking a new rhetoric for social realism, have a
clear view of the social reality that the series must both reflect and engage
with. Wheatley is also concerned with the ways in which television drama
embodies assumptions about its audience, and pursues this in a sophisticated way in relation to late twentieth-century television adaptations of
'the female Gothic'. Wheatley's essay draws on feminist approaches to
conceptualising the female audience in film and popular literature as well
as television to argue that there is an intriguing web of connections
between the programme makers (and behind them, the machinery of
pre-publicity and marketing), the text and its audiences, in which the
viewing context, the home, is of central importance. The main examples
here are *Rebecca* (Carlton 1997), *The Woman in White* (BBC 1997) and
The Wyvern Mystery (BBC 2000). Drawing on close textual analysis,
Wheatley uncovers the specific strategies used to identify the (largely
female) audience with (invariably female) protagonist, and explores the
ways in which this identification both acknowledges the domestic viewing context and renders it strange and troubling. The home, far from
being a place of security, is a dangerous and alien environment in Gothic
fiction, and in this analysis the explicit connection between fictional and
actual domestic locations is a major source of their audience appeal. The
explicit recognition of the viewing context within the texts themselves,
Wheatley argues, also challenges the assumption that because television
operates in the culturally sensitive arena of the home it must, by its
nature, be more consensual and conservative than the cinema.

There is a clear emphasis in much television analysis on the specificity
of television forms and genres, and this has been an inevitable, and welcome, response to both the maturity of Television Studies as a discipline
and the coming of age of the medium itself. However, this should not
mean that the relationships between television and other media should
be ignored, particularly when it has reworked genres originating elsewhere, and both Wheatley and Lacey draw useful connections to other
media and cultural forms. Wheatley's analysis of the female Gothic gains
both force and depth from the parallels drawn with popular literature
and cinema (especially melodrama). Lacey traces specific connections
between contemporary theatre practice and television, noting how they
run along different lines towards, on the one hand, the new experimental
drama of social realism and, on the other, popular situation comedy. In
an analysis of the specific historical conjuncture of the late 1950s and
early 1960s, Lacey notes the importance of critical terms drawn from the

theatre – naturalism in particular – in debates about the political dimensions of television forms, and suggests that the work of Bertolt Brecht, the German playwright, director, poet and theorist, was particularly significant. The view of Brecht at the time may not have been especially complex or theoretically rigorous, but he exerted a powerful emotional and political appeal, and his theory and practice provided radical practitioners in both media with important points of reference.

Brecht has been important to British television in other ways as well, and one of the themes running through both Cooke's and Lacey's essays (and it is also an implicit theme in Blandford's) is the interplay between the popular and the 'canonical' in television drama, which, for Lacey, receives a theoretical rationale in Brecht's writings on the popular and the realistic (Brecht 1977). Cooke's analysis of *Clocking Off* argues that a 'serious' drama series, of which this an important example, can nevertheless command a large popular audience (a point made explicitly by Lacey in his account of *Up the Junction* and *Cathy Come Home* and implicitly by Wheatley in her analysis of the positioning of adaptations of Gothic novels – sited firmly within the popular – as serious, 'quality' television). For Blandford, the reverse may also be true, and popular drama series can, despite the constraints of genre and the priorities of commissioners, express a complex, contemporary cultural identity (he cites, for instance, BBC Scotland's *Hamish Macbeth* (1995–98) in this context, arguing that it subverts, rather than endorses, cultural stereotypes).

Indeed, at both the theoretical and textual levels, the binary opposition between the popular and the legitimate, which maps on to older schisms between low and high culture that bedevil the discussion of other cultural forms, looks increasingly untenable and redundant. It is worth reiterating a point made in the General Introduction to this collection; television may well reproduce divisions between the popular and the canon, but it also challenges them. In the long term, it is probably the latter that is more significant for Television Studies.

Reference

Brecht, B. (1977), 'Against George Lukács', in Ronald Taylor (ed.), *Aesthetics and Politics*, London: New Left Books.

8

Haunted houses, hidden rooms: women, domesticity and the female Gothic adaptation on television

Helen Wheatley

Popular television drama produced for a specifically female audience has been thought about and discussed in relation to a number of key dramatic genres within British television. Perhaps the most influential area of television studies that has dealt with the importance of drama for women is that of 'soap opera studies' (cf. Brunsdon 1981 and 2000; Modleski 1982; Hobson 1982; Ang 1985; Seiter 1989; Geraghty 1991). This rich area of scholarship has discussed the soap opera variously as 'feminine text' and explored the idea that 'the competences necessary for reading soap opera are most likely to have been acquired by those persons culturally constructed through discourses of femininity' (Morley 1992: 129). It has also offered sustained analyses of the particular ways in which women watch and understand soap opera (Hobson 1982; Ang 1985; Seiter 1989), arguing that through programme publicity, scheduling, and advertising the soap opera industry in Britain and the US seeks to address a certain kind of expected female viewer (see Brunsdon 1981). In addition to this ground-breaking work on the soap opera, analyses of popular television drama for women have also examined dramas which, it can be argued, depict female characters in transgressive gender roles, particularly in the context of the tough female cops and criminals of the crime genre (cf. Baehr and Dyer 1987). A discussion of the post-feminist heroine of the crime drama in the UK has focused particularly on the *Prime Suspect* (Granada 1991–2003) mini-series (Brunsdon 1998; Hallam 2000; Creeber 2001; Thornham 1994 and 2002–3), and the debate which centres on the relationship between the gendered identities of the central protagonist, DCI Jane Tennison (Helen Mirren), the murder victims she investigates throughout the course of the narrative(s), and the viewer of the drama who watches her do so. In both of the above cases, the question of genre – and the representation of femininity within particular genres – is tied to the notion of gendered forms of viewing via practices and positions which are then either examined empirically (through audience study) or located in an examination of text and context and their address to an *assumed* female viewer.

The analysis of popular television drama for and about women is not solely confined to British television studies, however. For example, in the US, the study of popular television drama for women has been collected in a number of key edited collections (Spigel and Mann 1992; Rabinovitz and Haralovich 1999), covering subjects from soap opera to serial drama and sitcom. Several important works have focused on the articulation and transformation of feminist discourse in television drama – understood as 'post-feminist' television drama (Bathrick 1984; *Camera Obscura* 1994–95; Dow 1996; Mayne 1997; Press 1991; Probyn 1990). More recently, popular primetime dramas such as *Ally McBeal* (20th Century Fox 1997–2002) and *Buffy the Vampire Slayer* (20th Century Fox 1997–2003) have also received a considerable amount of critical attention (Moseley 2002; Moseley and Read 2002; Kaveney 2002; Wilcox and Lavery 2002), with debate again centring on questions of genre, representation and the relationship between feminist and 'feminine' discourses.

This connection between gender and genre is, of course, not specific only to television fictions. Aside from a wealth of critical literature on the woman's film and the interconnections between genre and the female viewer, there is also, for example, a long history of novel and short-story writing for and about women (and its associated scholarship), the 'female Gothic', the topic of this essay, being just one among many of these literary genres. It is hoped that this study of adaptations of popular female Gothic fictions on television will illuminate a sense of both continuity and progression between modes of readership and viewership for women of this genre, and the ways in which we might locate a specific gendered viewing position through the close analysis of a particular cycle of popular television drama.

Adaptation of female Gothic literature, a term which encompasses a broad range of sources from Daphne du Maurier's *Rebecca* to the work of Joseph Sheridan Le Fanu, Wilkie Collins and others, has always been popular on British television. It featured frequently in the anthology drama series of the 1950s and 1960s, such as *Hour of Mystery* (ABC 1957) and *Mystery and Imagination* (ABC/Thames 1966–70), and has enjoyed a recent renaissance in the form of the two-part Sunday night, 'feature' drama on both the BBC and ITV in Britain. Made as lavish co-productions with North American television companies, as well as with smaller independent domestic producers, these recent adaptations are evidently seen as a viable investment property within the industry, in that they offer a clearly defined, and therefore targetable, group of viewers; as such, the term 'popular television drama *for women*' can usefully be applied to them. Whilst it would be inaccurate to suggest that these television dramas have no male viewing contingent, or that there are not equally complex and interesting viewing pleasures for the male viewer, it is the case that television takes on traditions of distributing and consuming the female Gothic text which predate the last century, and which include a clear characterisation of a certain kind of female reader.

To begin this exploration, it may be useful to briefly summarise existing definitions of the particularities of this sub-genre of the Gothic, in both its literary and cinematic forms. A great deal of critical work has been undertaken on the female Gothic novel,[1] a sub-genre which is described in broad terms by Robert Miles as featuring narratives of 'a heroine caught between a pastoral haven and a threatening castle, sometimes in flight from a sinister patriarchal figure, sometimes in search of an absent mother, and often both together' (1994: 1). A number of key analyses have also been written about the female Gothic in film, particularly in relation to the woman's film of the 1940s.[2]

Michael Walker defines the generic narrative of these films as follows:

> The heroine's point of view; – the whirlwind courtship and marriage to the hero; – the return to his family mansion, arrival at which is traumatic; – a past secret of the husband's, which causes him to behave strangely towards the heroine, and which relates to a dead wife, whom the husband may have killed; – the heroine's investigation of this secret, which focuses in particular on a forbidden (locked) room, her penetration of which causes the husband to become murderous; – a jealous rival of the heroine already inside the house, who sets fire to the house at the end, seeking to kill the heroine. (1990: 18)

This definition, therefore, builds on the key narrative elements described above by Miles in relation to the female Gothic novel, by expanding upon key visual characteristics, such as subjective narration (point of view) and the importance of location to the female Gothic narrative (in the form of the ancestral mansion).

The question of subjective narration and point of view will be addressed more fully below: however, it is the significance of the domestic space in these narratives which must remain at the forefront of the introduction of this analysis of the female Gothic on television. The importance of the home in female Gothic fiction, in the form of the dilapidated Gothic mansion, is made most clear in Mary Ann Doane's analysis of the Gothic woman's film of the 1940s. Doane states that 'the paradigmatic woman's space – the home – is yoked to dread, and to a crisis of vision. For violence is precisely what is hidden from sight' (1987a: 134). This analysis addresses the representation of domestic space as the site of fear within these films, and goes on to outline the specificities of this representation (in relation to the appearance of the hidden room and the significance of the staircase, window etc.). Framing her analysis of the Gothic home, Doane makes the point that these films addressed a specifically female audience:

> In the first half of the [1940s], due to the war and the enlistment of large numbers of young men in the armed forces, film producers assumed that cinema audiences would be predominantly female . . . Furthermore, there is an intensity and an aberrant quality to the '40s films which is linked to the ideological upheaval signalled by a redefinition of sexual roles and the reorganisation of the family during the war years. (1987a: 4)

This critical analysis of the genre suggests that the popular Gothic woman's film of the 1940s *worked through* some of the crises and paranoias surrounding domestic space in the decade, and became a space in which gendered anxiety might be addressed. This argument is also taken up by Tania Modleski, in that she asserts that these films 'may be seen to reflect women's fears about losing their unprecedented freedoms *and* being forced back into homes . . . In many of these films, the house seems to be alive with menace' (1982: 21–22). However, what Doane fails to take into account, and what Modleski implicitly infers, but does not explicitly address, is that the cinemagoing, predominantly female, audience *had* escaped the confines of this 'dreadful' place in order to attend the cinema. Thus, a certain amount of the frisson built up around this paranoid depiction of the home is dispelled by its public viewing context.

This point therefore provides a segue in to the crux of this analysis of the female Gothic adaptation on television: by bringing the narrative of female paranoia or fear back into the home, understanding television as an inherently domestic medium, the closeness between the threatened heroine and the viewer of the text is re-established. Doane has argued that the female Gothic shifted medium at the end of the 1940s, with the popularisation of Gothic 'dime-store' paperbacks (1987a: 124); however, one could argue that this move into 'pulp fiction' was in fact a *return*, which accompanied the redomestication of the female Gothic narrative on television. What is certain is that in the decades that followed the end of the war, a number of female Gothic adaptations were broadcast on television in the UK, including three BBC adaptations of Du Maurier's *Rebecca* (in 1947, 1954 and 1956), and adaptations of *The Two Mrs Carrolls* (BBC 1947) and *The Woman in White* (Hour of Mystery) (ABC 1957).

Rather than offering a history of the female Gothic adaptation on television, this analysis of recent adaptations seeks to outline the ways in which these dramas are inherently medium-reflexive, and the ways in which they are evidently self-conscious as television adaptations. It will be argued that the adaptations in hand are eminently aware of both their domestic viewing context and the female domestic viewer. It is not the project of this analysis to argue that these dramas are somehow timely, in a similar fashion to those analyses of the woman's film of the 1940s. Current debates surrounding domestic violence and child abuse are clearly important discursive contexts for these dramas, however, as are those home-centred anxieties surrounding the ever-changing status of women's role within the home in a post-feminist society. Rather, this analysis will explore the processes by which these popular fictions for women address a female domestic viewer, recording her into the text itself and situating her viewing context (the home) at the centre of the narrative, thus exploring the relationship between text and context on television.

Popular Gothic fictions for women

From the end of the eighteenth century onwards, popular, inexpensive outlets for the female Gothic narrative attracted the female reader, who, it was presumed, avidly 'devoured' the serialised fictions of domestic terror, following the fates of a bevy of female victim-heroines. As Alison Milbank describes:

> Many Gothic tales first appeared in the pages of journals like *The Lady's Magazine*. Women's periodicals also encouraged submissions from their readers and in this way a reciprocity of female reading and writing of Gothic was established. Through the circulating libraries for the middle class, and the Gothic chapbooks of the lower classes, a new generation of women readers was able to enjoy [female Gothic fiction]. (1998: 53–54)

Furthermore, Kate Ferguson-Ellis suggests that the female novel reader was at the epicentre of the boom in female Gothic literature, 'whose newly created leisure allowed her to make use of the circulating library and whose "placement" in the home made her a reader eagerly courted by publishers' (1989: x). It is not entirely clear whether this characterisation of a predominantly female readership is legitimate; as Alison Milbank points out, 'whether the description of the devourer of Minerva Press productions as female was accurate is debatable, as men were extensive novel readers' (1998: 54). However, rightly or wrongly, the reader of these Gothic fictions was, on the whole, characterised as female by the 'Gothic industry', those producing and marketing the novels, and has subsequently been assigned a certain 'voraciousness' by those commenting on the phenomenon.

Joanna Russ's (1993) and Tania Modleski's (1982) work on popular female Gothic fiction in the twentieth century also places emphasis on the ways in which the novels of presses such as Ace Books (producers of female Gothic 'pulp' fiction) were marketed and distributed. In their work, the generic Gothic novel is described as being directed precisely towards a certain kind of middle-class, female reader: according to Terry Carr, ex-editor of Ace Books: 'the basic appeal . . . is to women who marry guys and then begin to discover that their husbands are strangers' (Russ 1993: 32). Subsequently, Russ spends much of her essay exploring the particular pleasures of the popular female Gothic novel for women who 'have a keen eye for food, clothes, interior décor, and middle-class hobbies (e.g. collecting sea shells, weaving, or collecting china)' (1993: 36), concluding that 'these novels are written for women who cook, who decorate their own houses, who shop for clothing for themselves and their children – in short, for housewives' (1993: 39).

In the twentieth and twenty-first centuries, this avid readership has also extended to the (supposed) equally avid viewership of television, and the consumption of female Gothic narratives through journals, chapbooks and 'dime-store' novels can be understood as prefiguring television as a form of domestic consumption by the female reader or viewer. Like the pulp fiction described above, television offers a private rather than a public space for the reception of these (often serialised) narratives. Just as the Minerva Press saw the Gothic as a viable investment in the eighteenth and nineteenth centuries, and Ace and Fawcett Books did the same in the late twentieth century, so television companies turned to the genre, with its pre-sold audience, as a safe bet for both domestic viewing figures and international sales.

This discussion of the sales and marketing techniques employed by the publishers of pulp Gothic fiction for women in the eighteenth, nineteenth and twentieth centuries provides an illuminating precursor to a discussion of the marketing of Gothic television for women. As well as offering particular acknowledgement within the programmes themselves of the presence of the female viewer (as I will argue below), the framing discourses surrounding the television adaptation of the female Gothic address the question of female viewership explicitly. To take a particular example; Carlton/Portman Production's *Rebecca* (ITV 1997) was an expensive international co-production which appealed to the pre-existing audience for the female Gothic and the already established audience for the Sunday-night costume drama (see Giddings and Selby 2001: viii) (though an adaptation of Du Maurier's novel clearly falls slightly outside of the parameters of the classic adaptation in its position as a 'popular fiction'). The two-part drama cost £4 million to make, and was obviously seen by its production companies as a viable investment in a pre-sold property, based on the popularity of the novel, Hitchcock's film version of *Rebecca* and the numerous earlier television adaptations. In a sense, by portraying *Rebecca* as a 'television event', Carlton attempted to lure a captive audience to its two-part adaptation, which was shown in the UK early in the new year (5 and 6 of January 1997) at the tail-end of the Christmas schedule. A Carlton press release issued in June the previous year detailed the 'greatness' of *Rebecca*'s stars, locations and budgets, emphasising both the event status of the adaptation and its exportability, as well as the drama's inherent appeal to a tradition of reader-viewers:

> Portman Productions executive producer Tim Buxton says: 'The wealth of talent which is working together to bring this du Maurier classic to the screen is certain to create a television "event" to be enjoyed by her fans, old and new, around the world.' (5 June 1996)

Scheduled on consecutive nights against two of the BBC's most popular serial dramas (*Ballykissangel* (1996–2001) and *EastEnders* (1985–)), *Rebecca* received, on average, an impressive 35 per cent audience share,[3] an audience inevitably drawn in by the drama's intensive pre-advertising campaign (from the previous summer onwards) and extensive coverage in the *TV Times* listings guide, as well as a number of tie-ins, such as the book which accompanied the adaptation (Tiballs 1996). This book offered a series of informative contexts, including information on Du Maurier, profiles of particular members of the cast, location information, and an illustrated chapter entitled 'Dressing for the part' on the costumes used in the adaptation. With its emphasis on the details of dressing up and home furnishings, the tie-in book clearly appeals to an assumed female audience, with the reader-viewer figure evoked above in Carlton's press release being explicitly referred to as women or girls within the text: for example, director Jim O'Brien states in an interview for the book, 'a lot of girls read the story and they can treat it as being entirely innocent if they want to, but older women can see what du Maurier is getting at' (Tiballs 1996: 54). Thus the female reader or viewer is addressed both as an avid fan of the genre and as a consumer of 'lifestyle' goods.

This continual conflation of the female reader, viewer and consumer therefore brings us back to the question of television's inherent suitability for the presentation of female Gothic narratives. As in the above instance, the programme makers clearly relied upon a continuum of female readership and viewership, implicitly occurring within the domestic rather than public sphere, in order to sell their product. In the case of *Rebecca* at least, Carlton and the programme's producers appealed to this female reader-viewer through the seductive discourse of 'lifestyle' (ideal homes, fantasy fashions etc.), precisely the pleasures of the popular female Gothic novel isolated by Joanna Russ (1993). Indeed, it is perhaps no coincidence that many of these adaptations reappeared on television at precisely the same time as an explosion in lifestyle programming and makeover shows in the UK (see Brunsdon *et al.* 2001). The irony of this congruence is that *Rebecca*, as with the other female Gothic narratives, also implicitly critiques the representation of the domestic space as ideal home, and in fact expresses a certain anxiety around the image of the perfected woman or wife.

Representations of domestic space: the imprisoned woman

The overarching narrative structure of the female Gothic adaptation is found in the heroine's removal from a place of safety to the threatening location of her husband's or employer's familial mansion, with many of the narratives finding resolution in her removal from this dangerous domestic space, and subsequent move into her own home. *Rebecca* is perhaps the exception to this, where the young Mrs De Winter moves into a new house *with* her husband, albeit in a disabled, perhaps emasculated, state. The following analysis will illustrate the notion that these programmes play upon certain anxieties focused on and experienced by women in the marital home through an investigation of the threatening, cage-like, labyrinthine and, ultimately, un-homely domestic spaces of the female Gothic television adaptation.

In addition to offering an idealised representation of heterosexual romance, the female Gothic narrative frequently begins with a representation of an idealised (most usually pastoral) domesticity. This configuration of the house, often the parental home, offers a stark contrast to the house that the heroine will eventually move to. For example, the opening of an adaptation of Joseph Sheridan Le Fanu's novel *The Wyvern Mystery* (BBC1 2000) finds the young Alice (Tamara Harvey) ensconced in her father's house, a modest image of domestic bliss (it is safe, warm and lit with mellow light). In this opening scene Alice is seen reading from a book of fairy stories, a present from her father. During this sequence, Alice's (Naomi Watts's) adult voice-over states, 'when I was very young, my father held me tightly and told me of witches and goblins; if only I had known how close they were'. Here, the dialogue sets up the central tension of the drama: the visual images establish an image of domestic perfection, whilst the voice-over simultaneously represents its impossibility through Alice's suggestion that threat or terror ('witches and goblins') is close at hand. Before the title sequence has ended, Alice's father dies (owing to his harsh treatment at the hands of his landlord and Alice's eventual 'benefactor', Squire Fairlie (Derek Jacobi)) and the young Alice is removed to Wyvern Hall, where she is locked into an attic room. However, even before this removal takes place, in the first five minutes of the adaptation, the opening sequence's mobile camera repeatedly encloses the young Alice through a series of diegetic frames (through the back of the wooden dining chairs and the square window frames), thus surrounding her with horizontal and vertical bars which visually prefigure her eventual imprisonment in the attic of her 'benefactor's' home.

Also central to the opening sequence is the presentation of a book of fairy stories to Alice by her father, which establishes the young heroine from the outset as a diegetic consumer of Gothic fictions. At this moment a closeness is established between the young girl and her fairy-story book, and this closeness is reiterated by the adult Alice's confessional voice-over, as well as the younger actor's physical interaction with the book (playing with it and tracing the illustrations with her finger). However, it is also implied that this is a closeness which is *shared* between the heroine onscreen (the diegetic viewer) and the television audience at home (the actual viewer) through the use of subjective photography which, during a zoom into extreme close-up of a line-drawn illustration of a girl running in the woods, places our eyes in conjunction with those of the young Alice. As this image of a young woman running through the woods is matched visually later in the drama, when the adult Alice runs away from

Wyvern Hall and the amorous advances of the Squire, the little girl might in fact be seen as the diegetic viewer or consumer of her *own* inevitable Gothic narrative, emphasised by the striking similarity between the two iconic images from the drama (the fairytale illustration and an extended sequence where Alice runs through the woods of Wyvern Hall).

This analysis of the opening sequence of *The Wyvern Mystery* thus reflects upon the ways in which the female Gothic on television is inherently reflexive of its domestic viewing context. Another BBC adaptation by the writer David Pirie, of Wilkie Collins's *The Woman in White* (BBC1 1997), also takes up the narrative preoccupations and presentational style of the female Gothic television adaptation as described above. Like all of the other female Gothic adaptations, this drama centres on the removal of the central female protagonists (in this case, Laura Fairlie (Justine Waddell) and her half-sister Marian (Tara Fitzgerald)) from the familial home of their uncle to the imposing Gothic pile of Laura's new husband, Sir Percival Glyde (James Wilby). This new home, initially approached with high hopes of domestic bliss, is soon discovered to be a space of internment, in which Laura is beaten, sexually abused and presumed to be murdered (but actually kidnapped and force-fed laudanum). No more emphatically is Laura's and Marian's imprisonment stated than in the mise-en-scène of the drama, which explicitly reiterates the imagery of the cage or prison (as did the barred frames surrounding the young Alice in *The Wyvern Mystery*). Throughout these adaptations, the houses on screen are represented as labyrinthine, cage-like, as closed spaces from which the heroine cannot escape and in which she finds no homely comfort. In *The Woman in White*, the space surrounding Laura is frequently depicted in these terms, even before she enters her husband's home. On her introduction in the drama, Laura is found standing at the window in her uncle's house, against and behind a number of objects which reflect the cage motif (wall panelling, furniture, window panes, bird cage), and all of which symbolise her potential position as a prisoner within the home. At this moment, Laura's position in front of the window is also significant, as it reflects upon the ambivalent position of the window as an interstice between the house and the outside world. Here, as elsewhere in the cycle, the window is a symbolic space which may be read as either benign (providing access to the outside world) or, in fact, malignant (withholding her from that world, somehow representing her anxiety about her current position).[4] As Mary Ann Doane describes, in her analysis of the female Gothic cinema of the 1940s, 'the window has special import in terms of the social and symbolic positioning of the woman –

the window is the interface between inside and outside, the feminine space of the family and reproduction and the masculine space of production' (1987b: 288).

One could perhaps extend this symbolic use of the window to embrace a wider metaphor relating to the television screen, in that it has also be seen as a 'window to the world' within the domestic viewing context. The programme makers of the female Gothic drama allow the female viewer a particularly fearful view of another domestic space by bringing the potential dangers of domestic space to television, thus affording the television screen both the properties of the window (a view of 'outside' the viewing space or home) and the mirror (a reflection of the viewing space or home). This kind of reading (television as simultaneous window and mirror) must, however, be treated cautiously as it clearly relies on a *metaphorical* reading of television broadcast and reception. As Jostein Gripsrud notes, 'while a metaphor is rarely entirely false, it does give prominence to some features of the phenomenon in question, and leaves others in the shade. This is why all metaphors [in Television Studies] should be regarded with a degree of suspicion' (1998: 17).

What this discussion of the female Gothic television adaptation has outlined thus far has been the ways in which the heroine negotiates her role or position within the domestic space of the Gothic narrative. As such, it has focused on the analysis of specific locales within the mise-en-scène of the female Gothic dramas on television (the house and its particular elements). However, what has not yet been made explicit is the importance of exactly how we enter this space as viewers; from which, or rather, whose position are the exploratory tracks, pans and zooms around this space taken? The question of subjective narration will be the main focus of the latter part of this analysis, as the connection between heroine and viewer, and their subsequent identification, is delineated.

On a fundamental level, the female Gothic television drama is taken from the point of view of the central female protagonist. This shared subjective position is understood as both optical and aural point of view (predominance of subjective camerawork and character-specific sound perspective) and narrative point of view (the viewer shares her basic knowledge of 'what's going on' throughout the drama, and, it is expected, is sympathetic towards the heroine's predicament). This conjoined position, between the heroine and the viewer, therefore has a great impact on the way in which the plot is perceived and organised. For example, once inside the dreadful house of the female Gothic, much of the audio-visual perspective, which the viewer shares with the heroine, is taken from an obscured position (cracks through doors, wind-whipped balconies, a shadowy window etc.). Tania Modleski notes the importance of this shared position of uncertainty in relation to the female Gothic in its literary form, when she states that 'the reader shares some of the heroine's uncertainty about what is going on and what the lover/husband is up to. The reader is nearly as powerless in her understanding as the heroine' (1982: 60). In the television adaptation, viewers, like the heroine, do not hear or see all they need to make sense of the plot from the outset, but rather are privy to snatches of dialogue and glimpses of visual clues to the central enigma of the drama (the secret which must be uncovered in order to achieve narrative resolution). This depiction of subjectivity on the verges of domestic space very much reflects the wife's position within the nineteenth-century home in general, and marks an exclusion from the understanding of events which comes from her husband's ability to move between the public and domestic worlds.

In David Pirie's adaptation of *The Woman in White*, it is Marian's subjective audio-visual perspective from which a large majority of the shots and sound recording are taken. This shared perspective is coupled with a predominance of facial close-ups of Marian throughout the drama, which also suggest a certain *closeness* between her and the viewer. Gareth Neane, producer of *The Woman in White*, has argued that this predominance of the facial close-up is what marks his production out from other literary adaptations on television: he describes the visual style of the adaptation as 'not sitting back in wide shot looking at costumes. There are big close-ups, shots tight on eyeline, and a camera that moves around with a slight untidiness that you don't normally see in period drama' (Ellis 1997: 22). This comment clearly marks female Gothic adaptations such as *The Woman in White* as being aimed towards the translation of *subjectivity* and *identification* over the more usual drive towards *spectatorship* and a detached sense of *visual pleasure* which, it has been argued, is found in the observation of heritage detail within other popular television adaptations (cf. Nelson 2001; Cardwell 2002). This difference also contributes to a reading of these female Gothic adaptations as potentially radical texts, providing a vicarious expression of the female viewer's domestic fears, through a close identification with the Gothic heroine.

Like Alice in *The Wyvern Mystery*, Marian is further linked to the viewer through explicit reference to the act of reading Gothic fictions at the beginning of the narrative, and thus the mechanisms of identification previously outlined are made all the more explicit. Shortly after the arrival of her tutor, Marian announces her interest in the female Gothic narrative, when she states, 'I am sorry if you caught me observing your arrival. My sister and I are so fond of Gothic novels that we sometimes act as if we were in them', to which he replies, 'you would certainly seem to have the perfect setting for your pretence'. This self-referential exchange demonstrates a certain knowingness in the young women's performance of their roles within the paranoid domestic drama, as well as highlighting the importance of the domestic location. It also clearly draws a parallel between the female protagonist as diegetic consumer of the female Gothic narrative and the female viewer as extradiegetic consumer of the same.

The frequent use of subjective camerawork and sound perspective does not only hold the viewer in the position of victimised or hysterical woman throughout the female Gothic narrative, however. On another level, the extent of subjective narration within the female Gothic television drama may be read as evidence of female empowerment and agency. One of the most striking changes made in David Pirie's adaptation of *The Woman in White* is the reassignment of the narrator's voice from the very beginning of the drama. Whereas Wilkie Collins's novel tells the story from the perspective of Laura's and Marian's art teacher, Walter Hartright, and the opening monologue or flashback is taken from his perspective, Pirie's adaptation of the text begins in Limmeridge graveyard and is accompanied by *Marian's* voice-over. The subsequent flashback following this voice-over is therefore taken from the central female protagonist's perspective, and indeed, her explanatory voice-over continues over the introduction of Mr Hartright at the railway station (even though Marian cannot have *actually* witnessed his arrival and his confrontation with Anne Catherick). This significant revision made to the female Gothic narrative thus inscribes female subjectivity from the start and frames the whole narrative as Marian's memory or flashback, marking the entire drama as originating from Marian's perspective. This unusual instance of female narrational omniscience (the fact that she recounts events to which she was not witness) is reaffirmed whenever expositional voice-over is used throughout the adaptation, always spoken in Marian's voice. In light of this significant variation of narration, female subjectivity is assigned an unanticipated strength within the female Gothic narrative, even though it also marks the heroine (and viewer's) exclusion from important information at various points in the narrative.

This reading of the flashback or interior point-of-view sequence as a sign of strength or resistance is in keeping with Susan Hayward's comments on the flashback as a potential moment of female potency: 'the flashback . . . can be a moment when the psyche has control of its unconscious. So flashbacks of whatever gender should represent an ideal moment of empowerment' (1996: 86). Hayward goes on to note, however, that many female flashbacks in classical narrative cinema are mediated by the male 'expert' protagonist (analyst, detective etc.), thus disavowing it as a moment of empowerment.[5] On the contrary, in the female Gothic television adaptation, mediation of memory or imagination is almost always associated solely with the female heroine. Ultimately, in these adaptations it is the desire to *view* her own Gothic narrative or location that drives the female protagonist on throughout the drama, towards the revelation of her worst fears and her ensuing escape from the threatening domestic space in which she finds herself. It is this 'will to view' which aligns the female Gothic heroine with the television viewer in no uncertain terms.

In conclusion, as in the resolution of the 1998 television version of *The Woman in White* (which centres on the recovery of the feminine text (Anne's diary), and therefore on the possibility of two equally victimised women making contact with each other through the act of reading), the female Gothic television drama may be seen as potentially radical, in that it allows for points of contact between the female domestic viewer and the dramatisation of anxieties converging on women's position in the home. Previously, Lynne Joyrich (referencing an argument made by Laura Mulvey) had argued that the sense of resistance or subversion often associated with cinematic melodrama is impossible within the realms of the television drama: 'As TV brought popular entertainment into the home, national consensus triumphed over potentially oppositional melodrama' (1992: 228). This analysis of the female Gothic adaptation, itself a form of television melodrama, challenges Joyrich's claim somewhat. What, hopefully, has been shown during the course of this discussion of popular television drama for women is that the impact of the domestic viewing context brings the female viewer's fears relating to her home and domestic relationships into stark relief, offering a textual space in which these anxieties may be exposed, and, perhaps, worked through. Through the emphatic depiction of the Gothic heroine on television as a diegetic reader-viewer, a sense of cathartic solidarity may be established between the victimised woman on screen and the viewer at home.

Notes

I would like to acknowledge the support and encouragement of Dr Rachel Moseley at the University of Warwick, to whom this work is dedicated.

1   Alison Milbank provides a thorough overview of the field of study in Mulvey Roberts's *The Handbook to Gothic Literature* (1998: 53–57).
2   For example, *Rebecca* (Alfred Hitchcock, US 1940), *Dragonwyck* (Joseph L. Mankiewick, US 1947), *Gaslight* (George Cukor, US 1944), and *The Two Mrs Carrolls* (Peter Godfrey, US 1947).
3   Based on AGB Programme Ratings (week ending 5 January 1997, p. 20, and week ending 12 January 1997, p. 2).
4   This is an idea that is explored also in Julianne Pidduck's work on Jane Austen adaptations (1998), although Pidduck does not discuss the Gothic genre directly.
5   For example, Mildred/Joan Crawford's narration in *Mildred Pierce* (Michael Curtiz, US 1945).

References

AGB (1997), *Programme Ratings*, 5 January.

AGB (1997), *Programme Ratings*, 12 January.

Ang, I. (1985), *Watching Dallas: Soap Opera and the Melodramatic Imagination*, London: Methuen.

Baehr, H., and G. Dyer (1987), *Boxed In: Women and Television*, New York and London: Pandora.

Bathrick, S. (1984), '*The Mary Tyler Moore Show*: women at home and at work', in J. Feuer, P. Kerr and T. Vahimagi (eds), *MTM: Quality Television*, London: BFI.

Brunsdon, C. (1981), '*Crossroads*: notes on soap opera', *Screen* 22:4, 32–37.

Brunsdon, C. (1998), 'Structures of anxiety: recent television crime fiction', *Screen* 39:3, 223–243.

Brunsdon, C. (2000), *The Feminist, the Housewife and the Soap Opera*, Oxford: Clarendon.

Brunsdon, C., C. Johnson, R. Moseley and H. Wheatley (2001), 'Factual entertainment on British television: the Midlands TV Research Group's "8–9 Project"', *European Journal of Cultural Studies* 4:1, 29–62.

Camera Obscura (1994–95), Special Issue 'Lifetime: a cable network for women', 33–34.

Cardwell, S. (2002), *Adaptation Revisited: Television and the Classic Novel*, Manchester: Manchester University Press.

Creeber, G. (2001), 'Cigarettes and alcohol: investigating gender, genre and gratification in *Prime Suspect*', *Television and New Media* 2:2, 149–66.

Doane, M. A. (1987a), *The Desire to Desire: The Woman's Film of the 1940s*, Bloomington and Indianapolis: Indiana University Press.

Doane, M. (1987b), 'The woman's film: possession and address', in C. Gledhill (ed.), *Home Is Where the Heart Is: Studies in Melodrama and the Woman's Film*, London: BFI.

Dow, B. J. (1996), *Prime-time Feminism: Television, Media Culture and the Women's Movement since 1970*, Philadelphia: University of Pennsylvania Press.

Ellis, M. (1997), '*The Woman in White*', *Televisual* (July), 20–22.

Ferguson-Ellis, K. (1989), *The Contested Castle: Gothic Novels and the Subversion of Domestic Ideology*, Urbana: University of Illinois Press.

Geraghty, C. (1991), *Women and Soap Opera: A Study of Prime-Time Soaps*, Cambridge: Polity Press.

Giddings, R. and K. Selby (2001), *The Classic Serial on Television and Radio*, Basingstoke: Palgrave.

Gripsrud, J. (1998), 'Television, broadcasting, flow: key metaphors in TV theory', in C. Geraghty and D. Lusted (eds), *The Television Studies Book*, London, New York, Sydney and Auckland: Arnold.

Hallam, J. (2000), 'Power plays: gender, genre and Lynda La Plante', in J. Bignell *et al.* (eds), *British Television Drama: Past, Present and Future*, Basingstoke: Palgrave Macmillan.

Hayward, S. (1996), *Key Concepts in Film Studies*, London and New York: Routledge.

Hobson, D. (1982), *Crossroads – The Drama of a Soap*, London: Methuen.

Joyrich, L. (1992), 'All that television allows: TV melodrama, postmodernism, and consumer culture', in L. Spigel and D. Mann (eds), *Private Screenings: Television and the Female Consumer*, Minneapolis: University of Minnesota Press.

Kaveney, R. (ed.) (2002), *Reading the Vampire Slayer: An Unofficial Guide to Buffy and Angel*, London and New York: Taurus Parke.

Mayne, J. (1997), '*L.A. Law* and prime-time feminism', in C. Brunsdon, J. D'Acci and L. Spigel (eds), *Feminist Television Criticism: A Reader*, Oxford: Oxford University Press.

Milbank, A. (1998), 'Female Gothic', in M. Mulvey Roberts (ed.), *The Handbook to Gothic Literature*, Basingstoke and London: Macmillan.

Miles, R. (1994), 'Introduction to special number: female gothic', *Women's Writing*, 1:2, 1–5.

Modleski, T. (1982), *Loving with a Vengeance: Mass Produced Fantasies for Women*, London and New York: Routledge.

Morley, D. (1992), *Television Audiences and Cultural Studies*, London: Routledge.

Moseley, R. (2002), 'Glamorous witchcraft: gender and magic in teen film and television', *Screen* 43:4, 403–422.

Moseley, R., and J. Read (2002), '"Having it *Ally*": popular television (post-)feminism', *Feminist Media Studies* 2:2, 231–249.

Nelson, R. (2001), 'Costume Drama', in G. Creeber (ed.), *The Television Genre Book*, London: BFI.

Pidduck, J. (1998), 'Of windows and country walks: frames of space and movement in 1990s Austen adaptations', *Screen* 39:4, 381–400.

Press, A. (1991), *Women Watching Television: Gender, Class and Generation in the American Television Experience*, Philadelphia: University of Pennsylvania Press.

Probyn, E. (1990), 'New traditionalism and post-feminism: TV does the home', *Screen* 31:2, 147–159.

Rabinowitz, J. and M. B. Haralovich (eds) (1999), *Television History and American Culture: Feminist Critical Essays*, Durham N.C.: Duke University Press.

Russ, J. (1993), 'Someone's trying to kill me and I think it's my husband', in J. Fleenor (ed.), *The Female Gothic*, Montreal: Eden.

Seiter, E. (1989), 'Don't treat us like we're so stupid and naive: towards an ethnography of soap opera viewers', in E. Seiter *et al.* (eds), *Remote Control: Television, Audiences and Cultural Power*, London: Routledge and Kegan Paul.

Spigel, L. and D. Mann (1992), *Private Screenings: Television and the Female Consumer*, Minneapolis: University of Minnesota Press.

Thornham, S. (1994), 'Feminist interventions: *Prime Suspect*', *Critical Survey* 6:2, 226–233.

Thornham, S. (2002–3), 'A good body: the case of /for feminist media studies', *European Journal of Cultural Studies*, 6:1, 75–94.

Tiballs, G. (1996), *Rebecca – Starring Charles Dance, Diana Rigg, Emilia Fox and Faye Dunaway*, London: Chameleon.

Walker, M. (1990), '*Secret Beyond the Door*', *Movie* 34/35, 16–30.

Wilcox, R. V., and Lavery, D. (eds) (2002), *Fighting the Forces: What's at Stake in 'Buffy the Vampire Slayer'*, Oxford: Rowman and Littlefield.

9

BBC drama at the margins: the contrasting fortunes of Northern Irish, Scottish and Welsh television drama in the 1990s

Steve Blandford

> Broadcasting Minister Kim Howells has criticised TV producers in Wales for taking themselves too seriously, claiming it led to a lack of success at network level. The MP for Pontypridd, South Wales, said that Scottish programme makers had achieved more because they were willing to treat their nation and its people in a light-hearted way . . . In an interview for the Royal Television Society's magazine Television, Dr Howells named the BBC Scotland drama series Monarch of the Glen as one of his favourites. (17 December 2001, http://news.bbc.co.uk/1/hi/wales/1716165.stm)

Dr Howells has developed a bit of a reputation for shooting from the hip but beneath the rhetoric it may be possible to discover in these remarks a potentially fruitful area for investigation in this chapter's quest to explain the differing network profiles of Northern Ireland, Scotland and Wales in the 1990s. In one of the key postwar British plays for the stage, *Comedians* (Trevor Griffiths, 1976), Challenor, a hard-bitten talent scout from the 'Comedy Artists and Managers Federation' arrives to see the members of an evening class for comedians perform in a local club. His verdicts on some of the group have, I would argue, continuing relevance for the kinds of judgements still made today about television drama originating in the UK's 'national regions'. Running through his notes on the comics he has seen earlier in the evening he turns to Mick Connor, originally from the Republic of Ireland:

> It mighta worked . . . if you'd taken something more up the audience's street. I mean, you might find being an Irishman in England fascinating, there's no reason we should, is there? *(Pause)* Had a sort of earnestness about it I didn't much take to. You know, as if you were giving a sermon. (Griffiths 1976: 55–56)

This is a recurrent motif throughout the play: when another of the novice comics does an immaculate impression of Frank Randle, the music-hall star from Wigan who died in 1957, Challenor sneers, 'Try it in Bermondsey, sonny. Try it in Birmingham even' (Griffiths 1976: 33). The thrust of these remarks forms one of the key themes of Griffiths's play, that is the extent to which the comics must make concessions to the metropolitan and class prejudices of those who control their industry in order to further their careers. To some extent, this kind of dilemma remains for the decision-makers in BBC Northern Ireland, Scotland and Wales today, and was certainly current in the 1990s.

What follows is an account of a number of the key popular series originating in the BBC 'national regions' in the 1990s, followed by a detailed account of the work of BBC Wales Drama department acting as a kind of case study of the impact of the pressures that were felt, to varying degrees, across the sector during this period.

BBC Northern Ireland

In his full-length study of screen culture both sides of the Irish border Lance Pettitt asserts that 'One of the BBC's most successful drama departments in the 1990s was that based in Northern Ireland under the leadership of Robert Cooper' (Pettitt 2000: 229). Pettitt does not attempt to deal with that slippery term 'successful', but let us assume for a minute that one of his criteria might be the presence of Northern Irish work on the network. In this respect he is partially right, though in the sphere of popular drama the reputation of the department rests pretty firmly with one peak-time show, the spectacularly popular *Ballykissangel* (1996–2001)

The series became the golden goose as far as BBC Northern Ireland was concerned, attaining the kinds of viewing figures more commonly associated with straightforward soap opera and running eventually to six series, though the final one showed a rapid decline in its audience. It certainly had an impact way beyond any other series from Northern Ireland, Scotland or Wales in the 1990s, and is therefore worth considerable attention in this context. *Ballykissangel* was, in fact, made for BBC Northern Ireland by Tony Garnett's Island World Productions. The 1990 Broadcasting Act's imposition on both the BBC and ITV of a quota system for independent production had introduced what Lez Cooke terms 'a postmodern shift away from the idea of a producer-led culture . . . towards a consumer-led culture where the broadcasters were forced to compete with an increasing number of competitors for a share of the audience'

(Cooke 2003: 162). *Ballykissangel* is, on the face of it, a classic product of such a shift, though Cooke goes on to identify Tony Garnett as one of the very few 'progressive' producers able to respond to such a shift in ways that retained their ability to remain inventive within such a problematic television environment. Garnett himself has described his methods as creating 'Trojan Horse drama' (Cooke 2003: 162). It is therefore interesting to look at *Ballykissangel* in this context: on the one hand, a prime-time long-running series in the era of market-led commissioning; on the other, the product of a company also responsible for innovative work such as *Cardiac Arrest* (1994–96) and *This Life* (1996–97).

For a series that stuck around for so long in a decade that saw so much attention to an Irish agenda in British politics, *Ballykissangel* has received remarkably little serious critical attention. What exists has tended to consider the series, not unreasonably, in relation to the 'heritage' tradition that has received so much attention within film studies. In the context of work such as Ronan Bennett's *Love Lies Bleeding* (BBC 1993) and lesser examples from three decades of 'troubles' drama, the view of Ireland and the Irish presented by *Ballykissangel* is striking and tends to accord far more with older cinematic traditions than anything produced for television in the recent past. As Ruth Barton puts it in one of the few lengthy academic articles on *Ballykissangel*:

> The sense of 'pastness' which the series exudes is an ahistorical, apolitical past; it relates to an Ireland that never was and which does not exist now. *Ballykissangel*, with its pretty country houses, litter-free streets, simple grocery shops, its unspoilt countryside (not a rusting car in sight) and its constant sunshine, is pure confection. It is also increasingly a simulacrum in the Baudriallardian sense. Tourist buses travel not to Avoca [the 'real' location where the series is filmed] but to Ballykissangel. (Barton 2000: 423)

At one level, of course, the series's popularity is relatively simple to explain – it fits easily within a tradition that gradually took hold in the 1990s and, as indicated above, is perhaps best personified by ITV's *Heartbeat* (1992–). That is, drama that is undemanding (even by the standards of television drama in general) in terms of both the narrative structure and the moral dilemmas it attempts to deal with, and which relies firmly on certain kinds of nostalgia for its visual identity. What makes *Ballykissangel* slightly different, perhaps, is both its origins in a 'national region' that had previously been principally associated with a wholly different set of dramatic iconography (urban, deprived, paramilitary) and its attitude to the notion of the 'visitor' within the series itself.

If we take the latter point first, Barton (2000) compares the portrayal of rural Ireland in Ballykissangel to earlier misty-eyed film versions such as *The Other Eden* (1959) and concludes that 'in Ballykissangel, the sense that the Irish way of life is superior to the British is much stronger. The notion of Irish idleness has equally become a positive one; in late twenti-eth-century society, pleasurable idleness is one of the working popula-tion's ultimate fantasies' (2000: 415). She exemplifies her argument with reference to one of the series's key storylines, which concerns a long-run-ning battle between a father (Padraig played by Peter Caffrey) and mother (Finnuala played by Frances Tomelty) over their son (Kevin played by John Cleere). As Barton intimates, Finnuala is depicted as the archetype of the woman who has sacrificed not only her child but also her sense of humanity to the demands of a successful career and big-city lifestyle. The oppositions here are clear enough and are echoed in various comic guises throughout, such as the gentle mockery of one of the central characters', Quigley's, pretensions to be a big-time businessman. There is a sense, then, that for all its appeal to tourist instincts the narrative thrust of *Bal-lykissangel* means that it is operating from a position of confidence. This also relates to the earlier point, which is that *Ballykissangel* originated from a place that had previously offered the BBC network a kind of drama overwhelmingly dominated by the 'troubles'. For all its froth and slightly queasy association with Web-based gimmicks such as *The Ballykissangel Examiner* (a BBC-maintained cod local newspaper site), the series represented an unwillingness for television in the North of Ireland to be defined in ways associated entirely with political violence. The problem is that, in doing this, there has clearly been a resort to some-thing close to an older comic Irishness – though the series's creators clearly saw it very differently. On the official website of World Produc-tions, information is given about the intentions of the series's original creator, Kieran Prendeville: 'He was determined that the stories would not be those considered stereotypical of the Irish – no "Oirishness", no begorrahs, shillelaghs or Little People' (www.world-productions.com/wp/content/shows/ballyk/info/history.htm).

To be fair to the series, the wholesale commodification of its central tropes has exaggerated its worst excesses in ways that are little to do with the programme itself. In the first three series at least there was more of a tendency towards a kind of low-key black humour. There was also much made of the strong central female role of Assumpta Fitzgerald (Dervla Kirwan) and her almost-relationship with the local priest, Father Peter Clifford (Stephen Tompkinson). The playing out of the tensions between

Clifford's socially concerned brand of religious vocation and the sexual chemistry between him and Fitzgerald gave the series a central narrative thrust able to take it beyond the quaintness of village life. In addition, the central female role was also used at times as a strong opposition to the ultra-masculine, small-time entrepreneur Brian Quigley (Tony Doyle). Add to this mix Assumpta Fitzgerald's open atheism, and we begin to see perhaps at least some trace of Garnett's influence.

Clearly, though it would be wrong to make a case for *Ballykissangel* as in any sustained sense 'progressive', in a decade of very different kinds of devolution for all three Celtic nations it represented both a major presence on the BBC network and a popular drama that had some semblance of a refusal to be too easily defined. Having said this, as the series progressed into its fourth recommissioning the 'simulacrum' dimension tended to take hold, and it became hard to see through the coach tours, the ever-proliferating websites and the tabloid fascination with the fact that the two leading actors had an offscreen relationship to match their onscreen, 'forbidden' flirtations. Of particular significance was the fact that at the end of the third series Assumpta Fitzgerald was dispatched by fire and water in the cellar of her own bar, in the manner of so many strong women before her, and the priest she so nearly led astray followed her out of the series. Up to this point, however lightly handled, a drama had been built around two strong performers playing out some of the central dilemmas of a changing rural life on the twin battlegrounds of gender and the Catholic faith. Once they were gone, it was harder to ignore the heritage aesthetic. It is perhaps significant that the only producer credit given to Garnett himself is on series two.

BBC Scotland

Unlike either Wales or Northern Ireland, BBC Scotland's drama department entered the 1990s in a position of some strength. A key series of the 1980s, *Tutti Frutti* (1987), as Hugh Herbert said, had 'looked set to break the network's resistance to regional drama played in heavy accents' (Herbert 1993: 178), and Bill Bryden's tenure at the drama department in Glasgow had made space for genuinely innovative work to be shown on network television. The first attempt by BBC Scotland to follow the success of *Tutti Frutti* was also written by John Byrne and set around a touring music scene, though in *Your Cheatin' Heart* (1990) he turned his attention towards country music. As Cairns Craig has argued, this second series continued Byrne's interesting exploration of the problematics of contemporary Scottish identity, particularly in relation to an increasingly globalised culture in general, and an American-dominated one in particular:

> The characters of *Your Cheatin' Heart* live in a constant process of double-take as they switch between the real and metaphorical environments of Scotland and America, equally at home and equally foreign in each, inhabitants of a culture which can no longer be defined by the boundaries of its own geography or past history. (Craig 2002: 1)

Though to some extent it attempted to repeat a formula – by using Byrne again so quickly – *Your Cheatin' Heart* still sees BBC Scotland Drama at its bravest in relation to popular forms, particularly in the way it attempts to deal with the question of the nation. Hugh Herbert sees first *Tutti Frutti* and then its follow-up as part of a concerted effort by Bryden, supported by Michael Grade (then Controller of BBC1), to establish a specifically Scottish power base for drama and new writing, though he also notes Byrne's resistance to being delineated in this way (Herbert 1993: 192). Whatever the specific motivation, however, across the two series a rare trick had been pulled off in the matching of strong national or regional identity with little compromise (the series was accompanied by the usual boring and predictable discussion of subtitling) to a narrative form with a claim to be genuinely popular.

However, from this point on, and through the rest of the decade, BBC Scotland Drama, despite a fairly strong network presence, was more often forced to compromise and, in particular, treat questions of identity in less complex ways. It is therefore appropriate to see Byrne's two series as the end of something rather than a beginning: the end, that is, of popular drama commissioning in Scotland with some faith in a strong, contemporary regional identity, and the start of a trend towards an altogether more sanitised product with so-called broad appeal. It would be unfair, though, to present this decline in unqualified terms, as the discussion below of the most popular series of the 1990s to come out of Scotland attempts to demonstrate.

In terms of commissioning and popularity, BBC Scotland's biggest success by far in the 1990s was *Hamish Macbeth* (1995–98). If the title suggested a parodic, cartoon Scotsman then the producers of the show clearly had other ideas. The publicity notes for the Zenith/Skyline production stress both the central character's off-beat nature and the show's 'contemporary' look at Highland life: 'Andrea Calderwood, Head of Television Drama at BBC Scotland says, "Hamish is a very exceptional police-

man and the goings-on in his village of Lochdubh offer a fresh and entertaining view of contemporary life in the Highlands"' (http://members.
ozemail.com.au/~blinda/hmpub1.htm).

However, earlier in the notes there is a passage which is perhaps even
closer to the series's heart:

> Hamish Macbeth was filmed entirely in and around the beautiful village of
> Plockton on the North West Coast of Scotland. Previously famous for the
> palm trees which unexpectedly fringe its pretty harbour, Plockton is now set
> to become much better known as television's fictional village of Lochdubh.
> (http://members.ozemail.com.au/~blinda/hmpub1.htm)

Like *Ballykissangel*, *Hamish Macbeth* undoubtedly gave rise to a simulacrum through its creation of 'the apparently sleepy Highland village of
Lochdubh'. The BBC's own publicity again talks proudly of the coach parties to Plockton and the World Wide Web has sprouted sites with contents
ranging from adoring fan material on Robert Carlyle to photos of 'Wee
Jock', the policeman's West Highland terrier.

There is, however, evidence to suggest that perhaps there is a little more
to *Hamish Macbeth* than an inducement to tourists to go in search of this
contemporary *Brigadoon*. Firstly, there is the casting of Robert Carlyle in
the title role. Although probably his best-known role, Begbie in *Trainspotting* (1996), was still to come when the first series of *Hamish Macbeth* was
made, Carlyle had already begun to acquire a particular set of associations as a British 'star' figure through his appearances in feature films such
as *Riff-Raff* (1990) and television dramas such as *Cracker* (Granada 1993)
and *Safe* (BBC 1993). These are very different films and dramas, but all
had Carlyle's characters as capable of explosive violence as well as various
kinds of sensitivity. This accumulated persona was key to an attempt to
position *Hamish Macbeth* as more 'quirky', even slightly 'difficult', in relation to other possible equivalents including ITV's *Heartbeat*.

Apart from the contribution of Carlyle's onscreen and offscreen image,
it would be reasonable to argue that the characterisation and, to a limited
extent, the narrative thrust of *Hamish Macbeth* had some degree of distance from the more anodyne offerings in the Sunday-night slot that it
occupied. To begin with, the show has at its heart a reversal that is the
foundation of the eponymous central character; that is, the local policeman Macbeth's lack of ambition and traditional masculine 'drive'. If
career-orientated power struggles have been at the centre of police drama
from its early days, *Hamish Macbeth* makes it clear that its central character is driven by the avoidance of promotion and the inevitable disrup-

tion to his life of rural solitude that this would bring. This is also a policeman who likes to live on the fringes of the law he is paid to uphold, and smokes cannabis and deals in older kinds of justice when necessary. However, if *Hamish Macbeth* is the centrepiece of BBC Scotland Drama's contribution to the network in the 1990s, it is undoubtedly more blandly palatable to a UK and overseas 'tourist' market than *Tutti Frutti* was at the end of the 1980s.

We can, perhaps, see *Hamish Macbeth* as representing Scotland's first response to what seemed a decisive shift in commissioning policy from the 'national regions' in the 1990s; by the end of the decade, *Monarch of the Glen* (2000–) had taken the trend a stage further. The series properly belongs to the decade that follows the one under consideration, but as the logical conclusion to what seemed to have begun in the 1990s it is worth a brief mention here. The BBC Scotland Annual report for 2002/3 is understandably proud of three drama series for the BBC1 network in the previous year. These were the fourth series of *Monarch of the Glen, Two Thousand Acres of Sky* (2001) and *Rockface* (2002), and what they all had in common was an attitude to place that undoubtedly owes more to the discourses of tourism than of drama. The satirical Scottish website 'The Jaggy Thistle' has taken a keen interest in this particular trend, and a 2000 story puts the following into the mouth of a fictitious BBC executive:

> We should have made it clear that the show is for Southern English con-sumption only, people who like watching things where deeply complex class and national conflicts are magicked away by making all the characters lovely, and setting the 'story' in a beautiful natural setting with not an Arndale Centre in sight. (www.thejaggythistle.co.uk/monarch.htm)

Even allowing for the excesses of the genre, the above is uncomfortably close to what appears to have become a trend for network commission-ing for BBC1 in relation to Scotland (and Northern Ireland, to some extent, through *Ballykissangel*) – a trend that is unlikely to be reversed, given the relative success of the key series in terms of ratings, overseas sales and the web-related tourism spin-offs.

BBC Wales

The depth of the desperation over Wales's lack of a BBC popular network presence in the 1990s was, some of us thought, truly reflected in a *Western Mail* article celebrating the emergence of a character from a popular 1995 advertisement who became known as Terry the 'Pot Noodle Man', played by a Welsh actor, Peter Baynham. 'Baynham's alter ego must take the credit for adding to the Welsh presence on network primetime television', the paper asserted bathetically, adding later that '[Terry] is, it seems, one of the few figures who has made the Welsh accent acceptable viewing' (9 November 1995). The key word in this context is, of course, 'acceptable'. As I wrote at the time, Terry is the epitome of a 'twp Taffy'[1] and many would argue that this is the only kind of Welsh representation regularly available in popular television (see Blandford and Upton 1996), a tradition that is still maintained through Rob Brydon's character in the excellent *Marion and Geoff* (2001).

Throughout the 1990s it appeared to be an impossible struggle for a succession of Heads of Drama in Cardiff to find Welsh drama 'acceptable' to the BBC network, particularly in the sphere of popular recurring series of the kind represented by *Ballykissangel* or *Hamish Macbeth*. What follows will attempt to examine some of the reasons why this was so and consider the wider implications for all drama production in the 'national regions'.

If we look at some facts about BBC Wales Drama in the early 1990s, its later failure to establish a network presence on a par with Northern Ireland and Scotland looks all the more surprising. To start with, in 1992 Ruth Caleb was appointed Head of Drama with a strong track record and, one supposes, the clout in London to have her department taken seriously. Two years later she was able to claim an enormous increase in network presence from two hours to over thirty-one hours (see Blandford and Upton 1996). However, the reality behind these figures is at the heart of one of the key problems that Caleb and her successors were to face. Eighteen of those thirty-one hours were accounted for by an experimental networking of the long-running Welsh-language soap opera *Pobol y Cwm* (1974–), an extremely bold move by Caleb's department, but one which was destined not to pass the only test that mattered in John Birt's BBC. However, although the challenge to the traditional British dislike of subtitles was bold, the fact remained that the BBC Drama budget in Cardiff was, like it or not, stuck with *Pobol y Cwm* as part of its commitment to supply S4C with a quota of Welsh-language programming. On the one hand, the programme provides a regular source of employment for directors, actors and technicians who in turn stay in Wales and help make it a significant broadcasting centre. Equally, Alison Griffiths has made a strong case for *Pobol y Cwm*'s contribution to national and cultural identities (Griffiths 1995). On the other hand, there is no denying that BBC Wales's commitment to *Pobol y Cwm* has contributed to its difficulties with the network in both real and symbolic terms. In real terms, the soap is a continuous and inflexible demand on resources in an era that has seen fierce new competitors drive down drama budgets to levels unimaginable even a decade before. In symbolic terms, *Pobol y Cwm* is perhaps the embodiment within BBC Wales Drama of what Dai Smith (former Head of English Language Broadcasting in Cardiff) has called the 'cultural settlement'[2] as far as London is concerned. Since S4C's inception in 1980, there has been a series of bitter exchanges between English-language filmmakers based in Wales and London-based commissioners over what some have seen as an openly hostile resentment at the existence of one of the most expensive (in terms of public subsidy) television stations in the world. The result, as Karl Francis and others have argued, has been a denial of opportunities for those working in the English language in Wales that has had serious cultural consequences (see Blandford 2000).

It is important to make clear at this point that this chapter offers no criticism of either S4C (though until comparatively recently its sense of its own audience produced a rather limited range in drama) or the BBC's commitment to supply the channel with Welsh-language drama. The problems that have arisen are much more the product of a crude assessment by the metropolitan centre of the role of S4C and Welsh-language programming. If any programming from the 'periphery' has a difficult task in the brave new producer-led world of television drama, then the perception of Wales as needing to be satisfied with its lot having got S4C has seemingly made it almost impossible to get popular programmes from there on to the network, or at least – if they make it that far – to get them recommissioned.

In its section on 'Regional Broadcasting', the BBC Annual Report and Accounts for 1997/8 acknowledges what an important year it had been for this particular part of the Corporation's remit:

> This has been a momentous year for Regional Broadcasting. The political landscape was transformed by votes in favour of a parliament for Scotland, a national assembly for Wales and an assembly for Northern Ireland . . . The BBC won all three of the Society's Regional Programme Awards this year. (www.bbc.co.uk/info/report98/regional.shtml)

For BBC Wales Drama however there is a sorrier tale to tell only a page later:

> BBC Wales continues to provide music coverage of outstanding quality . . . *Visions of Snowdonia* was a welcome springboard for increased factual output from Wales . . . To enjoy such levels of advancement across all pro-

gramme genres presents a greater challenge. These successes cannot disguise the fact that a number of drama series – *Drover's Gold, Tiger Bay* and *Mortimer's Law* – did not have sufficient audience appeal to be re-commissioned.

The last sentence here is remarkable for at least two reasons: first is the fact that Wales has three series on BBC1 inside a year after a decade of neglect, but second is the fact that none of them was recommissioned. *Drover's Gold* (1996) and *Mortimer's Law* (1996) are perhaps rather different cases to *Tiger Bay* (1996). Although it is clear that all three were made with the hope of some degree of longevity, it was only *Tiger Bay* that had the structure to suggest a genuinely long-running popular serial. Its initial run introduced audiences to a large cast of characters with the usual range of ages and backgrounds designed to maximise the breadth of the audience. *Tiger Bay's* strength lay in the potential tensions arising from its setting in the old docklands area of Cardiff, which has undergone a radical transformation in the last twenty years. To some extent, *Tiger Bay* attempted to reflect these tensions, sometimes in rather clumsy ways, and there was a sense of a shifting contemporary reality about it that was certainly a long way from a tourist-board vision of an 'emerging' Cardiff. As ex-BBC producer Adrian Mourby put it: 'the Welsh EastEnders clone, *Tiger Bay*, has been accused of putting off inward investment' (Mourby 1997)

Mourby's throwaway remark is revealing: unlike *Hamish Macbeth* or *Ballykissangel, Tiger Bay* made few concessions to the idea of popular television as being part of a total package that would also see increased sales of Shirley Bassey dolls and tourist buses pointing out the authentic docklands pub inhabited by old sailors. Instead, the so-called 'Welsh EastEnders' (BBC 1985–) depicted characters involved in similar sets of squabbles, adulterous relationships and comic confusions as their London counterparts. Arguably, in the process some of the distinctive possibilities of the location were lost and the end result was an anonymous urban landscape without a fraction of the budget of *EastEnders*. This is perhaps unsurprising in a climate where producers consistently either complain of ideas being 'too Welsh' or, if not Welsh at all, require a justification for programmes being made in Wales.[3]

Tiger Bay was probably BBC Wales's biggest play for a genuinely mass appeal popular drama in the 1990s, though it was by no means the only one. Ruth Caleb's time at BBC Wales was probably most notable for a number of single dramas for the now-defunct Screen One and Screen Two slots (for example Andrew Davies's *Filipina Dream Girls* (1991)), but she also tried a number of different ways to overcome what seemed to be a very deep-seated antipathy to a strong Welsh presence at the heart of prime-time BBC1. One of these was an attempt to use the experience and track record of Lynda La Plante to 'create' series through the Cardiff department, although in the case of both *Civvies* (1992) and *The Lifeboat* (1996), the series were commissioned but not repeated amidst a certain amount of acrimony.

Though much was done to discourage this view during the 1990s, it is difficult to discount entirely the idea that one of the contributory factors behind Wales's lack of network success is the kind of cultural antipathy that was at its most vicious during the 1992 general election campaign. The day after the election, *The Sun*'s triumphalism was at its most hubristic, claiming it was their coverage 'wot won it'. A key element of this coverage, of course, was the character assassination of Neil Kinnock, the then leader of the Labour Party, which made much of his Welsh identity. More recently, Anne Robinson demonstrated (on the popular BBC2 show *Room 101*) how easy and acceptable it is to dislike 'the Welsh' en masse in a way that would simply not be tolerated if the target were almost any other nation or ethnic grouping.[4] Hugh Herbert quotes Alan Watkins writing in *The Observer* on Neil Kinnock's destruction by tabloid: 'The truth is that the English regard the Scots as industrious and honest, the Irish as charming and feckless, but the Welsh as mendacious and disloyal' (Herbert 1993: 193). Whilst it would be foolish to overplay them, it would also be remiss to ignore these deep-seated attitudes as one factor in the way that BBC1 in particular has consistently either ignored Welsh television drama or publicly humiliated its department in Cardiff by not recommissioning series that appeared to have at least a modest shelf-life.

From the middle of the decade onwards, a number of key decisions seem to signal that, while Wales had not entirely given up on having a major network presence, it was making bold statements about not relinquishing its independent stance in order to pacify London. First of all, the combative Karl Francis, most famous for social realist films set in the deprived post-industrial landscapes of the South Wales valleys, was appointed as Head of Drama. Secondly, much of the effort spent on popular programming went in to developing series that played very hard to the Welsh audience first (and a south-east Welsh audience at that) and the network could either embrace it or not. Out of this strategy came, for example, *Belonging* (1999–), *Satellite City* (1996–69) and *The Bench* (2001–), none of which has been taken up by the network despite attracting strong regional audiences.

Of these three *Belonging* is perhaps closest to the formula most likely to produce a long-running popular series. The programme is set in a small town in the South Wales valleys, and its storylines generally revolve around the usual diet of infidelities and family crises, though arguably there is a greater sense of economic reality and, in the background, of the area's past than is commonly found in British soap opera. One of the central characters was made redundant as the last of the mines closed, and there is a pervasive sense of 'new' short-term jobs associated with the volatile global marketplace (one key location is a mobile-phone shop) replacing those that accompany a long-term investment in the locality. There is perhaps a case for saying that it is *Belonging*'s determination to display both its strong local roots and at least a passing acquaintance with economic realities that has excluded it from any serious consideration for the BBC network. Since Channel 4's *Brookside*'s (1982–2003) change of direction in the late 1980s, there has been little to suggest that the commissioning of popular series on any of the major channels has been able to countenance these kind of concerns in any sustained way. *Belonging* is now in its fourth series and popular in Wales, but highly unlikely to been seen in the rest of the UK despite a cast of relatively well-known faces, including Charles Dale, Gwen Watford and Eve Myles.

Conclusions

The second edition of Robert Murphy's *The British Cinema Book* (2001) contains a welcome addition to the range of concerns covered in the first edition in 1997, namely Martin McLoone's chapter on recent cinema from Northern Ireland, Scotland and Wales (McLoone 2001: 184–190). While the first edition seemed to regard the idea of 'British' as relatively unproblematic, McLoone's chapter gives the book a more balanced post-devolutionary sensibility. McLoone, in fact, goes a stage further and joins those who see the 1990s as the start of a postcolonial period for Scotland, Ireland and Wales, something that is beginning to emerge from the screen culture of the three nations:

> The tendency in recent films emanating from the Celtic periphery is to attempt to move cinematic representation beyond the dominant imagery and traditional iconography that has defined it. The re-imagining that is taking place in Scotland, Wales and Northern Ireland involves a reworking of national or regional tropes and stereotypes . . . Film-making in Britain's Celtic periphery suggests that a process of internal decolonisation is well underway and that peripherality has moved towards the edge of contemporary cultural debate. (McLoone 2001: 190)

To set against this, in terms of the variously devolved powers to the new bodies in Belfast, Cardiff and Edinburgh, broadcasting is barely affected. The BBC remains, in a sense, a major instrument of what some would see as enduring colonial power. In turn, its popular channel's vision of the new devolved nations remains resolutely wedded to 'dominant imagery and traditional iconography' or, in the case of Wales, precious little representation at all. Unlike the cinematic tradition that McLoone sees emerging (*Trainspotting* (1995), *Human Traffic* (1999), *Divorcing Jack* (1998)), popular BBC television drama emanating from 'the Celtic periphery' in the 1990s has tended, with some minor reservations, to retreat to the iconography of other cinematic eras. When it has not done so, it has rarely been recommissioned by the network controllers in London.

Homi Bhabha's description of the tendency of postcolonial cultures to aspire to the 'elevated condition of the coloniser' (quoted in Owen 2001: 101) is given a new twist here. It is not so much that writers, directors and producers from the three nations under discussion are attempting to ape an English-style product, rather that, in broadcasting at least, the idea of any postcolonial, or even post-devolutionary, sensibility remains invisible, at least on the network. When it has flickered into life in, for instance, BBC Northern Ireland's *Give My Head Peace* (1998–), it has remained firmly on the margins and broadcast only in the nation where it originated.

This leads us finally to the question as to whether any of this matters. One view is that the devolved nations have the limited 'local' programming that is proportionate to their various levels of 'independence', and the BBC is not obliged to do more. For many this will be a seductive line of argument, even within the Celtic nations, where many are understandably heartily sick of the implicit obligation to be perpetually concerned with 'identity'. However, there is a potentially broader question at stake about the future of the UK as a whole and the role that the BBC has to play within it. That is: how far are we able to be grown up about 'British' identity, not simply inclusive of 'Celtic' variations, but all the other enriching inflections that have come from, and will continue to come from, voices marginalised by their strong identification with issues of ethnicity and gender? It would be foolish to pretend that nothing changes: digital radio and television, for instance, promise to provide a host of spaces for so-called 'special interest' groups. What is under scrutiny here is genuinely popular television drama, about which, in the context of Scotland, John Caughie wrote:

> Dramatic forms seem to me to occupy a particularly prominent place within the discourse of television which constructs a notion of Scottishness. It is the fictional and dramatic representations of Scotland . . . which seem to offer the points of identification for a Scottish identity. (Caughie 1982: 120)

What devolution has drawn to our attention is that Caughie's concern for Scottishness should really be a concern for a contemporary revaluation of Britishness, which would, of course, include ever-changing ideas about Scottish identity. In some of the key feature films of the last decade or so there have been signs of this happening. As well as the 'Celtic' features already mentioned, films such as *Bhaji on the Beach* (1994), *East Is East* (1999) and *Bend it Like Beckham* have problematised identity in popular forms, in terms not only of race but also of gender and sexuality. In popular television drama there have been isolated and well-publicised moments when similar shifts have taken place. However, this brief look at popular television drama from Northern Ireland, Scotland and Wales in the 1990s appears to suggest that the BBC's faith in the need for a broader, more flexible idea of Britishness does not yet extend to its commissioning of programmes that they hope will have genuinely broad appeal.

Notes

1   'Twp Taffy' – a term widely understood in Wales to describe derogatory portrayals of Welsh people as 'simple' or stupid.
2   Interview with the author, 2003.
3   An example is Peter Edwards who was Head of Drama Development at HTV Wales, who complained in an unpublished interview with the author in 1997: 'We have sent ideas to them [London-based commissioning editors] which get sent back saying they're too Welsh. Somehow they want the opposite . . . If your idea is more universal they say "Well, why should we do it in Wales?" You're Welsh, you deal with Welsh things, your humanity stops there. To fully express your humanity, you've got to be English.'
4   *Room 101* is named after George Orwell's vision of totalitarian hell, in which Winston Smith, the central character in *Nineteen Eighty-Four*, is placed in a room containing his worst fears and phobias. In the programme, the idea is treated ironically, and guests are invited to nominate their 'pet hates' to go into the eponymous room and discuss them with the series's host, the comedian Paul Merton. Anne Robinson nominated the Welsh.

References

Barton R. (2000), 'The Ballkissangelization of Ireland', *Historical Journal of Film, Radio and Television* 20:3, Autumn, 413–426.

Bhabha, H. K. (ed.) (1990), *Nation and Narration*, London: Routledge.

Blandford, S. (ed.) (2000), *Wales on Screen*, Bridgend: Seren.

Blandford, S., and J. Upton, 'Courting the network', *Planet* 117 (1996) 70–76.

Caleb, R. (1994), Broadcasting Council Paper (Unpublished).

Caughie, J. (1982), 'Scottish television: what would it look like?' in C. McArthur (ed.), *Scotch Reels: Scotland in Cinema and Television*, London: BFI.

Cooke, L. (2003), *British Television Drama: A History*, London: BFI.

Craig, C. (2002), 'Displacements – the theatrical art of John Byrne', *International Journal of Scottish Theatre* 3:1, June. Online journal accessed at: http://arts.qmuc.ac.uk/ijost/volume3_no1/default.html.

Griffiths, A. (1995), 'National and cultural identity in a Welsh-language soap opera', in R. C. Allen (ed.), *To Be Continued . . . Soap Operas Around the World*, London: Routledge.

Griffiths, T. (1976), *Comedians* London: Faber and Faber.

Hebert, H. (1993), 'Tutti Frutti', in G. W. Brandt, (ed.), *British Television Drama in the 1980s*, Cambridge: Cambridge University Press.

McLoone, M. (2001), 'Internal decolonisation? British cinema in the Celtic fringe', in R. Murphy (ed.), *The British Cinema Book*, 2nd edn, London: BFI.

Owen, R. (2001), 'The play of history: the performance of identity in Welsh historiography and theatre', *North American Journal of Welsh Studies* 1:2. Online journal, which can be accessed at: http://spruce.flint.umich.edu/ellisjs/volOne.html.

Pettit, L. (2000), *Screening Ireland*, Manchester: Manchester University Press.

Internet sources

http://news.bbc.co.uk/1/hi/wales/1716165.stm (Accessed October 2003)

www.world-productions.com/wp/content/shows/ballyk/info/history.htm (Accessed October 2003)

http://members.ozemail.com.au/~blinda/hmpub1.htm (Accessed October 2003)

www.thejaggythistle.co.uk/monarch.htm (Accessed October 2003)

www.bbc.co.uk/info/report98/regional.shtml (Accessed October 2003)

Mourby A. (1997), 'View from the Valleys' www.welshdragon.net/resources/Articles/valley.shtml

Further reading

Anderson, B. (1991), *Imagined Communities: Reflections on the Origin and Spread of Nationalism*, London: Verso.

Ashcroft, B., G. Griffiths and H. Tiffin (eds) (2000), *Postcolonial Studies: The Key Concepts*, London: Routledge.

Basnett, S. (1997), *Studying British Culture: An Introduction*, London: Routledge.

Berry, D. (1996), *Wales and Cinema: The First Hundred Years*, Cardiff: University of Wales Press.

Corner, J. (ed.) (1991), *Popular Television in Britain: Studies in Cultural History*, London: BFI.

Curtis, T. (ed.) (1986), *Wales: The Imagined Nation*, Bridgend: Poetry Wales Press.

Dick, E. (ed.) (1990), *From Limelight to Satellite*, London: BFI.

Hill, J., and M. McLoone (eds) (1996), *Big Picture, Small Screen*, Luton: University of Luton Press.

Hjort, M., and S. Mackenzie (eds) (2000), *Cinema and Nation*, London: Routledge.

McLoone, M. (2000), *Irish Film, The Emergence of a Contemporary Cinema*, London: BFI.

Murphy, R. (ed.) (2003), *British Cinema of the Nineties* 2nd edn, London: BFI.

Petrie, D. (2000), *Screening Scotland*, London: BFI.

Richards, J. (1997), *Films and British National Identity*, Manchester: Manchester University Press.

10

The new social realism of *Clocking Off*

Lez Cooke

The first episode of *Clocking Off*, the factory-based drama series created by Paul Abbott, was transmitted on 23 January 2000 at 9.00 pm on BBC1. A new drama series for a new century, yet *Clocking Off* was an unlikely success with its northern industrial setting, its focus on working-class relations in a Manchester textiles factory and its issue-based storylines. This description might, in fact, suggest a 'serious' television drama from the 1960s or 1970s, written perhaps by Jim Allen or Jeremy Sandford and directed by the likes of Jack Gold or Ken Loach, the kind of drama which would have been shown as a Wednesday Play (BBC 1964–70) or Play For Today (BBC 1970–84). The comparison is not superfluous. Nicola Shindler, whose Manchester-based Red Production Company produced the series, made the allusion directly: 'It was an opportunity to write really big quality stories for a massive populist audience. We talked a lot about *Play For Today* and the *Wednesday Play* which more often than not were good blue-collar stories, told properly. They used to get the nation talking' (Ogle 2000: 6).

That *Clocking Off* was shown on BBC1 was significant given the BBC's track record in producing realist, issue-based drama, from *Up the Junction* (BBC 1965) and *Cathy Come Home* (BBC 1966) to *Boys from the Blackstuff* (BBC 1982). That there had been little such drama produced since *Boys from the Blackstuff* was a result of the shift towards a more commercial, competitive climate in television in the late 1980s and 1990s, resulting in an aversion to risk-taking on behalf of the television companies and a preference for drama series and serials designed primarily to maximise audiences. This led the BBC to try to emulate ITV's success with bland, middle-of-the-road dramas such as *Heartbeat* (Yorkshire 1992–) by commissioning equally unadventurous soap-star vehicles such as *Harbour Lights* (BBC 1999–2000) and *Sunburn* (BBC 1998–2000). *Clocking Off* provided the BBC with an opportunity to return to its traditional strengths with a northern working-class drama intent on updating social realism for a new 'postmodern' television audience.

In the ratings-driven climate of the late 1990s when *Clocking Off* was being developed (under its original title of *The Factory*), Paul Abbott recognised that the BBC was the more likely home for such an unfashionable concept than ITV, for whom he had previously worked as a writer on *Coronation Street* (from 1989 to 1994), *Cracker* (two stories in 1995), *Reckless* (1997) and *Touching Evil* (1997). Not only did the BBC have a track record of producing social realist drama but the series needed a backer prepared to spend enough money to ensure it was both stylish and original: 'I took the idea to the BBC because at that time, if you mentioned northern working-class textile drama to anyone else, each word knocked the budget down by about 50 grand per episode. I knew it had to be done on a large scale, otherwise the stories would look like soap' (Naughton 2001: 26).

Clocking Off as series drama

Part of the originality of *Clocking Off* as a series (and one of the ways in which it revived an earlier tradition in series drama) was that it offered self-contained stories in each episode, rather than conforming to the increasing tendency in drama series towards serialisation, carrying storylines over from one episode to the next. Although a number of guest actors (John Simm, Christopher Eccleston, David Morrissey, Marc Warren, Denise Black, Tom Georgeson) made one-off appearances in the series, taking leading roles in single episodes, one of the novelties of *Clocking Off* was the way in which regular characters would also feature as the leading character for an episode while other factory employees played secondary or subsidiary roles. In subsequent episodes a background character might take the lead while the previous week's leading character would slip into the background.

The first series began with John Simm making a guest appearance as Stuart Leach, one of three Leach brothers working for Mackintosh Textiles. Paul Abbott's opening sequence provided an intriguing, attention-grabbing premise, with Stuart arriving home from a normal working day only to be met by the shocked and puzzled reactions of his wife and young son who have not seen him for thirteen months. Abbott gradually reveals that Leach has lost his memory and his bemused response to what has happened is conveyed so naturalistically that a series of enigmas are established without the expositional predictability one might find in a more formulaic drama. Abbott adds layers of complexity to the plot as it is revealed that Leach, a lorry driver with Mackintosh Textiles, had, during his long absence, met and married a woman in Sheffield with whom he has had a child, only to be found out by the woman's brother who viciously beats him up, causing the loss of memory. On coming round he leaves hospital and goes home but, in a narrative twist typical of Abbott's writing, Leach, remembering nothing of the last thirteen months, goes to his old home in Manchester, not his new one in Sheffield, thus initiating the events which motivate the plot. To add a further complication, Leach returns to find that his older brother Martin (Jason Merrells) has, in his absence, developed a relationship with Stuart's wife.

John Simm disappeared from the series after the first episode, the absence of his character being explained in episode two when Stuart's wife and child move to Sheffield, where he has been imprisoned for bigamy. Meanwhile, both Jason Merrells as Martin and Jack Deam as the third Leach brother Kev remained as central characters, with Kev featuring as the leading character in the first episode of series two, while Martin was to feature as the leading character in the final episode of the second series where his relationship with Sue, Stuart's wife, is reprised when she returns from Sheffield eight months pregnant, bearing Martin's child. Both of these episodes were written by Abbott, who shared the writing on the second series with three other writers, having written all six episodes of the first series himself.

In episode two of the first series Christopher Eccleston was brought in to play the leading role alongside factory worker Yvonne Kolakowski (Sarah Lancashire). While Lancashire had been a background character in episode one, and would continue as such in subsequent episodes in the first series, Eccleston made only one further appearance. That such a recognisable television actor as Sarah Lancashire, best known at the time for her role as sexy barmaid Raquel in *Coronation Street*, was prepared to appear in episodes of *Clocking Off* as a secondary character, a machine-worker who might simply be glimpsed in the background, was one of the features of the series which greatly enhanced its appeal. Referring to Eccleston's walk-on part in episode four of the first series, Abbott stressed that such appearances were important in lending weight to the drama, even if it meant a star actor appearing only briefly in the background: 'It must have cost 10 grand for him to do that but it's really important because he dignifies the story that is currently being told. It's the opposite of what normally happens and it's great' (Ogle 2000: 7).

The first series of *Clocking Off* attracted an average audience of 8.2 million, winning Bafta and Royal Television Society awards for Best Drama Series, while Paul Abbott won the RTS Writer's award for the series. The support of Nicola Shindler, founder of Red Production Company, for writer-led (rather than producer-led) drama was crucial to *Clocking Off*'s success. Red was founded in 1998 as a Manchester-based company, working out of offices rented from Granada TV, and its commitment to producing innovative regional drama was confirmed with its first commission, *Queer As Folk* (C4 1999–2000), a colourful, fast-paced drama about Manchester's gay community. Russell T. Davies's groundbreaking series established Red as a progressive company which was prepared to champion risk-taking, writer-led drama with a strong regional flavour. *Clocking Off* was to cement that reputation.

Television and social realism: defining a tradition

Regional television drama, whether produced by a regionally based company, such as Granada or Merseyside TV, or set in the regions, such as *Z Cars* (BBC 1962–78), *Boys from the Blackstuff* and many Plays For Today, has often taken social realism as its defining aesthetic. Social realism has a long history in British culture, dating back to the 1930s documentary film movement and manifesting in different forms at different historical moments. A celebrated moment was that of the British 'new wave' in the late 1950s and early 1960s, when many plays and films were awarded the dubious accolade of 'kitchen sink drama'. In television drama this tradition can be seen as early as June 1956 when Ted Willis's *Woman in a Dressing Gown* (Associated Rediffusion 1956) was screened as a Television Playhouse production on ITV. ABC's Armchair Theatre also specialised in 'kitchen sink' drama with plays such as Ray Rigby's *Boy with the Meat Axe* (ABC 1958), Clive Exton's *Where I Live* (ABC 1960) and Alun Owen's *After the Funeral* (ABC 1960).

Northern working-class realism was popularised in the early 1960s in Granada's new twice-weekly serial, *Coronation Street* (Granada 1960–). In an article on 'Realism and convention' in a monograph on *Coronation Street* Marion Jordan proposed a definition of social realism, before proceeding to describe how the conventions of social realism had been adapted to the soap opera form:

Briefly the genre of Social Realism demands that life should be presented in the form of a narrative of personal events, each with a beginning, a middle and an end, important to the central characters concerned but affecting others only in minor ways; that though these events are ostensibly about *social* problems they should have as one of their central concerns the settling of people in life; that the resolution of these events should always be in terms of the effect of social interventions; that characters should be either working-class or of the classes immediately visible to the working classes (shop-keepers, say, or the two-man business) and should be credibly accounted for in terms of the 'ordinariness' of their homes, families, friends; that the locale should be urban and provincial (preferably in the industrial north); that the settings should be commonplace and recognisable (the pub, the street, the factory, the home and more particularly the kitchen); that the time should be 'the present'; that the style should be such as to suggest an unmediated, unprejudiced and complete view of reality; to give, in summary, the impression that the reader, or viewer, has spent some time at the expense of the characters depicted. (Jordan 1981: 28)

This definition fits *Clocking Off* very comfortably, except perhaps for the suggestion that the 'narrative of personal events' should have 'a beginning, a middle and an end'. As the description of the first episode indicates, Abbott is not particularly interested in telling stories in a linear fashion. Neither do his stories have tidy resolutions, although each episode of the series was satisfactorily contained within its sixty-minute length, enabling the next episode to deal with a completely different story. All of the other criteria can be readily applied to *Clocking Off*, which uses the textiles factory as the backdrop against which various dramas are played out. It is worth noting that these dramas are invariably 'domestic' in that they involve the home life, family and friends of the factory workers. In this respect *Clocking Off* could be said to belong to the genre of the 'kitchen sink' drama, but the emphasis on the collective experience of the workplace opens the drama out to embrace a social dimension which some of the earlier kitchen sink dramas, especially the ones confined to studio sets, often lacked.

Further drama series, including generic ones such as *Z Cars*, can be located within the genre of social realism in the early 1960s, but it is in the Wednesday Plays and Plays For Today of Tony Garnett and Ken Loach that social realism in television drama achieved its fullest expression as a result of their preference for shooting on film and on location, enabling the 'lived reality' of working-class life to be shown with a documentary verisimilitude. *Up the Junction* was the first expression of this new social realism, transposing the northern industrial setting to the south but retaining the essential ingredients of working-class characters, 'ordinary' locations such as 'the pub, the street, the factory, the home', a kaleidoscopic narrative of personal events, involving social problems such as unwanted pregnancy and illegal abortion, conveyed through an impressionistic documentary style better suited to expressing an 'unmediated, unprejudiced and complete view' of working-class life in mid-1960s London, more complete at any rate than that which could be achieved in the television studio. Loach and Garnett developed this approach in *Cathy Come Home* and other dramas for the BBC: *In Two Minds* (1967), *The Big Flame* (1969) and *The Rank and File* (1971), the latter two written by Jim Allen, an ex-miner who first wrote episodes of *Coronation Street* before going on to write a number of militant television plays, nearly all with northern industrial settings.

Clocking Off can be viewed as an amalgamation of these two traditions. On the one hand, the ambition to present 'good blue-collar stories, told properly', the sort of stories that 'used to get the nation talking', locates the series in the Loach/Garnett/Allen tradition of The Wednesday Play and Play For Today. On the other hand, the 'domestic' qualities of *Clocking Off*, its emphasis on the camaraderie of the factory workers, the 'ordinariness' of the characters and their social situations, the element of serialisation that is present as a result of the personal relations between regular characters, all suggest an affinity with the popular social realism of a soap opera such as *Coronation Street*, a factor which may help to explain the popularity of such an unfashionable twenty-first-century concept as a drama series set in a northern textiles factory. The blending of these two traditions in *Clocking Off* is indicative of a postmodern shift in the representation of social realism in twenty-first-century television drama. The cultural divide between the 'serious' social realism of The Wednesday Play and Play For Today and the 'popular' social realism of *Coronation Street* has been eroded in the last twenty years so that a series such as *Clocking Off* can now embrace both traditions, being at the same time both 'popular' and 'serious'.

Clocking Off: social realism for the twenty-first century

Perhaps the nearest equivalent to *Clocking Off* on British television was *Bull Week* (BBC 1980), a six-part serial written by Ron Hutchinson and produced by Michael Wearing for BBC Birmingham. Like *Clocking Off*, *Bull Week* was based in a factory, in this case in the Midlands, and involved an ensemble cast including, in an interesting parallel to the first episode of *Clocking Off*, three brothers, two of whom work in the factory while the third is a union official there. *Bull Week* differed from *Clocking Off* in that it had a plot which developed over its six episodes, set on the six days of 'bull week', the week before the factory's two-week holiday when all of the employees 'work like bulls' to earn some extra money. Its storyline is more 'political' than those of *Clocking Off* but its factory setting, with scenes also in 'the pub, the street and the home', clearly identifies it as a drama of social realism.

A comparison of the two dramas is revealing, indicating not only what *Clocking Off* has in common with the earlier tradition of British social realism but also the ways in which Paul Abbott's series reworked social realism for a new conjuncture and a new 'postmodern' television audience. As Robin Nelson (1997: 30–49) has argued, the television audience of the 1990s was characterised by a preference for stories told with a faster tempo and delivered in easily digestible narrative segments, a postmodern preference which militated against the protracted, single-issue narratives of social realism. These changes in television consumption resulted in the emergence of new narrative forms which Nelson has characterised as 'flexi-narratives', indicating their ability to accommodate a number of different stories within episodes and the flexibility to move quickly between them, allowing some stories to continue over episodes in order to retain an audience while other stories are resolved within the episode. Nelson traces these changes back to American television in the 1970s and 1980s and the development of a new kind of television drama better suited to the shorter attention spans of the television audience. The independent production company MTM is credited with pioneering this new style of drama with programmes such as *Hill Street Blues* (MTM/NBC 1980–87), 'sophisticated adult programming which could nevertheless hold the attention of an audience whose powers of concentration were diminished' (Nelson 1997: 30).

In trying to present 'sophisticated adult programming' for a twenty-first-century audience, *Clocking Off* reworked social realism in a number of ways. Firstly, instead of the politics of the workplace which feature in *Bull Week*, *Clocking Off* presents a series of 'morality tales', eschewing the overt politics of classic social realism and focusing instead on the moral dilemmas of the central characters as they confront a variety of social problems that impinge on their personal lives, problems such as alcoholism, drugs, male violence, paedophilia and racism. For Paul Abbott, the variety in the episodes was one of the series's strengths, distinguishing it from other series where the pursuit of ratings success tends to result in a generic uniformity: 'I love the fact that one strand will be a romantic comedy, then the next week is more like a thriller. It has that flexibility' (Holman 2001: 23). This variety and difference between episodes, while dealing with single-issue storylines within them, is one way in which *Clocking Off* departed from the 'flexi-narrative' approach adopted in other contemporary drama series, placing it more in the single-play tradition of anthology series such as The Wednesday Play or Play For Today.

A concession to postmodernity in *Clocking Off* was the introduction of a number of stylistic changes which differentiate the series from its more sombre and sometimes pedantic social realist predecessors. The greatly increased tempo of *Clocking Off* is immediately evident. The thirty-second title sequence sets the tone: a colourful visual montage of images from inside the factory, including hand-held camera shots moving past factory machines, cut together with abstract images that provide a blur of colour and movement, an effect creating the impression of frenzied activity, reinforced by a driving rhythm'n'blues soundtrack.

After the title sequence each episode followed a similar pattern, usually a montage of factory scenes: employees arriving for work, or already occupied in the factory, or sometimes knocking off at the end of the working day, the familiar music track reinforcing the mood of activity prior to the initial equilibrium being disrupted and the week's story put into motion. The first episode is typical, starting off at a cracking pace with scenes at the factory taking place at some undisclosed time during the working day, intercut with Stuart Leach travelling on the metro in Manchester on his way home. After the shock of his unexpected reappearance, Sue, his wife, telephones the factory and we see Trudy, the assistant to Mack the factory owner, taking the call and delivering a message to Martin who rushes off to Sue's house. Martin comes face to face with his brother almost exactly five minutes into the episode, in which time there have been eighty-one shots, with an average shot length of 3.7 seconds. This is very fast for British television drama and while the pace inevitably slows after this brisk opening the narrative tempo of the episode as a whole is considerably faster than that of a drama such as *Bull Week*, made twenty years earlier.

To give another example: the first episode of the second series (featuring Stuart's brother Kev, who develops suspicions that a workmate who moves into the house opposite may be a paedophile) has only forty-eight shots in the first five minutes, an average shot length of 6.25 seconds. Yet the opening sequence of this episode seems just as fast as that of the first episode of series one because of the amount of camera movement within it. In *Clocking Off* the camera is rarely still and in the opening sequence of 'Kev's Story' (episodes in the second series were given such titles) the camera is very restless, its perpetual movement contriving to create the same impression that rapid editing did in the opening episode of the first series, generating a mood of ceaseless activity and capturing the attention of the viewer through the sheer vitality of its exposition.

Traditionally, social realism has been associated with a dour look, especially when the location has been the factories and terraced houses of the industrial north, as if this iconography was synonymous with dark colours and an absence of vitality. The role of cinematographer Peter Greenhalgh was crucial to the creation of a more colourful mise-en-scène for *Clocking Off*, executive producer Nicola Shindler asking him 'to make it look "beautiful" not grimy and industrial as one would expect' (Anon. 2001: 22). Among Greenhalgh's previous credits was the stylish contemporary vampire series *Ultraviolet* (C4 1998), and Shindler wanted a similarly glossy look for *Clocking Off*. According to Greenhalgh, 'She was looking for a lot of colours, tight shots and moving images', while for the second series he went 'a little further in trying to achieve an enhanced look. I've gone for a lot of out of focus colours. I would often put a fluorescent tube with a colour on it, well in the back of the shot, just to give the depth' (Anon. 2001: 22). This enhancing of the colour scheme is clearly evident in the first episode of series two where the opening sequence is replete with colour, especially in the factory scenes where the fabrics are all vivid primary colours. Many of the factory employees are also dressed in brightly coloured clothes, with Kev, the focus of attention, wearing a bright orange T-shirt (with 'Sex-God' in large lettering on the front and back, a neat summation of his 'laddish' character, which Greenhalgh highlights with a camera movement drawing our attention to it). The enhanced colours of the factory interior are maintained as the shift comes to an end, Kev going out to his van – bright yellow with a blue stripe running along the side – and more brightly coloured clothing is in evidence as he drives past workers outside the factory.

The use of primary colours is one of the most distinctive features of *Clocking Off* and one of the several ways in which it 'updates' social realism for a new audience. While Peter Greenhalgh played an important part in enhancing the colourful, vibrant look of the series, it was production designer Chris Wilkinson who was primarily responsible for the colour scheme, having received instructions from Shindler to be as inventive with colour as possible: 'I went to him and said that just because these characters were working-class didn't mean their houses were all grey and small and horrible. These days everybody is obsessed with interior design and trying to make their surroundings as attractive as they can – just look at *Changing Rooms*. So he brought colour into every home and location' (Ogle 2000: 7).

Shindler has acknowledged the influence of American series such as *Ally McBeal* (Fox 1997–2002) and *ER* (NBC 1994–) in wanting to create a stylish look for *Clocking Off*, seeking to jettison the sombre look of classic social realism in a drama which is, nevertheless, set amidst the industrial heartlands of the north-west of England: 'I think sometimes English people have a fear of making things look too good because they think it will look glossy and unreal. What we've tried to do with this is make it look real, but also make it look good' (Ogle 2000: 7).

One way in which *Clocking Off* differs from contemporary drama series is in the use of film rather than video. Most popular British television drama series, including *The Bill* (Thames 1984–), *Casualty* (BBC 1986–), *Coronation Street, EastEnders* (BBC 1985–), *Heartbeat* and *Holby City* (BBC 1999–), are shot on video but in order to achieve the glossier look for *Clocking Off* that the production team required it was essential that the series was shot on film. As Greenhalgh put it: 'I don't think they've perfected the technique yet of enhancing video to look like film. There have been very many brave efforts but there are always two or three shots where you can tell it was shot on video. You can't get that feel on video that you can get on film' (Anon. 2001: 22).

The desire to shoot on film, rather than record on video in the studio, had been considered essential by Loach and Garnett when making *Up the Junction* and *Cathy Come Home* in the mid-1960s, and these two Wednesday Plays set the standard for subsequent social realist television drama. Shooting on location was essential in order to achieve a 'sense of place' in the industrial towns and cities of the Midlands and the North, while shooting on film, rather than video, was essential for capturing the 'grainy reality' of working-class life. Yet drama budgets would not always allow the use of film exclusively, and many plays and serials of the 1970s and early 1980s were forced to use video for interior scenes, often recorded in the studio, while the more expensive film stock was kept for exterior location shooting. This resulted in a very noticeable disjunction in visual style between interior and exterior scenes. Perhaps for audiences at the time it was less distracting than it now seems – the combination of film and video footage would have been more the convention – but the difference in visual quality between scenes shot on video and those shot on film in a drama such as *Bull Week* is very apparent today.

In 1982 Philip Saville shot four of the five episodes of *Boys from the Blackstuff* on video because the budget did not allow the whole series to be shot on film, the exception being the fourth episode, 'Yosser's Story'. As each episode of *Boys from the Blackstuff* dealt with a separate story, the switch to film for 'Yosser's Story' was less problematic; in fact film was more suitable for the fantasy sequences, which would indicate Yosser's impending breakdown. Switching from video to film for one episode sidestepped the problem of having to combine film and video in the same episode, a problem which *Bull Week* was unable to avoid.

While improvements in video technology and the enhancement of video to look like film have narrowed the gap between film and video today, there is still a noticeable visual difference between dramas shot on film and those shot on video. This is partly to do with budgets. Video is used on long-running serials because it is cheaper. More footage can be shot in a day using video than when film is used, partly because more time needs to be spent setting up each shot for film. This is especially true when the shots are as elaborate as they are in some of the factory sequences in *Clocking Off*, such as the opening scenes of 'Kev's Story', for example. For these reasons, film tends to connote 'quality drama' because of the higher production values involved, whereas video is more often associated with the lower production values of a multi-episode drama where less time and money is available for rehearsal and camera setups.

Another way in which *Clocking Off* is noticeably different from classic social realism is in its extensive use of music. While many single plays of the 1960s and 1970s used music, it was often utilised sparingly, usually to create a mood of authenticity for the drama, with a predilection for English folk musicians such as the Watersons (in Alan Plater's *Land of Green Ginger* (BBC 1973)) or The Oldham Tinkers (in Barry Collins's *The Lonely Man's Lover* (BBC 1974)), music which now seems very much of its time. The exceptions might be *Up the Junction* and *Cathy Come Home*, which both used 1960s pop music in order to evoke modernity rather than nostalgia. *Bull Week* does not use incidental music at all, with the result that the serial seems to acquire an almost documentary seriousness in its absence.

The new social realism of *Clocking Off* is far removed in this respect from the austerity of classic social realism, employing a strident rhythm'n'blues-style soundtrack, in which drums and bass are prominent, enhancing the pace of the drama with its pounding rhythm track. Invariably, the theme music is used to provide a musical bridge from one scene to another or to expedite the narrative by accompanying a montage of scenes, its fast rhythm serving to drive the narrative forward. Like the camerawork, editing and production design, the music in *Clocking Off* is designed to enhance the vibrancy and vitality of the drama, providing another example of the way in which the series reworks and updates social realism for the twenty-first century.

The 'renewal' of social realism in *Clocking Off* also extends to the representation of class and gender. While the series makes the working-class employees of Mackintosh Textiles its main focus, there is a concern to acknowledge the social changes that have affected the working class in the last twenty years and the diversity of lifestyles that has resulted from these changes. This is most obvious in the variety of houses lived in by the characters in the series, ranging from the *nouveau riche* mock-Tudor mansion that Mack lives in somewhere in Cheshire to the more modest houses of his employees: the two-up, two-down terraced house of forklift truck operator Suzie, the slightly run-down suburban semi of factory machinist Freda, the more upmarket Victorian terrace that Kev lives in, the city-centre apartment of his brother Martin, the smart semi-detached house on a new estate that Stuart Leach is seen going home to in episode one, and the spacious house in a leafy neighbourhood where black factory foreman Steve lives with his family, a suburban idyll which is threatened when a sacked factory worker, from a run-down council estate, comes seeking revenge. The variety of housing in *Clocking Off* signifies not only the social, financial and class differences between the employees of Mackintosh Textiles but also the ways in which the socio-economic status of the northern industrial working class has changed since the period of classic social realism in the 1960s and 1970s.

To counter the impression that may have been given from the episodes cited that there is a predominance of male-centred stories in *Clocking Off*, it should be noted that, unlike many classic social realist dramas, women feature very prominently in the series. While a number of social realist dramas from the 1960s and 1970s, including *Up the Junction* and *Cathy Come Home*, *In Two Minds*, *Edna, the Inebriate Woman* (BBC 1971) and *The Spongers* (BBC 1978), feature women as central characters these female-centred stories represent a small percentage of the dramas within the male-dominated genre of social realism, a consequence, no doubt, of the fact that male writers tended to specialise in the genre. When women did feature, they invariably suffered to a greater or lesser extent, being subjected, for example, to illegal abortions, homelessness, the loss of children and family, and mental illness.

In contrast, women in *Clocking Off* are portrayed far more positively. While many of the women working in the factory do encounter domestic and social problems, these problems are usually resolved favourably, or at least more optimistically than in classic social realism. At least twelve of the twenty-seven episodes have female-centred narratives, and women feature prominently in many of the other episodes. In addition, there is frequent evidence of female camaraderie in *Clocking Off*, with virtually every episode featuring scenes in the factory, the canteen or the pub showing women laughing, gossiping, singing and generally enjoying themselves.

In the fourth series, Mackintosh Textiles even acquires a female factory manager when Pat Fletcher (Pam Ferris) succeeds Mack (Philip Glenister) following his decision at the end of the third series to sell the company to new owners. Pam Ferris gives a strong performance as the new boss, complementing the several strong female characters who work on the factory floor. Four of the six stories in the fourth series are female-centred, including one in which Pat succeeds in persuading the factory staff to pull together and double production in order to overcome a financial crisis; at the same time she is trying to deal with a personal marital crisis involving her alcoholic, gambling-addicted husband (Keith Barron).

Losing the plot

Yet by the fourth series of *Clocking Off*, in 2003, the novelty of its new social realism seemed to be wearing off, with audiences for the series falling to just over four million. After the eight-million-plus average for the first series the ratings for series two fell to six and a half million and to less than five million for the third series. Paul Abbott initially blamed the decline on the BBC for moving the series around in the schedules, from Sunday night for the first series to Monday night for series two and Thursday night for series three. The fourth series was moved back to Sunday nights where it was scheduled against ITV's highly popular drama series *Cold Feet* (Granada 1996–2003), pitching two Manchester-based dramas head-to-head. In the ensuing ratings battle it was the lighter comedy-drama of *Cold Feet* that won out, attracting double the audience that *Clocking Off* achieved in this, its final series.

At the end of the first series Paul Abbott had claimed that 'Viewers want both entertainment and integrity . . . and they like it done with style' (Holman 2001: 23), and the large audiences for the first two series seemed to confirm this. So what caused the decline in the audience, leading to the decision by the BBC not to commission a fifth series? Abbott blamed its demise on the lack of writers able to cope with the demands of writing original stories: 'I felt there was a real shortage of writers who have something to say in the single drama format. You give them 60 minutes to tell a single story and a lot of the things we rejected felt like sub plots from *Playing the Field*' (Deans 2003). Although Abbott had himself started his career by writing for *Coronation Street*, he attributed the inability of writers to produce interesting stories for *Clocking Off* to the fact that writers today are forced to write for the soaps in order to break into television. This, he suggested, not only militates against originality but encourages a 'metronomic' writing style, one which is stylistically conservative because of the pervasive naturalism of television soap opera: 'I wrote for *Coronation Street* for 10 years and it took me two years to get over it. You find yourself still writing about someone walking from home to the pub, and you have to then write a buffer scene to fill in the time they are en route. Why not just cut?' (Deans 2003).

It was the stylistic inventiveness of the series – faster cutting, mobile camerawork, a creative use of colour in the mise-en-scène, together with a lively music track and energetic acting from its large ensemble cast – which had distinguished *Clocking Off* on its debut in January 2000, giving a new lease of life to social realism at a time when the issue-based narratives of the genre seemed to have gone out of fashion. Furthermore, *Clocking Off*'s 'single play' approach, within a series format, enabled original stories to be developed in a way that the 'flexi-narrative' structure of most drama series did not, giving scope for moral complexity in the storylines that was enhanced by the potential that the series format offered to develop a familiarity with characters over a period of time. Paul Abbott, in particular, was able to exploit this, writing some superb original stories for the series while also capitalising on the fact that the characters had histories which could be reprised in subsequent episodes.

However, with Abbott spending more time writing other original dramas in 2002–3 (*State of Play* (BBC), *Alibi* (ITV), *Shameless* (C4)), his contributions to *Clocking Off* decreased, with only two episodes in the third series and none in the fourth. Meanwhile, the lack of writers capable of producing original stories in the style that the series demanded contributed to its demise. Yet the achievement of *Clocking Off* was to revitalise a genre that had seemed obsolete, breathing new life into social realism and putting the northern industrial working class back on to British television screens.

References

Anon. (2001), 'Beautiful lighting and vibrant colours underpin gritty urban drama', *In Camera*, April, 22.

Holman, J. (2001), 'Doing the business', *TV Times*, 31 March, 23.

Jordan, M. (1981), 'Realism and convention', in R. Dyer, C. Geraghty, M. Jordan, T. Lovell, R. Paterson, J. Stewart *Coronation Street*, London: BFI.

Naughton, J. (2001), 'Start the clock', *Radio Times*, 31 March, 26.

Nelson, R. (1997), *TV Drama in Transition: Forms, Values and Cultural Change*, Basingstoke: Macmillan.

Ogle, T. (2000), 'It's glam up north', *Guardian*, 16 January, 6–7.

Internet source:

Deans, J. (2003), '*Clocking Off* axed from BBC', MediaGuardian.co.uk, 29 April.

Further reading

Abbott, P. (2001), 'Culture clash', *Guardian*, 28 May.

Cooke, L. (2003), *British Television Drama: A History*, London: BFI.

Hill, J. (1986), *Sex, Class and Realism: British Cinema 1956–1963*, London: BFI.

Hill, J. (2000), 'From the New Wave to "Brit-Grit": continuity and difference in working-class realism', in J. Ashby and A. Higson (eds), *British Cinema: Past and Present*, London: Routledge.

Lacey, S. (1995), *British Realist Theatre: The New Wave in its Context 1956–1965*, London: Routledge.

Laing, S. (1986), *Representations of Working-Class Life 1957–1964*, Basingstoke: Macmillan.

Lay, S. (2002), *British Social Realism: From Documentary to Brit Grit*, London: Wallflower.

Millington, B., and R. Nelson (1986), '*Boys from the Blackstuff*': The Making of TV Drama*, London: Comedia.

11

Becoming popular: some reflections on the relationship between television and theatre

Stephen Lacey

It might seem perverse in a book concerned with recent, if not new, perspectives on television drama to argue that it is worth returning to an older, now largely ignored, critical frame of reference derived from the theatre. It is now so long since television drama ceased to be the small-screen version of a stage play that the time when television drama of all kinds defined itself in relation to the theatre seems almost beyond memory. That is not to say that relationships between the two cultural forms have ended; there has been no formal separation, let alone a divorce. Television's relationship to theatre has been characterised as a combination of deference and debt; deference to a cultural form that has occasionally lent kudos to its fledgling junior cousin, and debt to an industry that satisfies television's voracious appetite for the writing, directing, technical and acting talent that provides its professional base (Ridgman 1998: 1). It is not as simple as that, of course, and the debt also goes the other way, although these arguments will not be rehearsed here. I am more concerned to trace other connections, in the belief that the relationship of theatre practice and theory to their television counter-parts has been, all too often, constructed in terms of the inherited categories of traditional dramatic scholarship (the contribution of individual writers, in particular), and that this construction has limited the way in which critical debate about both media has developed. The intention in this essay is not to consider these questions on a broad canvas, but is rather more modest, local and (in part) historical. I am concerned mainly with tracing some of the relationships between the theatre of the late 1950s and 1960s and television drama of the 1960s and 1970s. I am particularly interested in how some of the key terms in the development of television drama (especially 'Brechtian' and 'the popular') might be illuminated when placed in the context of theatre theory and practice, and to pursue some connections between Joan Littlewood's Theatre Workshop and popular television comedy.

Both the theatre of the late 1950s and the television of the mid-1960s have been characterised in terms of their relationship to social realism (see Lacey 1995). What is being discussed here is the moment of 'Anger' and 'Working Class Realism' in the theatre, symbolised by John Osborne's *Look Back in Anger* (1956), the plays of Arnold Wesker, Harold Pinter, Shelagh Delaney, Brendan Behan, John Arden and Edward Bond, much of the work of the English Stage Company at the Royal Court Theatre, and of Theatre Workshop at Stratford East: in television, it is it is largely, though by no means exclusively, the BBC Wednesday Play anthology that is the most visible symbol of this moment. The key texts are *Up the Junction* (BBC 1965), written by Nell Dunn (with Tony Garnett as script editor), produced by James McTaggart and directed by Ken Loach, and *Cathy Come Home* (BBC 1966) (written by Jeremy Sandford, directed by Loach with Garnett as producer).

In broad terms, social realism is not so much a form (and certainly not a specific dramatic method) but a *project*. It was not exactly the same project across theatre and television, but there were key elements in common; the concern to find ways of engaging directly with contemporary Britain, especially the social experience of those (largely working-class) people who lay beyond the consciousness of political debate, often with a direct ideological objective. Social realism was realist in the sense that it usually adopted the mimetic dramatic methods (in both theatre and television) that had become established within the realist tradition (see Raymond Williams 1977) and which foregrounded verisimilitude. It was also realist in that it offered an argument about, and analysis of, social reality; this kind of realism was particularly strong amongst the more politically engaged radicals working in television at the time. These two senses of realism were, at times, in tension with each other, since in order to achieve a more politically engaged drama, whether on the small screen or on the theatre stage, the constraints of the inherited dramatic tradition were rejected (the single domestic interior, the limitations of the 'photographic' approach to representation, the restricted 'real time' approximations of the condensed linear narrative). Paradoxically, for television radicals this meant accepting an agenda and vocabulary borrowed from the theatre, whilst at the same time rejecting the 'theatrical' as a model for social realism. The main enemy was naturalism, understood both as a shorthand for the theatrical in general and for the particular, socially

restricted forms of much postwar drama in particular (a proper interro-
gation of the ways in which naturalism has been used in the discussion of
both postwar theatre and television drama requires an essay to itself).

Tony Garnett has commented perceptively on the unacceptable restrictions that the inherited forms of stage drama imposed on television:

> One thing we were pissed off with was the way television drama almost
> exclusively used the kind of naturalism that emerged in the 1890s in the the-
> atre. It was drama seen as a group of people who would occasionally walk in
> or walk out of a door, but while they were together they would sit around
> and have a conversation. Occasionally, because you wanted a bit of action,
> they would pour a drink. (Hudson 1972: 19)

The restrictions were particularly acute for those, such as Garnett,
whose prime concern was to engage directly with social reality, and create
a specifically televisual form of social realism. Television, as Garnett and
others were quick to realise, could use the camera to solve the inherent
problems of live studio-bound performance. The film camera allows
much more of a given society to be *shown*, rather than simply indicated
metonymically through the four walls of the stage or studio set. Showing
a social situation directly, in its actual location, has been an important
means of authenticating the 'reality' of social realism in television drama,
and it is no surprise that film emerged as an available technology alongside the political desire to represent contemporary Britain for a mass
audience.

The opposition to naturalism found a theoretical focus in the 1960s,
and figures prominently in the critical writing of two of the most influential contributors to debates about the development of television drama
in the period, John McGrath and Troy Kennedy Martin (see McGrath
1977 and Kennedy Martin 1964). Both equated naturalism with an outmoded theatrical legacy, studio-bound, psychologised and static. The
alternative ('non-naturalism' in Kennedy Martin's formulation) was to
create a drama that would exploit the freedom of the camera to engage
directly with the flux of social reality: as McGrath noted, 'We placed a
conscious emphasis on narrative – society, real and recognisable [and] in
motion' (McGrath 1977: 103).

Naturalism was also the enemy for many working within the theatre as
well, and it is no coincidence that McGrath should have come to television from the Royal Court (and should, a decade later, return to live theatre) and that Kennedy Martin's influential 1964 critique of naturalism,
'Nats go home', should appear in *Encore*, a theatre magazine closely iden-

tified with the New Wave. *Encore* allied itself with a range of theatre practitioners and writers who were opposed to naturalism (especially when it
was conceived as a theatre practice, an approach to staging, as distinct
from a particular genre of play).

Non-naturalism and Brecht

Those seeking to chart the course of a new and progressive drama on both
the stage and the small screen had an ally in their struggles against naturalism: the German poet, dramatist and theoretician Bertolt Brecht
(1898–1956). Brecht cast a long shadow across the theatre of the late
1950s and 1960s (and has continued to do so, intermittently, since),
although his work was appropriated in particular and idiosyncratic ways.
There is not the space here to account for this in detail (see Lacey 1995 for
a fuller discussion), but it should be noted that for many theatre practitioners he provided an example of an alternative to naturalism that was
rigorous, socially critical and which could be registered across the range
of means of theatrical communication, from writing to acting and
design. This did not result in a strictly 'Brechtian' theatre, or even a recog-
nisably political one. One the one hand, Brecht became a reference point
in the theoretical discussions of 'committed', contemporary and anti-nat-
uralist theatre that filled the pages of *Encore* magazine and beyond; on the
other, his influence was refracted through other traditions and practices,
and can be traced in the work of dramatists such as John Arden and
Edward Bond. Brecht's influence has been dated to the visit to London of
his company, the Berliner Ensemble, shortly before his death in 1956, and
it is his plays and staging practices that have exerted the most influence.
Brecht's theory was largely misunderstood or ignored, partly because of
the anti-theoretical preferences of much theatre of the time, and partly
because the theory was not properly available in translation until 1964. As
John Arden noted wryly in a review of John Willett's *Brecht on Theatre*: 'A
dramatist who takes his work sufficiently seriously to compile a whole
series of theoretical essays about it is an un-English and (we may think)
an untheatrical phenomenon' (Arden 1977: 37).

On the radical wing of television, however, there was a much clearer
engagement with the theoretical implications of the work. Undoubtedly,
some of the most interesting experiments with dramatic form on television in the early 1960s were attempts to work through what a Brechtian
television drama might look like. A key example here is *Diary of a Young
Man* (BBC 1964). Directed by Ken Loach and written by Kennedy Martin

and McGrath, the six-part series was written to provide a practical example of 'non-naturalism'. The series included narration, a dense soundtrack, still images and filmed montage 'that were designed to involve the
viewer in the drama, in a way that the more pedantic naturalist drama
could not' (Cooke 2003: 65). *Diary* . . . was also the result of the collective
interest in Brecht's work at the time. Tony Garnett has commented on
this: 'we were hanging out with each other all the time . . . and there was
a loose school of people of that generation and we were arguing and talking about these things . . .cos there was some voiceover in *Diary of a
Young Man* . . . So it's not an accident that we were talking the same
language'.[1] The reference to voice-over is particularly interesting, since it
indicates one of the techniques that marked both *Up the Junction* and
Cathy Come Home as being distinctive compared to other contemporary
dramas (it was the subject of comment in both the reviews of the plays
and the BBC's own audience research). Voice-over was read primarily as
a technique borrowed from documentary, and can be related to other
strategies that foreground closeness to observable reality in general, and
documentary in particular: the use of 16mm film, which comes with a
prior connotation of news and current affairs; the casting of non-actors;
and the use of seemingly overheard, rather than scripted, dialogue – in
short, what John Caughie has referred to as the documentary look, 'hand-
held camera, the cramped shot, natural lighting and inaudible sound'
(Caughie 1981: 343).

   This strategy serves both to authenticate the 'truth' of what is being
represented (as it does in documentary-dramas generally) and, in the case
of *Up the Junction*, to anchor a range of more experimental techniques,
specifically a montage structure in the use of both sound and image that
evokes not so much contemporary television news as prewar European
modernist cinema and the modernist tradition within British documentary (Caughie 2000: 119). The tension this could produce in the viewer
was registered in the BBC's audience research. On the one hand, a dislocation occurred because the 'continual cutting from one scene to another
only emphasized the fact the Up the Junction was not "drama" in the
usual sense' (BBC WAC VR/65/619); on the other, viewers commended
both the 'truth' of the situation (even if they felt it should not be seen on
the television screen) and the 'reality' of the acting.

   This modernist strategy also connects specifically, and intentionally, to
Brecht's practice in its use of a variety of discourses, often montaged
against each other, to give a range of points of view of a situation. Here is
Tony Garnett again, talking about the use of voice-over in *Up the Junction*:

It wasn't because we thinking of documentaries. Ken and I were very influenced by Brecht at the time and we were interested in a sort of alienation effect on film where what was going on the screen would get the *feelings* of the audience, and what was coming on the soundtrack would get the *mind* of the audience – it was trying to do that.

This combination of 'thought' and 'feeling' is highly illuminating, and what lies behind it is a relationship to both Brecht and naturalism that is complex and symptomatic. On the one hand, the political strategies of the text, which include not only voice-over but also the fractured, multi-focused narrative structure, reflect a Brechtian intention that leads to explicit political argument and self-reflexivity. On the other, the observational stance of *Up the Junction*, manifested in its documentary strategies, rejects artifice and denies self-reflexivity. It also re-engages with naturalism at a different level, exploiting what Deborah Knight has termed (in relation to Ken Loach's films in general) 'naturalism's unnerving directness, which takes us from the discussion of art to the discussion of society, from the discussions of characters in a fiction to discussions of people in real life' (Knight 1997: 60).

This is clearly not the kind of appropriation of Brecht that a decade later would inform the academic debates about the 'classic realist text', advanced by Colin MacCabe and others in *Screen* (MacCabe 1974). This set of arguments settled eventually on another Loach/Garnett/Allen collaboration, *Days of Hope* (BBC 1975), in order to repudiate the critical naturalist discourses it embodied. In that conjuncture, Brecht was co-opted to argue for a politically progressive practice that would dismantle the authority of the coherent realist narrative and substitute a radical formalist aesthetic. However, the earlier debt to Brecht ran parallel to the ways that contemporary theatre practitioners were engaging with him as a way of solving their own quite specific problems, especially how to combine a political and analytical discourse with a realism of performance that made both analysis and emotion possible. It is this loose and undogmatic appropriation of Brecht that informs the plays of, for example, Arden and Bond, and, in a neat symmetry, the later work of John McGrath with 7:84, a touring socialist theatre company (or, more accurately, two theatre companies, one operating in England and Wales, the other in Scotland). McGrath rejected television in the mid-1960s for the freedom, localism and immediacy of live theatre, establishing in 7:84 the kind of radical popular theatre that had become associated with Brecht. However, McGrath's immediate influence was not so much Brecht himself as another figure of the New Wave, whose attitude to Brechtianism was simultaneously rigorous and irreverent: Joan Littlewood.

Theatre Workshop and popular performance

The rejection of naturalism discussed here is most often referenced in the discussion of legitimate drama and the single play, but it also has implications for popular drama, on both the stage and the television screen (McGrath's involvement with the ground-breaking BBC police series *Z Cars* (BBC 1962–78) being just one example), although this is much less often remarked upon. It also connects to the theatrical New Wave in a different way, via the work of Joan Littlewood and her company, Theatre Workshop. Littlewood was one of the most influential theatre directors of the late twentieth century, whose work was rooted in the specific traditions of British popular culture yet had international significance. Unlike the English Stage Company, which produced *Look Back in Anger* at the Royal Court, Theatre Workshop was rooted firmly in the 'illegitimate' popular workers' theatres of the 1930s, and was primarily a touring company playing mainly to working-class audiences in the regions (existing, therefore, largely beyond the consciousness of the established theatre industry). The Company settled in the Theatre Royal in Stratford East in 1953.[2] Although the plays were directed by Littlewood, whose distinctive signature was on all stages of the production process, the Company was probably most influential for foregrounding the role of the actor in performance, displacing the literary text as the centre of authority. In its heyday in the early to mid-1950s, Theatre Workshop ran an extensive training programme centred on the ethos of the actor ensemble. Littlewood's rehearsal methods, which included extensive improvisation (frequently leading to the re-writing of new plays in collaboration with their authors), were both distinctive in the postwar context and highly influential.

Theatre Workshop made its initial reputation in the early 1950s with a number of hard-edged productions of classical plays, often showcased at foreign festivals. However, it was the Company's work with new drama from 1956 to the early 1960s that placed it at the centre of the theatrical New Wave. Littlewood brought a variety of plays, and a number of relatively new writers, to the Stratford East stage: Brendan Behan's *The Quare Fellow* (1956) and *The Hostage* (1958), Shelagh Delaney's *A Taste of Honey* (1958), Frank Norman's *Fings Ain't Wot They Used to Be* (1959) and Stephen Lewis's *Sparrers Can't Sing* (1960). Although the plays may have been different from each other in their original form (Behan's *The Hostage*, for example, was a sober tragedy in its initial version), the Company's working methods ensured that a house style developed, which seemed all the more evident because it was markedly different from most other theatre at the time. The style may be characterised as: a willingness to cross and combine dramatic genres (particularly comic and dramatic forms) to include music, poetry and direct address; a realism in performance (evident in a 'naturalness' in the acting) within a theatrical context that constantly broke with the dominant convention of 'fourth wall' naturalism; and a gleeful borrowing of the techniques and conventions of British popular theatre, notably the music hall. In Littlewood's productions, such techniques were central to the overall performance aesthetic, and to the socialist-libertarian politics that underpinned it. Reviews of both *A Taste of Honey* and *The Hostage* compared the initial productions to music hall, and popular comedy generally: for Lindsay Anderson, the former was 'pure music hall' (Anderson 1970: 80), whilst for Ken Tynan, *The Hostage* offered an experience where 'phrases like "dramatic unity" are ruled out of court: we are simply watching a group of human beings who have come together to tell a lively story in speech and song' (Tynan 1984: 228). Theatre Workshop's productions were, therefore, resolutely anti-naturalistic, in ways that loosely paralleled the 'non-naturalism' called for by Kennedy Martin and others working in television at the time.

The results of this approach in Theatre Workshop's evolving acting style are of particular interest here. The combination of explicit comedy, direct address and 'truth to life', a veracity based on meticulous research and observation, produced acting that was self-referential, that drew attention itself as acting, and also, often at different moments within the same performance, was so 'real' (close to observable reality) that it seemed not to be acting at all. Commenting on a 'seemless' combination of acting styles in the performances of both the central character, the teenager Jo, and her mother, Helen, in *A Taste of Honey*, Goodwin and Milne observe that 'a more or less naturalistic sequence shows the mother and daughter together. Jo goes out to make some coffee, while the mother goes on talking to her. She turns her head quite casually, and suddenly you find she is talking directly to the audience' (Milne and Goodwin1960: 10). The point here is that 'front cloth' direct address exists within the context of a performance that is still 'convincing' at the level of characterisation and that continues to signify 'the real'. It is an effect that is achieved by being, at least partly, outside what are perceived to be the mannerisms of traditional acting – that is, it gains its 'reality effect' in contrast to expectation:

> This was a far cry from the polite restraint usually seen on the stage. The actors looked and sounded different. Gone were the hallmarks of mainstream English acting – the dignified poise, well-cut profiles, modulated tones. They didn't look like actors. They looked like people. (Milne and Goodwin 1960: 11)

In fact, Littlewood frequently recruited performers who had not received conventional training (sometimes no training at all), and who were not in this limited sense 'actors'. Milne and Goodwin's comments echoed frequent responses to the use of 'non-actors' in *Up the Junction* and *Cathy Come Home* (a strategy that has figured in nearly all of Ken Loach's work for the cinema). The connections were also more specific. In the course of describing the ultra-realism of the acting style of both plays, Garnett noted that it paralleled that of Littlewood's company, largely because many of the actors they were working with then (and later) were 'found and developed by Joan Littlewood'. Of course, this approach has other points of origin as well, since both Loach and Garnett were also influenced by broadcast documentary, Italian neo-realist cinema, 'New Wave' French cinema and (Loach especially) Czech cinema of the 1950s.

There is more that might be said about these connections in another context: it is more appropriate here to pursue the other aspect of the characteristic Theatre Workshop style indicated above, the popular and the comic – and its legacy for popular British television drama.

Theatre Workshop and sitcom

By the end of the 1950s, Theatre Workshop had begun to fragment under the economic pressures that had led to a series of financially successful transfers to the West End, which had the paradoxical effect of destroying both the ensemble ethos and the training programme that had made the work distinctive. Many of the original members left to pursue other options, and Littlewood herself left in 1961, returning briefly in 1963 to direct *Oh What a Lovely War* (which led to another West End transfer, and eventually a film). The demise of the Company occurred at the point that television output was expanding, especially drama of all kinds, and it is fascinating to note just how many actors associated with Theatre Workshop through the years went on to work in television and film, particularly popular television drama – notably sitcoms – from the mid-1960s to the early 1980s (and sometimes after). The list is impressive (see Goorney 1981: 211–213): Harry H. Corbett, Dudley Foster, Julian Glover, Clive Goodwin, Yootha Joyce, John Junkin, Roy Kinnear, Alfred Lynch, Brian Murphy, Bryan Pringle, Tony Selby, Victor Spinetti, Dudley Sutton and Barbara Windsor – and this is not exhaustive. Several of these names are at the centre of some most significant and popular drama series of the period (and the legacy continues through Barbara Windsor, as Peggy Mitchell in *EastEnders* (1985–)). To take two notable examples that will reoccur below: Harry H. Corbett played Harold in Galton and Simpson's *Steptoe and Son* (BBC 1962–65, 1970–74), and Brian Murphy and Yootha Joyce played the eponymous central characters in *George and Mildred* (Thames 1976–79).[3]

There is no simple reason why Littlewood's regulars figure so prominently in popular television drama of the time, but it owes something to a professional discipline based on creative independence combined with an ability to work within a team under pressure that underpinned the rigorous working methods of the Company. This was of considerable use in the context of the intense working conditions of long-running sitcoms, where actors receive little or no support from the director to discuss or develop their characters. In addition, the strict demands of the timeframe (in *George and Mildred* the writers worked to the fixed limit of twenty-four minutes per episode), and the need to play to both a television audience and a 'live' studio one, required both restraint and the ability to work independently. Murphy and Joyce were able to use their shared history in Theatre Workshop to create a strong working relationship that was picked up by the scriptwriters and was instrumental in the decision to develop George and Mildred from the subordinate characters in *Man About the House* (Thames 1973–76) into a series of their own.

There is also a common debt to the traditions of popular comedy that have strong theatrical roots. Critical writing about the sitcom has always acknowledged this debt. Raymond Williams, writing in 1974, remarked on 'the evolution of both the solo turn and the variety sketch into "situation comedy"' (Williams 1974: 66), and this tradition is referenced in both Cook (1982) and Creeber (2001). In their discussion of the sources of comedy in film and television, Neale and Krutnik note the extraordinary formal diversity even within the genre of comedy, whilst arguing that 'definitions and theories of comedy have their basis in the theatre' (Neale and Krutnik 1990: 14). They note the influence of both 'narrative' forms (derived in part from Aristotle's *Poetics*) and 'non-narrative' genres, where narrative is subordinate to character and 'routine', such as the *commedia dell'arte*, or where it is largely absent, such as music hall and variety. Added to this must be the way that these influences have been transformed and passed on via radio and film. Sitcom cannot be simply 'read off' as a product of these influences, as Mick Eaton has pointed out (Eaton 1978: 64), but it is particularly useful to note them when matters of performance are under discussion. It is the music hall in particular that is the strongest link between Theatre Workshop and popular television comedy, and it is no accident that it was in the 'narrative' end of the continuum of popular comic genres that its ex-members found a home.

Interviewed for the theatre journal *Theatre Quarterly*, Brian Murphy noted that 'The roots of the George and Mildred situation are there in the music-hall'. He was referring to the husband and wife 'double act' that is at the centre of the programme and that derived from the halls and the comic traditions that lay behind them, and continued, 'We don't have those double-acts on the stage any more, even in the clubs, and I think *George and Mildred* bridges the gap' (Murphy 1980: 23). He might have added that the work he and Yootha Joyce did at Theatre Workshop fulfilled the same function, though for a more local audience. Like sitcom, Theatre Workshop's productions reworked the familiar devices and routines of the music hall, such as the double-act, within the framework of a more traditional extended narrative. Behan's *The Hostage*, for example, has a clear – and highly dramatic – narrative line that concerns the kidnapping of a young British soldier by the IRA, his internment in a Dublin brothel, during the course of which he falls in love with a young Irish girl, and his eventual accidental death during the course of an abortive rescue attempt. In Littlewood's 1958 production (which included both Murphy and Joyce), this narrative progressed as much through gags, songs, routines and slapstick as through conventional dramatic devices (dialogue and exposition), and sought to balance comedy with pathos and politics. The inclusion of set-piece comic routines within a narrative that was essentially character-driven and serious also paralleled the incorporation of similar devices in certain sitcoms. As Neale and Krutnik have noted of *Steptoe and Son*, the agony of the central relationship between father and son, bound to each other in a 'prison of obligation', often explodes into comedy at the point at which the pain of the situation seems inescapable; 'Often behind the broadest comedy of the show are actions which would ordinarily be branded disturbing or cruel' (Neale and Krutnik 1990: 258).

The issue at stake here is that actors trained with Littlewood were familiar with an approach that required the simultaneous display of comic talent and psychologically and emotionally consistency. Theatre Workshop's productions were undoubtedly more challenging (certainly a lot more political, boisterous and rude) than was permissible within the ideological and aesthetic constraints of mainstream television, but the skills demanded of the actor were similar. The point of reference for Murphy was not so much the 'stand-up' comic as the 'character actors' who 'found a comic character, and then honed and sharpened and refined it, putting the character into different situations like we do in light entertainment today' (Murphy 1980: 25). This suggests a freedom of approach that is sometimes missed in critical discussion of the characters of popular television drama. Undoubtedly, the circular form of most sitcoms, which demands that, whatever happens within the frame of the individual episode, the basic situation must remain unchanged, constrains the development of character beyond a known typology; Harold Steptoe can never leave his father, though the viewer is asked to believe each week that it is possible; George is for ever locked into the cage of his sexual anxieties, and Mildred her fantasies of social betterment. However, as Murphy has perceptively noted, playing a lead character in a long-running series allows the writers to develop a working relationship with the actors and set challenges for them: 'in one episode he [George] is faced squarely with the fact that he *is* married to her [Mildred] and that he doesn't want to lose her, and we examine what his real thoughts are' (Murphy 1980: 26).

There is a parallel here between the playing of a character in different situations over time and one of the uses of improvisation that Littlewood developed with Theatre Workshop. According to the mythology, improvisation was the core of the acting process within the Company, replacing conventional methods of rehearsal and spilling over into performance. In reality, improvisation was used in a much more specific way (in the late 1950s, pre-performance censorship, which demanded that everything that appeared on stage be subject to prior scrutiny, severely constrained improvisation in performance). One of its main uses was as a tool to develop characterisation by playing a role in a context developed from, or analogous to, the dramatic situation of the play. The individual sitcom episode, though not in any sense improvised, offered a comparable experience for the actor by allowing him or her the freedom to explore the space within the character. It was akin to the working methods of another popular comic form, the *commedia dell'arte*, in which actors would 'know their characters and would react to the particular situation they were performing that night. In comic terms, that's probably still done in television sitcoms today' (Murphy 1980: 27).

The 'popular' and the 'canon'

Littlewood did not share the enthusiasm for television comedy, nor the sense of its place in the history of popular dramatic forms, that possessed many of her actors. Writing in her diary, she records idly turning on the television one night: 'A shock. Harry C's [Harry H. Corbett] filled the screen. He was talking in some stylised accent and there was a hideous old man with him . . . Harry, who had given us that incomparable Richard II and so many glorious moments of theatre; what had driven him to this?' (Littlewood 1994: 668). Littlewood was not alone in reacting to television in this way, since many theatre activists shared the widespread anxieties about the new medium that permeated cultural debates at the time (that it destroyed the family and bred a passive and inert audience, that it was a symbol of creeping Americanisation, that it destroyed 'authentic' working-class culture) (see Shiach 1989). It is ironic that more than forty years after its first appearance *Steptoe and Son* is now part of the 'canon' of television drama, legitimated by its enduring appeal to both viewers and academics.

That a programme such as *Steptoe and Son* can be both 'canonical' and 'popular' is a proposition likely to induce vertigo in those seeking fixed definitions of these fluid and difficult terms. The idea of a canon of television drama is, despite its convenience for publishers and academics, contestable, and is best thought of as a set of overlapping definitions (or notions if 'definitions' is too absolute a term) that describe different kinds of texts and practices from different viewpoints. Some of these are pragmatic (the canon of early television drama, for example, is often that which survives). Others are inherited from other cultural forms (the prestige accorded single-authored, 'literary' drama series or the single play, for example, and high-budget adaptations of classic novels), or are ascribed by academics (sometimes responding to the same cultural triggers). Most important in this context, however, is the use of the canon as a critical manoeuvre to validate drama that is seen to extend the political and aesthetic possibilities of the medium, and/or which has generated public debate about its significance. This is a controversial idea, since it can raise a priori assumptions about what that 'extension' might consist of (the devices of self-reflexivity, for example, in the plays of Dennis Potter); also, we tend to find such experiments more easily in the places where we are used to looking for them (that is, amongst the Wednesday Plays rather than, say, science fiction or popular comedy). However difficult such issues are, the worth of experimental and oppositional practice should be protected (in the opinion of this author), though it is debatable whether the erection of a canon is the best way to do this, not least because whenever the term is evoked it is immediately haunted by its opposite. The 'non-canonical', or rather the popular, has suffered too much from such polarisation, which always accords it a lower space in the cultural hierarchy. It has also meant that 'popularity' has often been denied to canonical texts in ways that limits discussion of them. In conclusion, I want to attempt to unravel some of the threads of this argument, by going back to theatre once more, this time to some of the ways in which the popular has operated as a critical and conceptual term.

Littlewood's engagement with, and deep knowledge of, popular performance traditions is an indication of the way that the term 'popular' plays differently in the context of theatre (and theatre studies) to the way it often does in public debate about television (and media and television studies, or cultural studies generally). Some of the key terms are visible in both, and the spectre of the binary opposition between popular and high culture hovers, as it does in all discussions of the popular, though it is viewed over a longer period of time, and at significant historical moments (Elizabethan or Jacobean theatre) the walls between the two terms dissolve. Popular genres are generally those that privilege the performance over the text, accessibility over difficulty, and visceral and emotional immediacy over literary worth. Though not restricted to the mimetic, popular forms often celebrate the connections between art and life (which may be one reason why naturalism, in the broadest sense of the term, has exerted such a strong pull over popular representation and culture in the twentieth century). As the sociologist Pierre Bourdieu argued, 'Everything takes place as if the "popular aesthetic" were based on the affirmation of continuity between art and life' (Bourdieu 1992: 32).

Louis James has noted that the epithet 'popular' has been attached to pre-industrial folk drama and the commercial urban drama aimed at the new proletarian audiences in the rapidly expanding cities in the eighteenth and nineteenth centuries (such as melodrama). The application of the term to the drama of the electronic media – radio, cinema and television – aimed specifically at a mass audience came later (James 1981: 1). He also notes another form of the popular: drama of the radical left that attempts to engage with a working class or popular audience as part of a process of ideological intervention. This is of particular interest, since it characterises the intentions of Brecht, McGrath and Littlewood, and recognises that there is space within the history of the popular for alternative, radical and formally innovative drama; it also, of course, captures the intentions of the combative and experimental work of Loach, Garnett, Sandford, Dunn, Kennedy Martin, McGrath and others working in television drama in the 1960s, and (as if these labels were not slippery enough) maps exactly on to one notion of the 'canon' outlined above.

In some ways, radical television drama at this time was uniquely placed in the history of popular dramatic forms, since it had the ability to reach a mass audience in ways denied live theatre (measured against the ability of television to mobilise national audiences – even within a multi-channel environment – live theatre will always fail). As Raymond Williams noted in his discussion of the Loach/Garnett/Allen *The Big Flame* (1969), the television audience was fully 'socially extended'; that is, it not only was a 'mass audience' in the crude statistical sense that is often used when assessing the popularity of broadcast drama but was also potentially, at any given moment, cross-class in its composition (Williams 1977). Both *Up the Junction* and *Cathy Come Home*, however, were also popular in the brute terms of audience maximisation, receiving viewing figures in the millions (the former reached 9.5 million people, and the latter 12 million).

As Brecht put it, it is possible to be both 'popular' and 'realistic', in the sense that one might create work that engages with, and provides an analysis of, a given society, yet is aimed at a popular audience. Writing in exile in the mid-1930s and commenting on political battles lost and still to be fought, Brecht argued forcefully that realism and the popular were inextricably linked; it was pointless to be realist without being popular, and popular forms without realist objectives were selling their audiences short (Brecht 1977). He also argued that there was not only the state of 'being popular' but also the process of 'becoming popular', and this emphasis on a dynamic process of change is an important one. From this perspective, the strategies that shape both *Up the Junction* and *Cathy Come Home* (the conscious use of documentary techniques to create a Brechtian 'complex seeing' and to position the dramas alongside news and current affairs) are not obscure modernist devices but good examples of attempts to 'become popular' and in so doing expand the definition of what a television play might be.

Notes

1   I am indebted to Lez Cooke for access to an unpublished interview with Tony Garnett for all the otherwise unattributed quotations from him included here.

2   For a full account of the history of Theatre Workshop see Goorney 1981.

3   *Steptoe and Son* began life as a one-off play in 1962, and became a series a year later. Four series were produced in the 1960s, and five more in the following decade (1970–74), each gaining very large audiences: in 1964, it was the most popular programme of the year, reaching 9.7 million viewers. Repeats of selected episodes in the 1980s regularly made the top-ten weekly viewing figures. *George and Mildred* began in 1976 as a spin-off from *Man About the House* (ITV 1973–76), and was written by the same writing team (Johnnie Mortimer and Brian Cooke). It ran over five series until 1979, regularly making the top-ten in the weekly ratings.

References:

Anderson, L. (1970), 'Review: *A Taste of Honey*', in C. Marowitz, T. Milne and O. Hale (eds), *The Encore Reader*, London: Eyre Methuen. This book is also known as *New Theatre Voices in the Fifties and Sixties: Selections from 'Encore' Magazine*, London: Eyre Methuen, 1981.

Arden, J. (1977), in 'Brecht', *To Present the Pretence*, London: Eyre Methuen.

BBC WAC VR/65/619 Audience Research Report for *Up the Junction*.

Bourdieu, P. (1992), 'The aristocracy of culture', in *Distinctions*, London: Routledge.

Brecht, B. (1977), 'Against George Lukács', in Ronald Taylor (ed.), *Aesthetics and Politics*, London: New Left Books.

Caughie, J. (2000), *Television Drama: Realism, Modernism, and British Culture*, Oxford: Oxford University Press.

Caughie, J. (1981), 'Progressive television and documentary drama', in T. Bennett (ed.), *Popular Television and Film*, London: BFI and the Open University.

Cook, J. (ed.) (1982), *Television Sitcom*, BFI Dossier 17, London: BFI.

Cooke, L. (2003), *British Television Drama: A History*, London: BFI.

Creeber, G. (ed.) (2001), *The Television Genre Book*, London: BFI.

Eaton, M. (1978), 'Television situation comedy', *Screen* 19:4, Winter, 61–89.

Goorney, H. (1981), *The Theatre Workshop Story*, London: Methuen.

Hudson, R. (1972), 'Television in Britain: description and dissent, interviews with Tony Garnett and John Gould', *Theatre Quarterly* 2:6, April–June, 18–25.

James, L. (1981), 'Introduction', in J. Bradby, L. James and B. Sharratt (eds), *Performance and Politics in Popular Drama*, Cambridge: Cambridge University Press.

Kennedy Martin, T. (1964), 'Nats go home', *Encore*, March/April, 5–14.

Knight, D. (1997), 'Naturalism, narration and critical perspective: Ken Loach and the experimental method', in G. McKnight, G. (ed.), *Agent of Challenge and Defiance: The Films of Ken Loach*, Trowbridge: Flick Books.

Lacey, S. (1995), *British Realist Theatre: The New Wave in its Context 1956–65*, London: Routledge.

Littlewood, J. (1994), *Joan's Book: A Peculiar History As She Tells It*, London: Methuen.

MacCabe, C. (1974), 'Realism and the cinema: notes on some Brechtian theses', *Screen* 15:2, 7–27.

McGrath, J. (1977), 'Television drama: the case against naturalism', *Sight and Sound* 46:2, 100–105.

Milne, T., and Goodwin, C. (1960), 'Working with Joan', *Encore*, July/August, 9–20.

Murphy, B., 'Acting in television comedy', *Theatre Quarterly* 10:37 (1980), 23–28.

Neale, S., and F. Krutnik (eds) (1990), *Popular Film and Television Comedy*, London: Routledge.

Ridgman, J. (ed.) (1998), *Boxed Sets: Television Representations of Theatre*, Luton: Arts Council of England/John Libby Media/University of Luton.

Shiach, M. (1989), 'As seen on TV: technology and cultural decline', in *Discourse on Popular Culture*, Oxford: Polity Press/Blackwell.

Tynan, K. (1984), '*The Hostage*', in *A View of the English Stage*, London: Methuen.

Williams, R. (1974), *Television, Technology and Cultural Form*, London: Fontana.

Williams, R. (1977), 'Lecture on realism', *Screen* 18:1, Spring; reprinted as 'A defence of realism', in R. Williams (1981), *What I Came to Say*, London: Verso.

Further reading:

Corner, J. (ed.) (1991), *Popular Television in Britain: Studies in Cultural History*, London: BFI.

Crowther, B., and M. Pinfold (eds) (1987), *Bring me Laughter: Four Decades of TV Comedy*, London: Columbus.

Macmurraugh-Kavanagh, M., and S. Lacey (1999), 'Who framed theatre? The 'moment of change' in British TV drama', *New Theatre Quarterly* 57, 58–74.

Rowbottam, S., and H. Benyon (eds) (2001), *Looking at Class: Film, Television and the Working Class in Britain*, London: Rivers Oram Press.

Strinati, D., and S. Wagg (1992), *Come on Down? Popular Media Culture in Post-War Britain*, London: Routledge.

Willett, J. (ed.) (1982), *Brecht on Theatre*, London: Methuen.

Editors' afterword: directions and redirections

As researchers and teachers in television drama studies, we have been concerned to include work in this book that reflects the dominant variety of the subject, comprising analytical study of television programmes as texts, the television industry as an institution along with its production practices and organisation, television in contemporary culture, the study of audiences and histories of television drama. The book aims not only to provide critical insights into specific problems and topics but also to encourage readers to consider the breadth of, and different emphases within, Television Studies. Rather than presenting Television Studies as homogeneous, or as a set of discrete and closed discourses, the book aims to show that Television Studies is an evolving and disputed field. At the close of the book, we decided to add this brief concluding overview of where we think studies in television drama might lead in order to develop strands of critical work included in the essays by our contributors, and also to suggest where the subject might go in the future.

In relation to published research on television drama, however, there are constraints on what researchers can bring to the public domain because of the political economy of academic publishing. The expansion of the teaching of television has led to a proliferation of books that discuss and summarise existing research, but the unpredicability and risk for publishers in presenting new research in specialist areas of the field has made it increasingly difficult for authors to gain contracts for new studies. This is exacerbated by the largely national character of television drama production and broadcasting, even in the global television economy of import and export of programmes and programme formats, and the consequent demand that academic work should have trans-national or cross-market appeal to the general reader or to television fans.

Although there are now more academic journals with a remit to publish new television scholarship, and Web-based publication also offers new possibilities for dissemination, academic institutions still expect university staff to centre their research activity on conventional paper publication and to give priority to the writing of books. This picture is a depressing one, and one that does not bode well for the creation of new ideas that texts for students can develop and explain.

However, a promising though relatively marginal opportunity exists for academic studies of television drama to grow by making further connections with the television industry. The role of the academic discipline of Television Studies in informing the production of television in Britain has always been peripheral, and the field's heritage from the 1960s and 1970s of making distinctions between progressive or conservative texts, and the highly theoretical arguments about form and meaning, had no real effect on writers and production staff in the business of making television drama. But as graduates from university degree programmes in Television and Media Studies now make up a significant proportion of the body of younger television industry professionals, this situation may change. There is also interest from academics and the funding bodies (such as the Arts and Humanities Research Board who fund some television scholarship) in how academic work can connect with and contribute to the television industry. Research into audiences has been funded by television companies and regulatory bodies, but so far there has been little concern with the aesthetic, historical and evaluative criticism that characterises work in the humanities disciplines where many of our contributors conduct their studies. We expect this to change, as new sources of funding for research are sought and television professionals feel more connection with academic work relating to their activities, having experienced it for themselves. We also think that the continuing public discussion about public service television in Britain will draw academics working on television drama into more public forms of debate. Television is now very much an industry (rather than an art or a service), and drama is being defended as a product whose high cost can be rewarded by high profile and large audiences (such as in the literary adaptations that continue to flourish and bolster the major terrestrial channels' claims to dominance). But public service is an attitude and not a genre of programme, so critical work in television drama studies should defend the claims both of high-budget and aesthetically demanding work but also the range of popular formats and genres, such as sitcom and soap opera, that fulfil the public-service remit of offering diverse kinds of form, topic and mode of audience engagement, and drama that addresses and deals with audience segments such as children or minorities that are identified by lifestyle choice and racial or sexual identity.

Broadcasters' interest in audiences also connects with academic studies of programme scheduling and intertextual relations, as well as the connections that viewers make between programmes. There is a long history of work in this field that includes the contributions by Raymond Williams (1974) and John Ellis (1982, 2002) whose interest was in the flow of programmes in the television schedule. Viewers rarely watch programmes singly but instead as part of a flow of material, usually over a period of hours. As Jostein Gripsrud (1997) and others have shown, the discussion of flow refers both to the concatenation of programmes and also to the viewer's experience. Viewers also switch from one programme or channel to another, composing their own 'texts' of television from these segments which do not exhibit the bounded and unified qualities which derive from thinking of television as a series of texts to be analysed singly. We think that academic work on these related issues may to some extent dissolve the disciplinary boundaries within which specialists in, for example, drama, documentary, news or light entertainment carry out their work. There is scope for studies that parallel the mixing and inter-relation of programming in scheduling and viewing by similar mixing in the objects of analysis and the theoretical frameworks that are used to analyse them.

Studies of television drama will also take greater account of the convergence of television with the interactive media of telephony, the Internet and cable and satellite transmission, since these recent developments in the means of reception suggest ways of thinking about television drama as a popular medium in which the notion of multi-accentuality (the different reception of the same material by different audiences) can be studied in new empirical and theoretical ways. This kind of research is already important to studies of interactive programmes in the factual genre of Reality TV (and especially *Big Brother* (C4 1999–)) where these technologies were first significantly developed (see Tincknell and Raghuram 2004, for example). This offers possibilities for updating the theoretical work begun in the 1970s on the relationship between television's mass broadcast to its audience and the television text's imbrication in popular culture, and finding out how television drama refigures and enables audience cultures and communities. In the context of Television Studies' critique of the forces of social control, and its valuation of ordinary viewers, an attention to new modes of delivery and interaction with television drama will develop the research into reception conducted in some of the essays in this book and in other ethnographic studies of the audiences of popular television drama. One aspect of this research will concern the segmentation of audiences, and how different audience groups enjoy and understand programmes differently. In fact, television drama means different things for different audiences. There are generational differences between the authors of the essays in this book and many of the students who may read it, for example, and what the category of television drama includes and what viewers expect from it is different for different age groups. In a multi-channel environment, it is often difficult for viewers to share viewing experiences with people of different generations and interests. For instance, in an example close to home for us, academics rarely have the opportunity to watch the daytime programmes that some groups such as the elderly, students and children see, because of the very long hours that academics now work in the catastrophically under-funded and over-regulated world of British higher education. New strands of work on reception and interaction will bear on the contexts in which programmes are watched, such as whether they encourage and reward family or individual viewing, and how they contribute to changes in viewing habits, as well as yielding interesting conclusions about the multiple possibilities for the meanings of programme texts.

Issues of quality, judgement and the canon run through many of the contributions to this collection (and were noted and discussed in our Introduction), and this is an indication that there will be a resurgence of evaluative criticism in Television Drama Studies. This is a political debate, because there are progressive or conservative kinds of pleasure, and Television Studies' refusal to judge good and bad programmes seems to distance its discourses from the valuation of the variety of pleasures that audiences gain from television drama. Producers of programmes, as well as actors, politicians or journalists, make taste distinctions in terms of popularity, value for money or the 'quality' status of their majority audience. The issues of whether there is more or less 'quality television' than there was, and the standards of taste and decency in television, have mostly been left to popular and journalistic opinion, industry reports and regulatory discourses.

Inasmuch as Television Studies involves the relationships between television and society, these problems may return on to the agenda. One aspect of this on which we think there will be much more work is in the evaluation and theorisation of performance (see Caughie 2000 for a statement of the issues involved here), and the popularity of drama in terms of its potential to offer a variety of viewing positions to a range of readers. Work on the performative aesthetics of television drama will develop ways of accounting for the range and significance of performance and the regulation of performative meanings, as well as the playful and subversive diversity of meanings and identities. Television drama has always been marketed to audiences in relation to performance, and work will consider the circulation of popular television drama personalities. For example, the capacity of the sitcom form to allow bravura perform-ance, tightly structured interlocking narrative strands in a thirty-minute time-slot and the development of character alongside moments of free-standing verbal play connect sitcom drama to the popular's association with performance and self-conscious 'effects'. But it also permits the exploration of such socially engaged and apparently canonical concerns as class and generational conflict, the pressures of change and consumer modernity, and passages of explicitly political and social commentary.

We gave significant space to work on genre in this book, and in the television marketplace, where the search for novelty is an imperative for drama producers, the genres of television drama have become highly unstable. Programmes and formats are characterised by generic leakiness, dismantling and recombining genres within and across episodes. Although we focused on the genre of sitcom in this book, we think that the exploration of generic instability and the stakes of genre as a delimit-ing and categorising force will continue to develop in work on such diverse television drama forms as contemporary urban drama, crime drama and the literary adaptation. We hope that historical analysis will further theoretical studies of how genres rise and fall in profile and pop-ularity. Situation comedy, for example, gave rise to popular programmes such as *The Rag Trade* (BBC 1961–63), *The Liver Birds* (BBC 1969–96), *Butterflies* (BBC 1978–83) and *Dad's Army* (BBC 1968–77). But other genres are less present today, such as the work-based series drama (*The Power Game* (BBC 1965–69), *The Troubleshooters* (BBC 1965–72), *The Brothers* (BBC 1972–76), *Triangle* (BBC 1981–83)), and might perhaps be understood alongside contemporary workplace docusoaps such as *Air-port* (BBC 1996-99) or *The Cruise* (BBC 1998). The historical study of children's drama such as *Changes* (BBC 1975), *The Tomorrow People* (Thames 1973–79), *Catweazle* (LWI 1970–71) and *Timeslip* (ATV 1970–71) hardly exists at present, although these programmes are fondly remembered and are occasionally the subject of nostalgic features in tel-evision theme-nights or on websites. As the field of television history becomes further established, popular programmes such as these could be addressed alongside popular adult programmes in, for example, the genre of fantasy drama and science fiction.

Some of our contributors made use of research on the memories of viewers, and this is likely to continue as a methodology for understanding popular television drama. This work also shares concerns with the consideration of television drama as a cultural heritage, without adopting an overly reverential attitude to programmes of the past or the present but aiming to open up programme archives to give access for the general public as well as to students and academic researchers. The BBC is already pioneering this 'public library' approach to television, as might be expected of a broadcaster funded by a licence fee, but at the moment the access to programme archives is restricted by technological and legal factors including the speed of Internet connections, the problem of copyright and the assumption that only students of programme content, rather than of television aesthetics, will be interested in it. We would argue that it is valuable to be able to re-view wildlife documentaries not only for their informational content but also for their aesthetic significance as television, and the same applies to the vast store of preserved television drama.

When we embarked on this book we of course had to consider questions of methodology. Some of these were practical, and included our contributors' and our potential readers' ability to access recent and historic programmes. Essays in this book address examples of television which are either widely known, still being broadcast or available through commercial or library sources in videotape form. As the retail availability of television in DVD and video form continues and is supplemented by digital access over the Internet, we expect that television drama studies will be able to address a wider range of issues and programmes. This, and the other developments mentioned in this Afterword, offer both new challenges and problems in the field, but also exciting opportunities.

References

Caughie, J. (2000), 'What do actors do when they act?', in J. Bignell, S. Lacey and M. K. Macmurraugh-Kavanagh (eds), *British Television Drama: Past, Present and Future*, Basingstoke: Palgrave Macmillan.

Ellis, J. (1982), *Visible Fictions: Cinema, Television, Video*, London: Routledge & Kegan Paul.

Ellis, J. (2002), *Seeing Things: Television in the Age of Uncertainty*, London: I. B. Tauris.

Gripsrud, J. (1997), 'Television, broadcasting, flow: key metaphors in TV theory', in C. Geraghty and D. Lusted (eds), *The Television Studies Book*, London, New York, Sydney and Auckland: Arnold.

Tincknell, E., and P. Raghuram (2004), '*Big Brother*: reconfiguring the "active" audience of cultural studies?', in S. Holmes and D. Jermyn (eds), *Understanding Reality Television*, London: Routledge.

Williams, R. (1974), *Television, Technology and Cultural Form*, London: Collins.

Index